Little Book of

SAFE SITES
INTERNET
yellow pages

THOMAS NELSON PUBLISHERS
Nashville

Copyright © 2000, 2001 by Thomas Nelson, Inc.

Published in Nashville, Tennessee by Thomas Nelson, Inc.

Library of Congress Cataloging-in-Publication Data

Little safe sites Internet yellow pages.
    p. cm.
   Includes index.
   ISBN 0-7852-4709-2
   1. Internet addresses—Directories.   2. Christians—Computer
network resources—Directories.

   ZA4201.S24 2000
   025.04—dc21   00-045221

Printed in the United States of America

1 2 3 4 5 — 05 04 03 02 01

Welcome to the SafeSites™
Internet Yellow Pages!

We are thrilled that you have chosen to explore the Internet with us. The SafeSites™ Internet Council has spent thousands of hours gathering and reviewing sites, each one with you in mind. There's a whole exciting world on the Internet that you are about to uncover: you can play exciting interactive games, study biblical archaeology, view live footage of earth from satellite cameras, read a novel, shop for a gift for a friend or family member, chat with Christian teens, and so much more. And you are able to do all of this with no fear of inappropriate Internet sites stumbling across your path.

We've already seen that the Internet is, without a doubt, going to be a significant part of the future. With every billboard, magazine cover, movie preview, and television show now listing a "dot.com" address, it is already a pervasive part of our culture. Learning to navigate the web safely is not an option for us and our families; it is a necessity.

The SafeSites™ Internet Council

The council consists of a wide spectrum of Christian Internet experts, including teachers, moms, dads, kids, lawyers, editors, Sunday School teachers, homeschoolers, ministers, teenagers, and everyday users of the Internet.

Their goal in searching and verifying sites was to find safe, informative and entertaining sites that you and your family would be comfortable visiting. These sites provide information on and help with Bible study, education, entertainment, counseling, family issues, history, cooking, ministry, pets, reference, games, travel, women's issues, and much more. They are considered safe because, at the time of selection, they did not contain questionable content including pornography, violence, gambling, crude language, astrology, or nudity.

Please note that all of these sites were considered safe at the time of publication. However, due to the changing nature of the Internet—banner ads, daily updates to websites, etc.— there is no way to guarantee that the sites will remain completely safe. Please check our periodic updates, and remember to alert us if you find a site that is not working or contains inappropriate material. Browse safely to protect your family!

The SafeSites™ Internet Council has reviewed every site in this book in the months and weeks before publication. At the time of review and in the opinion of the SSIC, these sites were not violent, racist, or pornographic. The sites did not use crude language or contain inappropriate adult content. At the time of publication they were considered appropriate for every member of your family.

The Internet is a constantly changing body of information, and we realize that selecting "safe" sites is a subjective process, as standards and convictions vary from family to family. Although these sites were carefully reviewed and approved at the time this book was published, they may have changed by the time you visit them. What was once appropriate may now be questionable. But the SafeSites™ Internet Council has done its best, as of the time of publication, to choose safe sites for families, not only because of their usefulness and interest value, but also because they maintained and encouraged a positive moral attitude.

The Publisher and the SSIC have gone to great lengths to select "safe" sites, but due to the ever-changing nature of the Internet, some sites may change their content or links. Obviously, the Publisher and the SSIC cannot be responsible for such changes and it is vitally important that parents monitor all Internet access in their homes. To assist families in safe Internet access, we have included filtered Internet access software from CleanWeb on the enclosed CD-ROM. If you discover a site listed in this book that is objectionable please notify us immediately at http://www.nelsonreference. com. We will delete objectionable sites from future editions.

Websites are added, moved, and deleted daily. Please check our periodic updates when you're on the web at www.nelson-reference.com and mark the changes in your book. Also, let us know if you find a problem that we haven't updated yet; you can also let us know at www.nelsonreference.com.

Search Engines

One of the best ways to begin navigating the net on your own is through the use of search engines, many of which are listed in this book. A search engine allows you to look for sites on the topic of your choice by entering a word or series of words into a search window.

Two tips will make your searching easier: Refine your search topic. The internet hosts over 800 million web pages, so a general search term like "Books" will result in literally millions of sites. Wading through such a list is virtually impossible. Narrow your topic. For instance, if you want to buy a book about George Washington, instead of "Books," enter "George Washington AND biographies NOT cherry tree," or if you're planning a vacation enter, "Beach OR mountains AND hotel reservations." Each engine provides tips for refining searches—look for "advanced search" options. The best way to learn is just to choose a favorite and become familiar with the way it works.

Remember to use caution when using search engines, as many have links to "unsafe" sites. Most search engines provide basic descriptions of the sites they find for you. Always study the title, description, and URL closely before linking to a site provided by a search engine.

Directories

Another good way to begin your web experience is with directories, which provide a list of sites divided topically. Some directories are already "family friendly," such as The Best of the Christian Web (http://www.botcw.com), Goshen (http://www.goshen.net/WebDirectory/), and 711.net (http://www.711.net/). Our search engine section lists directories that can help you choose sites that meet your needs.

In developing this book, we have teamed up with Best of the Christian Web, and the featured sites are from their database, or will be featured on their site soon.

Always Browse Carefully

A family computer with Internet access can be an incredible and beneficial tool for you and your children. But just as children best learn to drive from an experienced adult, they best learn to surf safely from someone who can show them the right way to go—someone to teach them how to avoid the pitfalls and dangers and how to use this tool to expand their knowledge, their perceptions, and their world. This book can be your guide—and theirs—to finding the Safe Sites™ on the World Wide Web.

Table of Contents

Adoption

Bethany Christian Services
http://www.bethany.org/
Christian domestic and international adoption agency.

Global Adoption Services
http://www.globadoption.com/
Non-profit Christian agency dedicated to the goal that
every child has a right to a caring environment.

Heartbeat International
http://www.heartbeatinternational.org/
Establishing, developing, and supporting effective help
centers all over the world. Heartbeat centers offer concrete services and support to people who are experienc-
ing or have experienced problem pregnancies, upholding
the intrinsic value of every human life.

International Adoption—Christian World
http://www.cwa.org/
One of the largest international child placement agencies.

other sites of interest

Adopt: Assistance for Adopting Children
http://www.adopting.org/ar.html
Waiting kids, waiting parents, birth family search, and
more links for people interested in adoption.

International Adoption Photolisting
http://www.precious.org/
View children by country, age, date they were added to
the list, or agency. Make donations, and other links.

National Adoption Information Clearinghouse
http://www.calib.com/naic/
Adoption, search, online databases, calendar, catalog,
and other resources.

Rainbow Kids
http://www.rainbowkids.com/
An international adoption agency providing resources
for parents and kids who desire adoption.

African-Americans

A Dictionary of African Christian Biography
http://www.dacb.org/
A continuing online research project to develop a comprehensive history of Christianity in Africa.

Black Christian Concerns Group
http://www.ccbi.org.uk/bccg/BCCG.HTM
A UK-based site for predominantly black Christians, including Afro-Caribbean, African, and African-American Christians on worldwide social justice issues.

Genesis Now
http://www.genesisnow.com/aboutGN.html
The leading Christian Resource on the web for African-Americans.

other sites of interest

African-American History Links
http://www.aristotle.net/persistence/weblinks.htm
Links to museums, organizations, and archival information on various aspects of African-American history.

African-American Resources on the Web
http://www.sscnet.ucla.edu/caas/projects/aawebsites.html
Links to dozen of historical and cultural sites.

Afro-America Online
http://www.afroam.org
Afro news from around the world, cultural information, history, history museum, and kids zone for African-Americans sponsored by the Afro-American Newspaper Company.

Afro-American Almanac
http://www.toptags.com/aama
An extensive online presentation of black American history and culture.

Black Facts Online
http://www.blackfacts.com
Black history Internet resource and search engine for facts related to black history events and dates.

Black Voices
http://www.blackvoices.com
Community and national issues, news, shopping, career helps, media, entertainment, black history quiz, and features by noted black columnists.

BlackMind
http://www.blackmind.com
Site features words of wisdom, books, downloads, artwork and other issues targeted to African-Americans. Free webhosting, and more.

Blackworld
http://www.blackworld.com
Internet directory and metasearch engine on a variety of subjects from arts and culture to technology.

NAACP
http://www.naacp.org
Official website of the NAACP with news and information on current activities and issues, as well as historical facts.

NetNoir
http://www.netnoir.com
Site features news, black issues, and information and resources on music, film, television, features, and Club NetNoir.

The Black World Today
http://www.tbwt.com
Local interests, commentaries, calendar, news, forums, reviews, reports and exclusives on issues affecting the black community.

Animals

Butterfly Website
http://butterflywebsite.com/gallery/index.cfm
Butterfly needs, nature education, articles and information, photo gallery, public education, and chatroom.

Endangered Animals of the World
http://www.geocities.com/RainForest/Vines/1460/index.html
A display of some of the many endangered species around the world.

Frogland
http://allaboutfrogs.org/froglnd.shtml
Frog of the month, stupid frog joke of the day, cool froggy stuff, frog radio, and more.

National Wildlife Federation
http://www.nwf.org/
News and articles about endangered species. Great kid's zone, too.

Seaworld/Busch Gardens Animal Information Database
http://www.seaworld.org/
Hundreds of sites on sea and land animals full of great pictures and information.

Tarantula Planet
http://www.tarantulaplanet.org/
Fact and picture filled site on keeping tarantulas as pets.

Turtletopia
http://www.turtletopia.com/
Turtle facts, turtle photos, turtle news. Everything turtle.

Art

A Religious Christmas in Art
http://www.execpc.com/~tmuth/st_john/xmas/art.htm
An extensive collections of fine art depictions of the Nativity and related themes.

Asian Christian Art Association
http://www.asianchristianart.org/
Galleries, exhibitions and programs to expand the presence of art in Asian churches.

Images of Medieval Art and Architecture
http://www.pitt.edu/~medart/menufrance/chartres/charmain.html

Images and floor plans of France's Notre Dame Cathedral.

The Omnilist of Christian Art
http://members.aol.com/clinksgold/omnart.htm
Links to top sites featuring Christian artworks.

The Sistine Chapel
http://www.christusrex.org/www1/sistine/0-Tour.html
A virtual tour with commentary of the magnificent artwork in the Sistine Chapel.

other sites of interest

Art History Network
http://www.arthistory.net/
A portal to many web resources on Art, Archaeology and Architecture.

Art in Context
http://www.artincontext.com/
Search for a particular painting, artist, style or theme here.

Art Safari
http://artsafari.moma.org/
An adventure in looking for children and adults.

Artcyclopedia
http://www.artcyclopedia.com/
A search engine with a database of more than 7,000 artists and their works.

Louvre
http://www.louvre.fr/louvrea.htm
Site text in English, Spanish, and other languages. Palace and museum, activities, information, purchase tickets online, and more.

Metropolitan Museum of Art
http://www.metmuseum.org/home.asp
Collections, exhibitions, events, site index, search the site, and more.

Museum of Modern Art
http://www.moma.org
Information on the collections, special events, educational resources, art news, e-postcards, etc.

National Gallery of Art
http://www.nga.gov/
General information, collections, exhibitions, online tours, programs and events, gift shop, and more.

National Portrait Gallery
http://www.npg.org.uk/index.htm
London's famous museum online. Links to exhibitions, education, research, gifts, donations, and more.

Virtual Library Museums Page
http://www.icom.org/vlmp/
Links to museums in Africa, Japan, Russia, Canada, Luxembourg, Switzerland, USA, and the rest of the world.

WebMuseum Paris
http://metalab.unc.edu/wm/
Art exhibits from Paris museums, plus a virtual tour of Paris—historical guided tour or self-guided tour.

Asian-Americans

Asian-American Christian Counseling Service
http://www.aaccs.org/
A non-profit organization dedicated to bring emotional healing and preventative education to families.

The Asian-American Christian Fellowship
http://www.aacf.org/
Dedicated to reaching the university and college community of Asian-Americans and spread the word of God.

other sites of interest

Asian-American Resources
http://www-personal.umich.edu/~lwu/asian.html
Asian-American resource center on the Internet.

Asian-American Health
http://www.baylor.edu/~Charles_Kemp/
asian_health.html
Asian-American health resources and cross-cultural care
and prevention resources. Includes full discussion and
quick reference information.

AskAsia Homepage
http://www.askasia.org/
An online source for K-12 studies on Asia and Asian-
Americans

Auctions
Ccbid
http://www.ccbid.com/
A full service Internet auction site serving the needs of
the Christian community.

Christian Auction.com
http://www.christian-auction.com/
Auctions, classifieds, and business-to-business connec-
tions for Christians.

ChristianWholesale.com
http://www.christianretail.com
The Christian Business to Business auction site.

other sites of interest
Amazon.com Auctions
http://www.auctions.amazon.com
Auction site for consumer goods and products sponsored
by Amazon.com.

Auction Warehouse
http://auction-warehouse.com/
Online auction bidding for computers, electronics, office
products, and more.

eBay.com
http://www.ebay.com
Person-to-person online trading and auction community
for the nation's bargain hunters.

Excite Auctions
http://outletauctions.excite.com/
Brand names, bargains, and collectibles all up for auction.

GeoAuction.com
http://www.geoauction.com/
A complete listing of the best online auctions the web
has to offer.

GSA Auctions
https://www.gsaauctions.gov/index.htm
The place to buy Federal surplus items.

Internet Auction List
http://www.internetauctionlist.com/
Web portal to online auctions.

Little Deals.com
http://www.littledeals.com/
Auction site for new and used baby clothes, products
and accessories.

UBid
http://www.u-bid.com
Internet auction site for computer products, consumer
electronics, apparel, jewelry and gifts, sports, recreation,
and more.

Yahoo.com Auctions
http://auctions.yahoo.com
Auction site for consumer goods and products sponsored
by Yahoo.com.

Bible Study Helps

All-in-One Bible Resources Search
http://www.bham.ac.uk/theology/goodacre/multibib.htm
Bible resources, Bible versions and translations, general,
academic and religious resources.

Bible Study
http://biblestuph.com
Daily online Bible readings, Bible search, trivia, puzzles,
and links to daily devotions and other Christian resources.

B

Bible Study Aids from ChristiansUnite
http://christiansunite.com/resources/index.shtml
Collection of Bible study and pastoral resources, including commentaries, church history, devotionals, autobiographies, Bible dictionaries, and other writings.

Bible Study Games
http://www.biblestudygames.com/biblegames/trivia
Trivia quizzes, study tools, and games.

Bible Study Tools
http://www.biblestudytools.net/
Searchable Bible versions, commentaries, concordances, dictionaries, and more.

Bible Study with a Kid's Heart
http://akidsheart.com/bible/bible.htm
An introduction to Bible study for kids.

Discover Bible Guides
http://www.iiw.org/discover/
Free online studies from the world's oldest and largest Bible correspondence school.

FreeBibleResources.com
http://www.freebibleresources.com
Free access to studies, and the ability to upload your own studies (or links to studies) for others to use in their teaching and study of God's Word. Daily devotional resources are available both on-site and as daily email subscriptions.

Goshen Bible Study Tools
http://www.worldchristian.net/bibletools.html
A resource for in-depth study and exploration of God's Word.

Indwelt
http://www.indwelt.com
Site contains a variety of helps for Bible study, books reviews, and more.

Logos Bible Software
http://christiansoftware.com/Mainmenu.htm
Bible study software, special book collections, teaching tools, screen savers, games, clipart, and more.

Matthew Henry Commentary on the Whole Bible
http://www.apostolic.net/bible/mhc/index.html
Site features the complete (not concise) Matthew Henry Commentary on the whole Bible.

Search the Bible
http://www.thechristian.org/default2.asp
Search the Bible in several languages and versions.

Thomas Nelson Publishers
http://www.thomasnelson.com
Honoring God and serving people since 1798, Thomas Nelson is the largest publisher of Bibles and Christian books and gifts, and is the tenth largest general trade publisher.

Biography

A Dictionary of Early Christian Biography
http://www.ccel.org/w/wace/biodict/htm/i.htm
Online text of a large work covering the lives of Christian leaders through the Sixth Century.

Christian Biography
http://www.livingweb.com/library/209_2.htm
Links to hundreds of biographical sketches from the Bible to the present day.

Christian Biography Resources
http://www.wholesomewords.org/biography/bio.html
Links to many pages on Christian figures in history.

other sites of interest

Biographical Dictionary
http://www.s9.com/biography/index.html
Dictionary covers more than 28,000 notable men and women.

B

Biography
http://www.biography.com/
One of the web's largest biographical sites, with more than 25,000 entries, plus 2500 video clips. Offers weekly features, and historical moments. Updated frequently.

Biography Center
http://www.biography-center.com
Indexes over 10,000 bios available on the web.

Distinguished Women of Past and Present
http://www.distinguishedwomen.com
Biographies of women who contributed to our culture in many different ways.

Lives, the Biography Resource
http://amillionlives.com
Links to thousands of biographies, autobiographies, memoirs, diaries, letters, narratives, oral histories, and more.

Presidents of the United States
http://www.whitehouse.gov/history/presidents/index.html
Biographies of all the Presidents of the United States.

WIC Biography Index
http://www.wic.org/bio/idex_bio.htm
The Women's International Center lists biographies of significant men and women from A to Z.

Books

Aliveworld
http://www.aliveword.com
Christian bookstore where fellow believers can save 30% or more off of retail prices on Bibles, books, videos, teaching tapes, children's items, music.

Awesome Christian Bookstore
http://awesomebks.hypermart.net/best1.htm
Online shopping for Christian books and music, with a search engine to help find out of print titles.

Berean Christian Stores
http://www.bereanchristianstores.com
Homesite of the Berean chain, with purchase and store information, church links, and ministry links.

Best in Christian Books
http://www.reflectionpublishing.com
Book store features bestseller list, information for writers, Christian links and a variety of Christian books.

Bible Store.com
http://www.light-n-life.com
Bookstore recommending Bibles, Christian books, and music. A comparison of Bible versions and a year-long Bible reading plan.

Book Nook
http://www.whitebuckpublishing.com/wbp/booknook.htm
Store offers a select collection of books which include Bibles, classics, commentaries, devotionals, fiction and general interest.

Charisma Book Warehouse
http://www.charismawarehouse.com
Offers books relating to children's ministry, youth ministry, children's education, Sunday School and leadership training, along with bestsellers.

CheapReads
http://www.cheapreads.com/
Christian books at bargain prices.

Christian Book Closet
http://www.concordant.org/Index.html
Store buys and sells used Christian books, features book reviews, author information, and a variety of other Christian titles.

Christian Book Exhange
http://www.cbe1.co.uk/
Site offers large range of Christian literature, including new books, used books, Bibles, book reviews.

Christian Book.com
http://www.christianbook.com

Online home of Christian Book Distributors, based in
Peabody, MA, offering over 70,000 different Christian
books, videos, CDs, cassettes, gifts, toys, home school
and academic resources, games, and other resources for
kids. Also features author profiles.

Christian Books USA
http://www.christianbooksusa.com

Discount Christian bookstore offers most Christian titles. Also offers a separate site for visitors outside of
North America.

Christian Focus Publications
http://www.familycentral.net/pk.wcgi/homecent

Provides bestsellers, children's books, and information
on Christian booksellers conventions.

Christian House.com
http://www.christianhouse.com

Bibles, books, music, software, and videos, along with a
Christian chatroom.

Christian Mezzanine
http://www.his-net.com/html/bookstores.html

Resources for hundreds of Christian books, Bibles, gifts,
music, videos, movies, Bible software and games.

Christian Poetry and Prose Resources
http://www.telusplanet.net/public/kwalden/writeart.htm

Site offers articles, samples, resources for writers interested in poetry and prose, links to other sites and arts
index.

Cokesbury Bookstore Online
http://www.cokesbury.com

Online bookstore that offers information and descriptions of available products and resources. Cokesbury is a
division of the United Methodist Church.

Colpoteurs House
http://www.tchbooks.com/

Offers a database of book titles searchable by author, title or keyword. Selections include devotionals/prayer,

Christian living, humor, reference, ethical investing, and pastoral care/counseling.

Encouraging Word Bookstore
http://www.ewbooks.com
Site offers Bibles, marriage and family books, music, videos, audio selections and apparel.

Faith and Grace
http://www.faithandgrace.com
Sells a vast selection of over 5,000 Bibles, including reference, print, electronic, audio and Bible software from over 60 vendors. Offers Bibles from Holman, Kirkbride, Nelson, Oxford, Tyndale, Word, World, and Zondervan.

Family Christian Stores
http://www.familychristian.com
Online bookstore sells the latest in Christian books, music, gifts, software, materials for children.

First Net Christian
http://www.firstnetchristian.com
Site offers best-selling Christian books, bargains, various kinds of Bibles, study resources, along with gifts and music.

Great Christian Books
http://www.greatchristianbooks.com/indexx.html
The best in Christian literature for the entire family.

Hallelujah Kids
http://www.hallelujahkids.com
Bookstore aimed at children offering Christian games, books, Bibles, kids' question area, and baby gifts.

Honor Books
http://www.honorbooks.com/
New releases, bestselling titles, product overview, exclusive brands, seasonal products, wholesale, and more.

Inspirational Media
http://www.inspirationalmedia.com
Online store specializes in Bibles, Bible commentaries, biographies, children's bestsellers, Christian literature and reference material. Also offers a number of free books.

James Drummond Used Books
http://www.jamesdrummond.co.uk
A variety of used Christian books and booklets available. Search for titles by author. Site also lists information about condition of the books.

Kregel Christian Books and Resources
http://www.gospelcom.net/kregel/
Offers more than 200,000 used books and other theological books and church resources, publications.

LifeWay Stores
http://www.lifewaystores.com/
Reviews of new releases, customer assistance, special services, search, store locations, and more.

Master Christian Library
http://www.online-bible.com/master_christian_library.html
CD-ROM product containing multiple volumes of Christian literature on 2 CDs.

Nelson Reference Books
http://www.nelsonreference.com/cgi-bin/SoftCart.exe/Home.html?E+catalog
Browse through the catalog of best-selling reference books and software. Site features free software, a daily devotional, free newsletter, and more.

Nelson/Word Direct
http://www.nelsonword.com/cgi-bin/SoftCart.exe/Home.html?E+catalog
Order Nelson/Word products online, register your Nelson software, and other links.

Only Believe Christian Book Distributors
http://www.onlybelieveonline.com
Variety of Christian books available on children, family, marriage, devotional, reference, study, ministry, and more.

Rare Christian Books
http://www.rarechristianbooks.com
Distributor and publisher of Christian books, particularly old conservative Christian books not available at modern Christian bookstores.

Renewal Christian Books
http://www.renewalcbm.com
Site features praise and worship CDs and books that encourage believers to be all that Jesus intends.

Virtual Christianity
http://www.internetdynamics.com/pub/vc/bibles.html
A comprehensive list of online English and foreign Bibles with a short description. Also introductory guidelines on reading the Bible also.

WorthyBooks
http://www.worthybooks.com
Sells top Christian bestsellers, Bibles, study resources, books for children, and gifts, along with music, and videos.

other sites of interest

Abebooks
http://www.abebooks.com
Search or browse for rare, used, and out-of-print books.

Alibris
http://www2.alibris.com/cgi-bin/texis/bookstore
Books you never thought you'd find from thousands of retailers at one source.

Amazon.com
http://www.amazon.com
This Seattle-based company sells and distributes books, music, DVDs, and sheet music, and more.

Barnes and Noble Online
http://www.barnesandnoble.com
Links to ebooks, music, ecards, prints and posters, software, and more.

Bartleby—Great Books Online
http://www.bartleby.com/index.html
Search through reference, verse, fiction, and nonfiction. Featured author, quote of the day, bookstore, and more.

B

Bibliofind
http://www.bibliofind.com
A major search engine for rare and out-of-print books.

Bonnie's Better Books
http://www.galaxymall.com/books/betterbooks
Online store offers a variety of wholesome children's books and literature.

Book Closeouts
http://www.bookcloseouts.com
Browse by author or publisher, bargains, catalogs, and more.

Book Pricer
http://www.bookpricer.com/
Find and compare prices on American or British books, in print or out of print.

Book Radar
http://www.bookradar.com
Search, compare, and buy books from all the major new and used book dealers.

Book Sale Finder
http://www.book-sales-in-america.com/
Click on your state and find the book sales, book fairs and auctions in your area.

Chicken Soup for the Soul
http://www.chickensoup.com/
Chicken Soup books, online stories, send in a story, speakers, seminars, and daily email signup.

HarperChildrens.com
http://www.harperchildrens.com/
Website for leading children's publisher with previews, contests and articles just for kids.

Meta Directory for the Omega 23 Books Page
http://www.omega23.com/Reference/
Links to art and artists, biographies, computers, economics, health, medicine, history, literature, music, math, science, and more.

Powell's Books
http://www.powells.com
Sale books, top twenty, rare book room, staff picks, events, and free stuff, plus much more.

Businesses

(see also Financial Information and Business Opportunities)

350+ Christian Businesses
http://www.christianet.com/christianbusinesses/
The Christian Businesses Directory is designed to assist Christians in locating products and services.

Banners4Jesus
http://banners4jesus.homestead.com/index.html
Custom-made worship banners and kits, lift up the name of Jesus indoors and out.

BBBOnLine
http://www.bbbonline.org
Better Business Bureau information for consumers and businesses.

Christian Advertising Network
http://www.christianadvertising.net
Christian Internet marketing advertising promotion using click throughs, banners, buttons, affiliates, newsletters, opt in email address lists, shopping links, etc.

Christian Business Directory
http://www.christianweb.org/direct.htm
Christian directory for businesses and ministry organizations. Contains links to Christian businesses.

Christian Business Mall
www.christianbusinessmall.com
A place for Christian businesses of integrity from A to Z.

Christian Business Marketplace
http://www.cbmarketplace.com
Homesite of the Christian Business Marketplace.

Christian Business Opportunities
  http://www.christianet.com/christianjobs/
  businessopp+.htm
  Christian business opportunities and jobs posted by
  Christian business opportunity companies across the
  United States.

Christian eBuy
  http://www.christianebuy.com/index.html
  A new online Christian business directory.

Christian Retailing
  http://www.christianretailing.com/
  An online magazine with news and advice for the Christian businessperson.

Findchristian.com
  http://www.findchristian.com/
  A service designed to help people locate businesses,
  groups, organizations, churches, etc. that follow and
  adhere to Christian beliefs.

Have Your Own Online Christian Bookstore
  http://www.majestee.com/bookstore/books.htm
  Business opportunity for online bookstore.

Charities

Christian Disaster Response International
  http://www.cdresponse.org/
  An international non-denominational disaster relief program.

Church World Service
  http://www.churchworldservice.org/
  Working in over 80 countries to relieve poverty, aid in development, provide emergency relief and assistance to refugees.

Compassion International
  http://www.ci.org/
  Program is Christ-centered through local churches to aid children in need.

Mission Without Borders
http://www.mwb-us.org/
A Christian nonprofit organization caring for people economically and spiritually.

Salvation Army
http://www.salvationarmy.org/
Operates in over 100 countries offering a wide range of social, medical, educational, and other community services.

World Concern
http://www.worldconcern.org/
An international Christian relief and development organization serving more than four million people in 27 countries each year.

World Vision International
http://www.wvi.org/
An international partnership of Christians working with the poor and oppressed.

other sites of interest

Breast Cancer Site
http://www.thebreastcancersite.com/cgi-bin/ WebObjects/CTDSites
Just click to donate for mammograms.

CARE
http://www.care.org/
10 agencies that deliver relief to over 63 countries each year.

FindIt
http://www.findit.org/html/fund_raising.html
Use their search engine to find information on over 50,000 foundations and grant-giving organizations.

FreeDonation.com
http://www.freedonation.com
Charity organizations fighting AIDS, cancer, hunger, and homelessness. Others receive support from sponsors when the site is visited.

Humanitarian Site
http://www.thehumanitariansite.org
Volunteer facts, frequently-asked questions, press and
media information, donations to date, contact information, and more.

Hunger Site
http://www.thehungersite.com
Donate to the fight against hunger, links to sponsors,
how you can help.

Make a Wish Foundation
http://www.wish.org/
The organization that has granted more than 73,000
wishes to sick and dying children around the world.

Operation Blessing
http://www.ob.org/index.asp
Providing short-term relief and development assistance
to economically disadvantaged people and victims of disaster throughout the world.

Rainforest Site
http://www.therainforestsite.com
Click on the icon to donate 16.2 square feet of land to
rainforest conservation, paid for by corporate sponsors.

Red Cross
http://www.redcross.org/
Provides disaster care, nursing, supplies, health care,
safety courses, and more on a worldwide basis to those
in need.

Second Harvest
http://www.secondharvest.org/
The largest hunger relief organization in the U.S.

Starlight Foundation
http://www.starlight.org/home.htm
Brightening the lives of seriously ill children by granting
wishes and providing entertainment to over 55,000 children each month.

Chatrooms

(see also Message Forums; Online Communities; Portal Sites)

711 Chat Café
http://www.cchat.net/
Christian chat network with rooms for kids and teens.

ABC AGC Christian Chat
http://netins.net/showcase/petpalace
Christian Bible study, Bible trivia, chat, Christian music links, etc.

Adult Christian Forum
http://www.delphi.com/kath
Christian discussions and Bible study with Christian chat rooms.

Bobbarooni Christian Chat
http://sites.netscape.net/bobthetomato40/bobarooni
Site features access to java based, monitored Christian chatroom. Site also offers links to other informative and inspirational sites.

Catspaws Spring-fed Well
http://www.catspaw.cjb.net
This Christian site features chatroom, prayer/testimonies message board, greetings, and links to other Christian sites.

Child of God Christian Chat
http://www.lodinet.com/webworks/cog/chat1.html
A monitored Christian chat room for fellowship, prayer and counseling.

ChristChat Network
http://www.holyscriptures.com/christchat.html
Christian chat membership network.

Christian Chat
http://www.christianchat.co.uk/
A global chat network for Christians with numerous categories.

Christian Chat Rooms
http://www.christianchatrooms.com/
Dozens of subjects, with special areas for teens and singles.

Christian Chat Rooms
http://www.churchusa.com/chat.shtml
Chat rooms for teens, Bible study, family talk, singles, prayer, music, and more.

Christians Online
http://conline.net
Site features interactives, chat rooms, message boards, testimonials, electronic postcards, an online arcade, resources, readings, and more.

Renewed Christian Chat
http://www.maxpages.com/renewchat
A place where believers can come for great fellowship and renewal.

The Christian Chat Network, Inc.
http://www.christian-chat.net/howto.htm
An IRC (Internet Relay Chat) for the Christian community.

UpWord Online Ministries Christian Chat
http://www.upword.org
Features coffee-lounge chat, and singles chat, and a Bible search engine.

Wilibrord's Christian Chat Sites
http://members.tripod.com/~Erala/chat.html
Links to numerous Christian chat rooms, and to other subjects as well.

Children

(see also Education, Families, Entertainment, Games, Homeschooling, and Youth)

At-Home Ministry
http://www.burlingtonpres.org/athome
Mazes, coloring, dot-to-dots, crossword puzzles and other activities that enable children to learn basic Christian messages while having fun at home.

Bible Birthday Party
http://www.biblebirthdayparty.com
Homesite for Bible Birthday Parties, with lessons and invitations to make your child's next birthday fun and an evangelistic outreach.

Christian Children's Page
http://www.cybercom.net/~ctm/
Facts and fun centered around God's word.

Christian Kid's Fun and Games On Line
http://www.angelfire.com/mt/BibleTruths/KidsFun.html
Hey Christian kids! Are you looking for a fun site to play safe games? Then this is the place for you. Many things to see and do. Safe surf site. Ages 1–10 years. It is worth a peek!

Christian Kids Links
http://home.netministries.org/kids.htmls
Christian kids' links, fun, educational stories, and much more.

GospelSoft—Bible software for Christian families
http://www.gospelsoft.com/christn/index.htm
Educational software for children and adults that reinforce positive Christian traits.

Just for Fun
http://www.geocities.com/EnchantedForest/Tower/9438/currentissue.html
An electronic magazine with a Christian focus for kids.

Keys for Kids
http://www.gospelcom.net/cbh/kfk/kfk.shtml
A daily devotional for children. Previous days' devotions are available to read as well as the current day.

Kidz Blitz
http://www.kidzblitz.com
Children's ministry and family events featuring games and challenges that illustrate the truths from God's word.

Links to Other Christian Games
http://www.oursalvation.com/links_games.htm
A list of Bible games for kids.

The Worldwide Christian Children's Website
http://church-of-christ.org/shrock/
Children's ministry with games, activities and bulletins
that teach Scripture.

other sites of interest

Enchanted Learning
http://www.enchantedlearning.com/
Dozens of projects for all ages, with hundreds of links.

FreeZone for Kids
http://www.freezone.com/
Links to advice, pop culture, sports, brainstorm, fun and
games, and more.

Gus Town
http://www.gustown.com/home/gustownsummer.html
Links to post office, toys, museum, library, café, cyber-
bud club, and more.

Headbone Zone
http://www.headbone.com
Links to friends, games, features, news, and more.

Kid's Domain—KIDS
http://www.kidsdomain.com/kids.html
Links to brain builders, holidays, online games, surf
safe, play place, and more.

Kid Positive
http://www.kidpositive.com
Feature stories, message boards, cultural entertainment,
games and activities, mailing list, weekly Webtoon, science, and other fun and educational activities for kids.

Kids' Space
http://www.kids-space.org
Submit drawings, story book, craft room, and more.

Otto Club
http://www.ottoclub.org
A safe place to play, coloring pages, and games for kids.

Christian Living

(see also Bible Study, Devotionals)

2001 ChristianBest Resource Index
http://christianbest.com
A comprehensive listing of Christian sites in a startling number of categories for both the average surfer and those looking to do research.

Born Again Network
http://www.bornagain.net
A website and chat server dedicated to Christianity. Worship daily and pray nightly in the main chatroom and fellowship through the web on the message boards. Also provides a great singles match-making service!

Christsite
http://www.christsite.com/home.htm
Membership site with resources, prayer, missions, and more for daily growth.

FaithSeekers
http://www.faithseekers.com/
Links to youths, music, devotion, and more on this Christian living website.

Gospel Trail Christian Resource Center
http://www.gospeltrail.com/
Links to hundreds of sites of interest to Christians.

JesusLovesU, Entrance Into the Lord's Holy Presence.
http://JLU.faithweb.com/
This site serves Christians and non-Christians. It includes, music, prayer, salvation, Bible study schedules, interesting links.

Peggie's Place
http://gospelcom.net/peggiesplace
Links to Christian pages, pastoral and Bible study pages, homeschooling, graphics, website building tips.

Waves of Glory!
http://www.geocities.com/SouthBeach/Pointe/9744
Articles, children's section, church history section, free newsletter, message boards, missions section, praise and worship section, prophetic insights and words, revival section, link, and more!

Wholesome Words
http://www.wholesomewords.org/
Family site with devotions and inspiration for children or parents.

Clipart and Downloads
(see also Art)

3D Revelations
http://lightning.prohosting.com/~noahweb/
Free Christian graphics, animated gifs, backgrounds, crosses, and clipart.

Animations Graphics Clipart
http://whytehouse.com
A Christian site offering free clipart, graphics, animations, screensavers, javascripts, java applets, MIDIs, etc.

Carol's Christian Graphics
http://www.fortunecity.com/millennium/newchurch/398/index.html
Free Christian graphics.

CFI: Free Christian Images
http://www.fci.crossnet.se/
Clipart, wallpaper and downloads with varied Christian themes.

ChristArt
http://www.christart.com/
Many selections in numerous Christian oriented categories.

Christ-Centered Graphics
http://www.giversministry.org/ccg/
Free Christian graphics, including backgrounds, sets, images, clipart, and text.

Christian Computer Art
http://www.CC-Art.com/
Over 6000 high quality clipart, line art, and color pictures.

Christian Graphics
*http://www.totalsurf.com/graphics/
christiangraphics.htm*
Christian graphics, clipart and icons with a huge wallpaper and screen saver collection.

Christian World Index Clipart
http://www.atlanticchristian.org/world/Clipart/
Comprehensive list of Christian clipart sites on the web. Bible text related, biblical themes, animations, icons, and miscellaneous.

Michele's Christian ClipArt
http://www.mcele.com/clip.htm
Christian clipart, animations, and backgrounds for personal or commercial use.

Spirit Christian Graphics
http://www.geocities.com/heartland/bluffs/5988/
Offers free original Scripture images for homesites.

The Omnilist of Christian Art
http://members.aol.com/clinksgold/omnart.htm
Links to top sites featuring Christian clipart and downloads.

wwjdpage free clipart
http://wwjdfree.homestead.com/index.html
Free WWJD Christian clipart for a website or homepage.

other sites of interest

Amazing Screen Savers
http://www.amazingscreensavers.com/
Download animal, cartoon, celebrity, holiday, nature, sports, and other screen savers.

Icon Bazaar
http://www.iconbazaar.com/
Animated icon clipart, as well as other categories of clipart: banners, arrows, cartoons, flags, molecules, road signs, and many more.

Web ClipArt

http://webclipart.about.com/internet/design/webclipart/mbody.htm

Links to chat, post a bulletin, and subjects from alphabets to web basics.

Clubs/Organizations

YMCA

http://www.ymca.int/

A worldwide Christian, ecumenical organization for men and women with an emphasis on youth and family.

other sites of interest

American Association of Retired Persons (AARP)

http://www.aarp.org

A nonprofit membership organization devoted to providing benefits for older Americans.

American Legion

http://www.legion.org/

The world's largest veteran's organization website.

Boy Scouts of America

http://www.bsa.scouting.org/

Questions and answers about scouting, scout history, shopping, news, etc.

Boys and Girls Clubs of America

http://www.bgca.org/

A safe place for kids to learn and grow. Find out here about their programs.

Campfire Boys and Girls

http://www.campfire.org

For 90 years Campfire has helped kids learn to grow and play together.

Girl Scouts of America

http://www.gsusa.org/

Questions and answers about scouting, scout history, shopping, news, etc.

Habitat for Humanity
http://www.habitat.org
Activities and information on international organization dedicated to making home ownership possible for those who otherwise would not.

Mothers Against Drunk Driving (MADD)
http://www.madd.org/aboutmad/default.shtml
Group dedicated to effective solutions to the drunk driving and underage drinking problems.

National 4-H Council
http://www.fourhcouncil.edu/
Information and links to the national youth development organization.

National Center for Missing and Exploited Children
http://www.missingkids.com
The official website for the organization dedicating to helping locate and retrieve missing and abducted children. Site includes child photo search, educational resources, success stories, news, and more.

Special Olympics
http://www.specialolympics.org/
Find out how to participate in the games, where the games are located, how to be a sponsor, and more.

Computers/Hardware

Christian Hardware
http://www.wordnet.co.uk/comphd.html
British Christian computer company offering honest advice and competitive prices.

Worldwide Computer Services
http://truthisblessing.com/wcs
Christian computer service to business/home networking.

other sites of interest

Adobe
http://www.adobe.com/
Graphic design, imaging, dynamic media, and authoring tools software enable customers to create, publish,

and deliver visually-rich content for various types of
media.

Apple Computer, Inc.
http://www.apple.com
Homesite for Apple/Macintosh computers peripherals,
etc.

Ask a Computer Expert
http://www.askme.com/cat/showcategory_483_hm_1.htm
Get detailed answers to your questions from real people
at no cost to you. Users also may share their expertise
with others to win cash.

Compaq
http://www.compaq.com
Homesite for Compaq computers peripherals, etc.

Computer Hardware Performance Page
http://www.cam.org/cam_org_eng/index.html
Site helps users to help gauge their hardware performance. Benchmark mania, video accelerators,
motherboards and updated news and information.

Dell Computers
http://www.dell.com
Dell offers custom configuration of personal computers,
portables and servers. Build your own PC—get the best
value with latest technology—order online.

Epson America, Inc.
http://www.epson.com/home.shtml
Homesite for Epson computer technology.

Gateway 2000
http://www.gw2k.com
Homesite for Gateway computers, peripherals, etc.

Guide to Computer Vendors
http://guide.sbanetweb.com
Links to thousands of the hardware and software vendors. In addition, lists of hundreds of other computer
companies on VARs. Added reseller links!

Hardware One
http://www.hardware-one.com
Site contains computer news and reviews with daily updates.

Hewlett-Packard Co.
http://www.hp.com
Homesite for Hewlett Packard computers, peripherals, etc. for home, home office, and small business.

IBM Corp.
http://www.ibm.com
Homesite for IBM computers, peripherals, etc.

InternetProductWatch.com:
http://ipw.internet.com
Internet computer hardware, software product reviews and information.

Lexmark
http://www.lexmark.com
Homesite for Lexmark computer peripherals.

Microsoft Corp
http://www.microsoft.com
Homesite for Microsoft, Inc.

NEC Corp.
http://www.nec.com
Homesite for NEC computer technology, etc.

Packard Bell,Inc.
http://www.packardbell.com
Homesite for Packard Bell computers, peripherals, etc.

PC Computer Reviews
http://www.smartcomputing.com
The magazine answers personal computing questions, including troubleshooting advice articles, computer hardware reviews, computer software reviews, tips guide, and tutorial help with personal computers.

PEP National Directory of Computer Recycling Programs
*http://www.microweb.com/pepsite/Recycle/
recycle_index.html*

PEP (Parents, Educators and Publishers) national directory of computer recycling programs and agencies that facilitate donations of used computer hardware for schools and community.

Sun Microsystems Inc.
http://www.sun.com
Homesite for Sun Microsystems computer technology, etc.

Symantec
http://enterprisesecurity.symantec.com/Default.cfm?PID=na
Product info, reviews, support, resource centers, service and support, and more.

TipWorld
http://www.tipworld.com
Site offers free daily tips, expert advice, email news, and free email newsletter.

User Evaluations of On-Line Computer Hardware Vendors
http://www.resellerratings.com
This survey includes evaluations of over 600 mail-order/Internet PC Hardware merchants, performed by over 5,500 Internet users to date.

Computers Software

Bible Believers Fellowship, Inc.—Christian Screen Savers
http://www.prisonministry.org/screensavers/saver.htm
Freeware and shareware religious screensavers with Scriptures from King James Version in English or Spanish.

Bibles Online Directory
http://www.angelfire.com/mt/BibleTruths/Bibles.html
A range of Bibles that you can download from the Internet.

CEBible for Windows
http://www.slsoftware.com
Entire Bible on your handheld Windows PC in NIV, NASB, KJV, and ASV.

Christian Shareware
http://shareware.crosswalk.com/ReferenceMaterial/
Christian shareware in categories: reference, Christian games, study tools, Bible translations, and more.

CVS Network Free Services
http://www.cvsnetwork.com/free
Free Internet evangelism tools, Christian web puzzles, referral service, and more.

E4 Group
http://www.e4.net/
Free giveaways of Logos library system Bible study software.

Free Bibles
http://members.spree.com/sip/fbible/ea1.htm
Downloadable Bibles (including in Greek).

FREE Computer Bibles!
http://kingdomnet.com/freebibles/
A collection of free Bibles to use on your computer. Each is rated, reviewed, and includes links to download, homepage, screen shots, etc.

Free Christian Software Directory
http://www.seriousd.com/freeware.htm
Dozens of links to sources for free Christian software.

Free Scriptures Screen Saver
http://www.prisonministry.org/screensavers/saver_free.htm
Religious freeware screensaver contains 12 pictures including scenics, random transitional special effects, 2 MIDI files for background Christian music with sound enable/disable. Scriptures are from Old and New Testaments of the King James Bible.

Gospel Soft
http://www.gospelsoft.com/christn/index.htm
Quality Christian software for family and children.

other sites of interest

Annoyances.org
http://www.annoyances.org/
Computer problems? This site has plenty of tips to improve performance.

Bug Net
http://www.bugnet.com/
Links and articles on computer bugs from a leading debugging company. Search, report a bug, FAQs, and order online.

Cyberian Outpost
http://www.chambec.com/outpost/index.html
Virtual computer store which has expanded its wares to include over 130,000 items both for PC and MAC .

Jumbo
http://www.jumbo.com/
Thousands of free and "shareware" for PCs and MACs.

MacCentral Online
http://www.maccentral.com/
Macintosh software, shopping, games, and book guide.

MacHome
http://www.machome.com/
Interactive news, software center, downloads, product reviews, and more.

MacWarehouse
http://www2.warehouse.com/default.asp?home=mac
PC and Macintosh products, networking, and supplies.

Opera Web Browser
http://www.operasoftware.com/special.html
Special software to increase computer accessibility to the disabled.

Search 4 Free Stuff
www.search4free.com
A fully-loaded searchable freebie directory including most standard topics plus: what's new, what's cool, top 10 sites, and most popular listings.

Consumer Information

Better Business Bureau System
http://www.bbb.org/
Check out a company or file a complaint. Learn to protect yourself and your family from scams.

Blacklist of Internet Advertisers
http://math-www.uni-paderborn.de/~axel/BL/
blacklist.html
Who are the junk emailers and spammers, and what you can do to stop them.

Consumer Review
http://www.consumerreview.com/cr1
Comparative reviews and ratings of a wide variety of products.

Consumer World
http://www.consumerworld.org/
Product reviews, price comparisons and bargains and news for the informed consumer.

Federal Consumer Information Center
http://www.pueblo.gsa.gov/
Hundreds of publications to order (for free) or read on line. Special kid's pages, too.

National Fraud Information Center
http://www.fraud.org/
National Consumers League site dedicated to Internet fraud.

Safety Alerts
http://www.safetyalerts.com/
Do you own a dangerous product? Find out here, and find out what to do about it.

U.S. Consumer Gateway
http://www.consumer.gov/
A portal to government sources of information vital to consumers.

U.S. Consumer Product Safety Commission
http://www.cpsc.gov/
Product recall notices, complaint procedures and advice
for kids.

U.S. Postal Inspection Service
http://www.framed.usps.com/postalinspectors/
What you can do about mail fraud.

Crafts

(see also Hobbies and Collectibles, Needlework, Sewing)

Christian Crafting
http://www.geocities.com/Heartland/6580/
Showcase, forums, resources, links and a newsletter for
the Christian crafter.

Danielle's Place of Crafts and Activities
http://www.daniellesplace.com
Craft and activity resources for Sunday school, VBS, and
homeschoolers. Teaching children about God through
crafts and activities.

Making a Difference (Crocheting for Christ)
http://ads.xoasis.com/rotate.pl
An all-volunteer program to provide homemade blankets
to premature and low birth- weight infants.

other sites of interest

Arts N Crafts
http://www.inmotion-pcs.com/amass/theboss/artsn.htm
Lots of craft ideas, most of which can be done by pre-
schoolers.

Aunt Annie's Crafts
http://www.auntannie.com/
Craft software, web books, downloads, and products.

Bluebonnet Village Craft Network
http://www.bluebonnetvillage.com
Provides a craft network of find suppliers, kids projects,
news, and information on crafting and the craft business.

ChildFun.com
http://www.childfun.com/hot.html
Ideas for family activities on dozens of subjects.

Craft Outlet
http://craftoutlet.com/projects.htm
Projects and crafts for all seasons.

Craft Sites
http://www.craftsites.com/
Home decorating, fabric crafts, country candles, and teddy bears.

Crafter's Community
http://crafterscommunity.com/
Chatroom, discussion boards, craft projects, instructions, and resources.

Crafts.org
http://www.crafts.org/
Books, craft shop, ads, tutorials, and events.

Crafts Galore
http://www.massachusetts.net/nozzle/crafts
Craft links galore on this huge site for parents looking to create fun for the kids or experienced crafters looking for supplies.

Crafts Index
http://www.familyfun.com/filters/mainindex/ crafts.html
Project ideas for the whole family, from Family Fun Magazine.

Creative Crafts
http://www.ideacraft.com
Crafts for all seasons.

Family Crafts
http://craftsforkids.miningco.com/mbody.htm
Crafts for kids, craft project index, chatroom, newsletter, and membership.

Free Craft Projects Depot
http://www.angelfire.com/on2/freecraftprojects
Offers links to sites with free craft projects.

Hands On: Crafts for Kids
http://www.crafts4kids.com/helping.htm
Projects, book order, and message board.

Jana's Craft Connection
http://www.wyomingcompanion.com/janacraft
Easy craft ideas and lots of links.

Mary's Crafts
http://www.net5000.com/crafts
Craft news and reviews. Mary answers craft questions in a public forum. Links to craft sites and free craft classified ads.

Top 100 Crafts Sites
http://crafters.net/cgi/topvlog.cgi?944041965
A directory of links to sites on crafts of all kinds.

Cultures

English and Foreign Bibles Online To Use
http://www.angelfire.com/mt/BibleTruths/Bibles.html
Bibles available to use on the Internet in every language in the world. Also includes free download of over 100 different Bible programs for your home computer.

History, Culture, and Christian Heritage Links
http://ic.net/~erasmus/RAZ32.HTM
Information on the effects the infusion of different cultures have had on the Christian faith in England.

The Global Gang
http://www.globalgang.org.uk/
An introduction for kids to the world around us from Christian Aid.

other sites of interest

Bowers Kidseum
http://www.nativecreative.com/kidseum/frames.html
An interactive museum introducing kids to cultures from around the world.

Cultural Connections
http://library.advanced.org/50055/index.shtml
Click on the world map and take a virtual tour of dozens of countries.

Culture Finder
http://www.culturefinder.com
Search engine of cultural events by date, city, event name, composer, or organization.

Cultures.com
http://www.cultures.com/
Devoted to cultures, modern and ancient, and the promotion of world communication.

Exploring Ancient World Cultures
http://eawc.evansville.edu/
Extensive site with information and photographs divided by region.

Multiculturalpedia
http://www.netlaputa.ne.jp/~tokyo3/e/
What we do alike, and what we do differently around the world, from sneezing to weddings, and more!

United States of American History
http://www.neta.com/~1stbooks/index.html
Links to Hispanic-American cultural sites.

Dictionaries and Encyclopedias

Baker's Evangelical Dictionary
http://www.biblestudytools.net/Dictionaries/
BakersEvangelicalDictionary/
Use the searchable database to look up the meanings of Christian words and terms.

Catholic Encyclopedia
http://newadvent.org/cathen/
Search the Catholic Encyclopedia and other links.

Easton's Bible Dictionary
http://www.monastereo.com/dictionary/
Contextual definitions of over 3,000 words.

Hitchcock's Bible Names Dictionary
*http://www.biblestudytools.net/Dictionaries/
HitchcockBibleNames/*
Look up meanings of biblical names.

King James Dictionary
*http://bible.crosswalk.com/Dictionaries/
KingJamesDictionary/*
Features 800 words that have changed in meaning since
the King James translation of 1611.

Smith's Bible Dictionary
*http://www.biblestudytools.net/Dictionaries/
SmithsBibleDictionary/*
Search one of the most famous Bible dictionaries.

other sites of interest

American Heritage Dictionary
http://bartleby.com/61/
Search over 350,000 entries and word meanings.

Answer Sleuth's Encyclopedias
http://www.find11.com/words/e/encyclopedias.shtml
Links to encyclopedic information on a variety of topics.

Children's Dictionaries and Encyclopedias
*http://aabra-kadaabra.com/
dictionaries-and-encyclopedias.htm*
Dictionaries, encyclopedias, games, cartoons, and other
information for kids.

Columbia Encyclopedia
http://www.bartleby.com/65/
Full text online and searchable.

CompConsult
http://compconsultant.com/Reference.htm
Dictionaries, encyclopedias, and other reference sites.

Encyberpedia
http://www.encyberpedia.com/cyberlinks/links/
Links to dozens of categories of information online.

Encyclopedia Brittanica
http://www.britannica.com/
Searchable site for magazines, books, and the complete *Encyclopedia Brittanica.*

Encyclopedia.com
http://encyclopedia.com
Online database and search engine sponsored by Electric Library. Site contains alphabetical listing of over 14,000 articles from the *Concise Columbia Electronic Encyclopedia,* Third Edition.

Fact Monster
http://www.factmonster.com/
Dictionary, encyclopedia, atlas, almanac and other homework resources.

Funk and Wagnalls Online Encyclopedia
http://www.funkandwagnalls.com/
Searchable encyclopedias, dictionaries, thesaurus, atlas, and much more.

OneLook Dictionaries
http://www.onelook.com
A search engine and database of over 3 million words in over 600 dictionaries.

Pedro's Dictionaries
http://www.public.iastate.edu/~pedro/dictionaries.html
English, multilingual, and a variety of foreign language dictionaries.

Research-It
http://www.itools.com/research-it/
Wide variety of searchable dictionaries and language tools, including a translator.

Schoolwork.org
http://www.schoolwork.org/encyc.html
Links to online encyclopedias.

Thesaurus.com
http://www.thesaurus.com
An online thesaurus, dictionary and search engine. Site also includes crossword puzzles, categorial outline, translator, alphabetical index, and more.

THOR: The Online Resource
http://thorplus.lib.purdue.edu/reference
An award-winning, virtual reference desk sponsored by
Purdue University, with links to a variety of dictionaries,
almanacs, thesauri, maps, government documents, phone
books, travel information, and general works on science
and information technology.

Webster's Dictionary
http://work.ucsd.edu:5141/cgi-bin/http_webster
Webster's Dictionary online.

WordCentral.com
http://www.wordcentral.com
An online *Merriam-Webster®* dictionary with daily
buzzword and teacher resources as well as other homework helps.

Wordsmyth English Dictionary-Thesaurus
http://www.lightlink.com/bobp/wedt/wedt-artfl.html
Search and find the meaning, pronunciation, and usage
of words.

Disabilities

D.E.A.F. for Christ
http://www.d-e-a-f.com
Site for Deaf Evangelical Agencies for Christ—a coalition of organizations serving the deaf community.
Site contains links to information about affiliated agencies.

Prospects
http://www.prospects.org.uk/
A British Christian voluntary organization that values
and supports people with learning disabilities.

Visually Impaired
http://www.wels.net/sab/csm/see.html
A wide variety of doctrinal study and other Christian materials for the visually impaired.

other sites of interest

Access 20/20
http://www.access2020.com/
Directories to online purchasing of Braille documents, audio recordings, and more.

All DisABILITY Links
http://www.eskimo.com/~jlubin/disabled/all.htm
Hundreds of links of interest to those with disabilities.

Amyotrophic Lateral Sclerosis Association
http://www.alsa.org/
Resources, referrals, information, links, and more.

Asperger Syndrome Coalition
http://www.asperger.org
Nonprofit organization committed to providing the most up-to-date information on Asperger Syndrome available.

Big Pages of Special Education Links
http://www.mts.net/~jgreenco/special.html
Links to websites with information for the handicapped.

Blindness Resource Center
http://www.nyise.org/blind.htm
Directories to organizations and universities with braille programs.

Bobby
http://www.cast.org/bobby
Links to download Bobby—a program that rates a website's accessibility for the disabled.

Cerebral Palsy
http://www.speechtx.com/cpalsy/cp.htm
Simple explanations of the complex disease known as cerebral palsy.

Children's Vision Concerns
http://www.el-dorado.ca.us/~lois/
Site dedicated to addressing needs of blind and visually-impaired children.

Cystic Fibrosis Foundation
http://www.cff.org/
News, facts, research, publications, donate, get involved, and more.

Deaf Resource Library
http://www.deaflibrary.org
An online collection of reference material and links intended to educate and inform people about deaf cultures in Japan and the United States.

Developmental Disabilities Resources
http://www.mcare.net/resourcA.htm
News, references, resources, and more.

Disabilities Information Resources
http://www.dinf.org/
A nonprofit corporation that collects information on disabilities and related subjects and makes it available on the web.

Disability Central
http://disabilitycentral.com/activeteen/
A place for disabled teens to find encouragement, a new disabled teen ezine, and more.

Disability News Service
http://www.disabilitynews.com/
News site that is Bobby-approved, and accessible to the disabled.

Disability Pages
http://disabilityinfo.org.au/dir0146/div/
divsite.nsf/pages/
Links to disability information, including fast facts on disabilities.

Internet Resources for Special Children
http://www.irsc.org
Disability links, news, search, and more.

Multiple Sclerosis Association of America
http://www.msaa.com/
Programs, services, membership, information, and more.

Muscular Dystrophy Association
http://www.mdausa.org/
Diseases, research, services, experts, programs, and more.

National Federation of the Blind
http://www.nfb.org/
Links to many sites for the blind including sites for jobs, technology, services, and much more.

Sign Language Dictionary
http://dww.deafworldweb.org/sl
Dictionary of ASL words, numbers, and alphabet with pictures, as well as International SL and other countries.

Special Education Resources on the Internet
http://www.hood.edu/seri/serihome.htm
This site is a collection of Internet accessible information resources of interest to those involved in the fields related to special education.

Seeing Eye Homepage
http://www.seeingeye.org/
Site dedicated to seeing eye dogs.

Drama, Dance and Puppetry

Christians in Theatre Arts
http://www.cita.org/cita.htm
Impacting the world and furthering the kingdom of God by equipping and encouraging Christians in the theatre arts.

Church Drama Letters
http://www.dramaletters.com
Site of an ezine that features a series of church drama letters focussing on "how to" build a church drama ministry.

DramaQuest
http://www.dramaquest.com
Christian drama website.

DramaShare Christian Drama Resource
http://www.dramashare.org
Supporting 3,800 ministries in 49 countries with royalty-free scripts, manuals, workshops and resources.

On Stage—Drama Ministry Page
http://www.angelfire.com/mi/drama
This site is great for anyone who uses drama as a ministry! Networking, resources, graphics, and fresh ideas!

Orion's Gate Christian Drama
http://www.tagnet.org/orion/Scripts.html
A site for Christian directors, producers, and actors seeking drama resources of a spiritual nature, including free scripts, tips, and techniques.

The African-American Christian Theater Connection
http://www.aactc.com/
Free skits, plays and musicals with a Christian perspective written by African-Americans.

The Omnilist of Christian Art
http://members.aol.com/clinksgold/omnart.htm
Links to top sites featuring Christian dramatic and dance troupes.

Worship Drama
http://www.wordspring.com/
Wordspring is a forum for artists, teachers, and ministers who desire to see the concept of grace communicated in such an extraordinary way that it transforms our culture.

other sites of interest

Alvin Ailey American Dance Theatre
http://www.alvinailey.org/
Homepage for the acclaimed modern dance troup.

American Ballet Theatre
http://www.abt.org/flashindex.htm
Comprehensive ballet site with artist biographies, schedules and an amazing video dictionary.

Children's Creative Theater
http://tqjunior.thinkquest.org/5291/
Links to history, terms, games, resources, try a skit, or visit a children's theater.

Dance Links
http://www.dancer.com/dance-links/
Large directory to dance related websites, focusing on ballet and pointe.

Dancescape
http://www.dancescape.com/
Extensive directory of ballroom dancing resources on the web.

InterActive Theater Company
http://www.hern.org/interactivetheater/
Actors, call board, map, shows and times, sponsors, and more.

Theater/Drama Resources
http://www.library.wwu.edu/ref/subjguides/ theater.html
A selective guide for locating plays, play reviews, literature criticism, and other theater resources.

Theatre.com
http://www.buybroadway.com/
Links to what's playing on Broadway, shopping, clubs and communities, official sites, and more.

Drug Stores and Pharmacies

No specifically Christian sites in this category.
The following sites are provided for your convenience.

AARP
http://www.rpspharmacy.com/
Members of AARP can shop and save here.

At-Cost-Drugs
http://www.at-cost-drugs.com/
Offers prescription medications, over the counter products, and drugstore items.

Cyber Pharmacy
http://www.cyberpharmacy.cc/
Large and convenient online pharmacy.

Drugstore. Com
http://www.drugstore.com/
Your online store for beauty, health, wellness, personal
care, and pharmacy products.

Eckerd
http://www.eckerd.com/
Health and beauty aids, prescriptions, and information.

FDA
http:///www.fda.gov
Homepage for the food and drug administration; ensures
that products are labeled truthfully and are safe for consumers.

iPrescription
http://www.iprescription.net/
An online store for drugs, beauty, health, prescriptions,
wellness, personal care, and pharmacy products.

Pharmacy Links
http://www.mnnice.com/pharmacy%20links.html
Designed with the handicapped and new Internet user in
mind.

Pharmacy.org
http://www.pharmacy.org
Links to pharmacy sites.

Pharmacy Store
http://www.pharmacystore.com/
Mail order prescription pharmacy offering no-cost prescription service.

Planet Rx.com
http://www.planetrx.com
Prescription drugs available online with a prescription.

Rite-Aid
http://www.riteaid.com/home_frameset.html
Online pharmacy and shopping service.

Rx Network
http://www.therxnetwork.com/pharmacy_listing.htm
Drugstore and pharmacy links are found on this site for people looking for a convenient place to pick up their prescription.

Rx.com
http://www.rx.com/
Online pharmacists, Rx magazine, and lots of health information.

Virtual Drugstore
http://www.virtualdrugstore.com/
One-stop reference guide to pharmaceuticals, the newest research, and the latest reports with details on side effects and drug interactions.

Walgreens
http://www.walgreens.com/
Online shopping with directories to pharmacy and prescriptions.

Wal-Mart Pharmacy
http://www.heartlandmall.com/wal_mart/pharmacy.htm
Pharmacy provides advice and fills prescriptions.

WebRx
http://www.webrx.com/
Easy shopping and good prices. Use their online price comparison chart.

YesRx
http://www.yesrx.com/
Online pharmacy and store, purchase prescriptions, or seek expert opinions.

Education—Christian

Catholic Schools on the Net
http://www.microserve.net/~fabian/files/school.html
A listing of catholic schools with homepages, categorized by country.

Christian Books—Eclectic Homeschool Bookstore
http://eho.org/Bookstore/chbookst.htm
Classics, history, Bible study tools and more.

ChristianCollegeSearch.com
http://ccs.gospelcom.net/
Searchable directory of all member institutions of the Council for Christian Colleges and Universities.

Summit Bible College
http://www.serve.com/exjw/userpages/Summit.html
Bible college offering theology degrees.

The Christian Connector
http://www.christianconnector.com/index.htm
Advice on college selection, applications, and interviews, as well as financial aid information.

Education—Colleges and Universities

Baker's Guide to Christian Distance Education
http://www.bakersguide.com
An online reference center for those interested in Christian distance education featuring program lists, student advising, and a monthly newsletter.

Bob's Canadian Christian Colleges
http://www.geocities.com/heartland/prairie/7391/christian.html
A compilation of sites of Christian colleges and universities or other post-secondary institutions from across Canada.

ChristianCollegeSearch.com
http://ccs.gospelcom.net/
Searchable directory of all member institutions of the Council for Christian Colleges and Universities.

Council for Christian Colleges and Universities
http://64.224.113.246/
Find jobs, scholarships, or application process on this Christian education site.

E

Edu.com
http://www.edu.com
Offers discounted prices to college students via partnerships with corporations on computer hardware/software, books and magazines, telecommunications, financial services and other products and services.

Online Bible College
http://www.online-bible-college.com/
An online ministry training program equipping Christians for the 21st century.

Seminary Links
http://www.geocities.com/Athens/Acropolis/3370/
This site contains links to over 70 Christian seminaries, with links to Christian sites.

Seminary Viewer
http://wwcol.com/con/drj/semview.html
Frames page that allows viewers access to 200 different international Christian seminary and higher education sites (colleges with religion degree programs) for the prospective seminary student.
http://www.summit1.edu
School offering degree programs via independent learning.

The Christian Connector
http://www.christianconnector.com/index.htm
Advice on college selection, applications and interviews, as well as financial aid information.

other sites of interest

Classmates
http://www.classmates.com
Find old classmates or find out what they are doing on this people-locating site.

GoCollege
http://www.gocollege.com/
Match your grades and test scores against college requirements. Scholarship searches and more, too.

Web U.S. Higher Education
http://www.utexas.edu/world/univ
Page sponsored by UT Austin, with links to web primary central servers at universities and community colleges in the U.S.

Education—Scholarships

Cooperative Baptist Fellowship Scholarships
http://www.cbfonline.org/classroom/scholarships.cfm
Assists Baptist students called to a vocation in the church.

United Methodist Loan and Scholarship Programs
http://www.gbhem.org/
A churchwide service to provide financial aid to tomorrow's leaders.

other sites of interest

101 Top College, University and Scholarship Websites
http://www.college-scholarships.com/100college.htm
Colleges, scholarships, and financial aid links.

Best College Scholarships, Grants, Loans, Financial Aid
http://rusty.hypermart.net/college.htm
Order a guide to college scholarships and financial aid.

College Connection Scholarships
http://www.collegescholarships.com
Free college scholarship information every month since 1995.

CollegeQuest Gateway
http://www.collegequest.com/cgi-bin/ndCGI/CollegeQuest/pgGateway
College information, financial aid helps, apply online—for students and parents.

FreSch!
http://www.freschinfo.com/index.phtml
Information on over 2,000 free scholarships. Searchable database.

Scholarship News
http://www.free-4u.com/index.html
Extensive resource listing information on scholarships available around the country.

Education—Resources

Daronda Blevins Education Center
http://www.darondablevinsedu.com
Site offers creative homeschool, secular and Christian education materials for ages preschool—adult.

other sites of interest

A+ Math
http://www.aplusmath.com/games/index.html
Matho, Concentration, Hidden Picture, worksheets, homework helper, flashcards, and more!

APlus Research and Writing for High School and College Students
http://www.ipl.org/teen/aplus/
A step-by-step guide to writing research papers, from topic selection through research and execution.

B.J. Pinchbeck's Homework Helper
http://school.discovery.com/students/homeworkhelp/bjpinchbeck/
Links to art, computer science, current events, English, foreign languages, health, p.e., and other school subjects.

Blue Webs Learning Library
http://www.kn.pacbell.com/wired/bluewebn
A library of blue ribbon learning sites on the web.

Bluedog Can Count!
http://www.forbesfield.com/bdf.html
A fun, interactive way to learn arithmetic.

College Board: Educational Excellence for All Students
http://www.collegeboard.org
Homesite of organization seeking to help high school students make a successful transition to higher education.

This site provides information, services, and products for students and parents as well as for professional educators.

Collegeview
http://www.collegeview.com
College site helps high-schoolers learn about schools they might like to attend.

E

Cool Math
http://www.coolmath.com
An amusement park of mathematics with links to kids, adults, students, teachers, and more.

Dave's Math Tables
http://www.sisweb.com/math/tables.htm
Heaps of math here!

Education
http://www.quikbuy.com/scholarships.html
A resource for scholarships, grants, and financial aid, including several dedicated search engines and databases, plus information on scholarship myths, tips, and advice.

Education 4 Kids
http://www.edu4kids.com
This is an Internet educational resource sponsored by CANITech, featuring the edu4kids network of educational drill games for kids pre-K-12 and beyond covering math, science, social studies and more.

Education Index
http://www.educationindex.com
This site is a search engine for educational information and links in over fifty categories.

Education Place
http://www.eduplace.com
An education online community with centers for reading, mathematics, social studies, science as well as educational games, and other interactives.

Educational Software
*http://www.worldvillage.com/wv/school/html/
download.htm*
All the programs here are shareware so they are free for
use. Want to teach your infants the alphabet and count-
ing? Check out the "Preschooler's Top Ten" or perhaps
you would like to learn a foreign language or brush up
on your history or geography?

ExploreMath.com
http://www.exploremath.com/
Lesson plans, and activities for math students and
teachers.

Flashcards for Kids
http://www.edu4kids.com/math/
Interactive math flashcards to test a student's skills.

FunBrain
http://www.funbrain.com/
Sections for kids, teachers, and parents, as well as links
to numbers, words, culture, and more.

Funschool.com
http://www.funschool.com
Interactive educational games for all ages preschool
through fifth grade.

Grammar Gorillas
http://www.funbrain.com/grammar/index.html
Grammar questions with a gorilla theme, a fun, interactive, game.

Homework Central.com
http://www.bigchalk.com/
A collection of homework helps for browse or search. Resources for parents, students and teachers include discussion groups, mail, homework help, advice, toolkit, and
much more.

Idea Box
http://www.theideabox.com/
Early childhood education and activity resources.

Knowledge Adventure
http://www.knowledgeadventure.com/home/
Directories for parents, kids, and educators, on subjects
such as math, science, and more.

Learn2.com Homepage
http://www.learn2.com
Educational site that contains tutorials for school or
business.

Library Spot
http://www.libraryspot.com
Libraries, reference desks, lists, must see sites, genealogy
helps, and more.

Little Explorers
http://www.EnchantedLearning.com/Dictionary.html
Picture dictionary with links for children, multilingual,
and other information.

Martindale's "The Reference Desk"
http://www-sci.lib.uci.edu/HSG/Ref.html
Links to hundreds of academic subjects, world news,
and much, much more.

Martindale's The Reference Desk: Online Calculators
http://www-sci.lib.uci.edu/HSG/RefCalculators.html
Formulas and calculators to solve any
problem.

MathStories.com
http://www.mathstories.com/
Math word problems—mother's day problems, Harry Pot-
ter problems, and more.

Mickey's Place in the Sun Educational Resources
http://people.delphi.com/mickjyoung/educ.html
Links to adult education, children and youth, clearing-
houses, stay-in-school networks and information, financial aid, scholarships, internships, grants, grammar
resources, organizations, policy and research, publications.

E

Peterson's
http://www.petersons.com
A web resource on education and careers. Users can research and connect to the schools, camps, colleges, study abroad programs, graduate programs, or jobs.

Reading Skills—Your Child's Greatest Asset
http://www.reading-comprehension
This site offers resources to help children to succeed in school by improving their reading comprehension.

SBG Mathematics
http://www.sbgmath.com/
Math and teacher tools for grades 1 through 6.

Special Education Resources on the Internet
http://www.hood.edu/seri/serihome.htm
This site is a collection of Internet accessible information resources of interest to those involved in the fields related to special education.

Study Abroad Information Center
http://247malls.com/OS/cj/studyabroad1.htm
Site offers listings for study abroad and language school programs worldwide.

Think Quest
http://www.thinkquest.org
Links to Internet challenge, junior, tomorrow's teachers, conference, library of entries, and more.

You Don't Have to Play Football to Score a Touchdown
http://www.mtsu.edu/~studskl/hsindex.html
A dozen ways to study smarter in less time, time management, be a good listener, memory principles, study web, and more.

Egreeting Cards

ChristianGreetingCards.com
http://www.christiangreetingcards.com/
A wide variety of inspirational cards and devotionals to share over the Internet.

EternalTalk
http://www.eternaltalk.com/ecards/
Free ecards created for Christians, by Christians. Links
to egames, etalk, echat, and ethoughts.

Ministry Cards
http://bibleverseart.com/
Help spread the Word of God over the Internet using free
electronic postcards. Allow this site to help open up the
doors to witness to other people or to let someone know
you are thinking of them.

other sites of interest

123 Greetings
http://www.123greetings.com/
Free postcards and screensavers in categories including:
birthdays, holidays, food and drink, weddings, love, kids,
sports, and more.

Awesome Cyber Cards
http://www.marlo.com
Card site allows browser to find cards for any occasion
and send them via email.

Card Boulevard
http://www.cardblvd.com
Electronic animated, musical greeting cards for all occasions.

Forever Yours
http://www.zworks.com/forever/index.html
Free musical greeting cards sent over email.

Free Electronic Christian Greeting Card and Florist Service
http://postcard.adventistbookcenter.com/
Send virtual cards or flower bouquets to a friend with Internet access.

Virtual Flowers
http://www.virtualflowers.com/
Send a free virtual flower bouquet or order gift products
online.

E

Employment

Christian Career Center
http://www.gospelcom.net/ccc/
A "one-stop" website for resume development, job searching, etc.

Christian Jobs and Employment
http://www.church2000.org/
Classifieds/jobs.htm An online forum for those seeking positions, and seeking candidates to fill positions in Christian employment.

Christian Jobs Online
http://www.christianjobs.com/
A service dedicated to placing Christians in Internet-oriented positions with Christian companies.

other sites of interest

America's Employers
http://www.americasemployers.com.
Site for persons seeking employment via the Internet.

American Jobs
http://www.americanjobs.com
Employment site for job, resume, and career management information.

America's Job Bank
http://www.ajb.dni.us/
Links for employers and job seekers, translations, partners, and more.

Career Builder
http://www.careerbuilder.com.
Mega job search site.

Career Path
http://www.careerpath.com/index.html
Find a job, post a resume, or manage your career on this site for job seekers.

Career Shop
http://www.careershop.com.
Career enhancement helps and job search information.

Careers on the Web
http://www.CareerWeb.com.
Information on professional, technical, and managerial jobs.

Cool Works
http://www.coolworks.com
Find a summer job or winter job working in a park or vacation resort.

Headhunter
http://www.headhunter.net
Job site with more then 200,000 jobs listed. Jobs range from technology to education.

Hot Jobs
http://www.hotjobs.com/
Search for jobs by keyword, location, or company. Jobs from accounting to transportation at entry-level and above.

Job Hunt.com
http://www.jobhunt.com
The ultimate free online guide to net employment resources.

Jobs.com
http://www.jobs.com
Online guide to employment resources.

Riley Guide
http://www.dbm.com/jobguide
Surveys, job searches, and more in this employment guide.

Work Seek
http://www.workseek.com/
Career research, career expos, create a profile, work-life stuff, and more.

Entertainment

Catholic Community Television Network
http://www.cctn.org
Broadcasting Sunday mass and other audio selections.

Christian Entertainment
*http://www.christian-radio-1.com/christian_
entertainment.htm*
Information on Christian entertainment resources on the
web.

Christian Radio and Television on the Web
http://www.vanguardmag.com/radio.htm
Homesite of information and resources on the Internet.

Christian Spotlight on the Movies
http://www.ChristianAnswers.Net/spotlight/home.html
A movie rating review site for Christians. Contains current movie reviews and archival search by title or by
"moral rating."

Christian Television Network
http://www.nmtv.org/
National Minority Television Network features 24-hour
Christian television programming, including educational, instructional children's programs.

Christian-Search.Net LinkSearch—Entertainment/
Television
http://christian-search.net/Entertainment/Television
Entertainment/television section of Christian-
Search.Net.

Church 2000: The Christian Information Source for the
New Millennium
http://www.church2000.org/Search/search_radio.asp
Site allows users to find Christian radio and television
stations, add or upgrade a listing.

Cornerstone TeleVision
http://www.ctv.org
Homesite of a Christian television network broadcasting
over 100 Christ-centered programs, 24 hours a day, 7
days a week.

Crosswalk Movies
http://movies.crosswalk.com/
Christian reviews of blockbuster movies.

Dove Family Approved Movies and Videos
http://www.dove.org
Family-safe entertainment resources.

Ducky Movie Reviews
http://www.killerducky.com
Site offers Christian movie reviews.

Gateway Films Vision Video
http://www.visionvideo.com/vv/home.asp
Wholesome family entertainment, Christian entertainment, Christian video, Christian film, Bible video, Christian history, classics, and more.

G-Rock
http://www.grock.com
Music and sports television network with a message of
truth.

Kidz Quest Video Clips
http://www.christiananswers.net/kids/vidclips.html
Fun videos centered around life in a rain forest.

Living Word World Outreach Center
http://www.lwwoc.org/ramcitv.htm
Christian Internet television website, including radio
broadcasts.

**PhAt pHiSh!—Your Authority For Youth Oriented Christian
Entertainment**
http://phatphish.com
This is a youth-oriented Christian website.

Premier Christian Radio UK
http://www.premier.org.uk
Christian music and talk radio station broadcast live
from the UK plus information presenters and schedules.

The Most High Place—Christian Entertainment
http://www.mosthighplace.com/entertainment.htm
Movies, music, games and more!

The Way Home
http://www.lumen2000.com/twh/index.htm
Catholic Christian television program hosted by Bobbie

Cavnar, coordinator of a catholic, charismatic covenant community.

TVGuardian
http://tvguardian.com
TVG silences profanity and exclamatory uses of God, Jesus, and Christ from TV, Videos and DVDs. It makes TV time, family time again!

other sites of interest

AtNZone
http://www.atnzone.com/
Interactive forums, television, music, and movie links.

BONUS.COM® the SuperSite for Kids
http://www.bonus.com
Features over 900 fun, free, online activities for kids. Games, puzzles, brain teasers, build things, explore and more!

Culture Finder
http://www.culturefinder.com
Search engine of cultural events by date, city, event name, composer, or organization.

Eakle's Family Entertainment Site
http://www.eakles.com
Clean jokes, applets, heart-warming stories, great music, cyber cards, and more.

Family Entertainment
http://www.familyentertainment.net
Details on the content of family entertainment from a parent's perspective.

Family Entertainment Links
http://www.edgamesandart.com/famtainmentlinks.html
Family entertainment site, linked sites include, amusement parks, games, art, books, international recreation, and attractions homepages.

Family Internet
http://www.familyinternet.com
A service for parents offering comprehensive, high-quality, customizable information for children, family, and parenting.

iCulture
http://www.infoculture.cbc.ca/
Links to dance, film, theatre, cultural politics, books, music, visual arts, and other cultural sites. Use discretion when viewing entertainment sites.

E

Internet Movie Database
http://www.imdb.com/
Search database for over 200,000 movie and TV titles and over 400,000 actors and actresses.

Kid Explorers
http://christiananswers.net/kids/home.html
Adventures in the rainforest! Fun for the whole family with games, activities, stories, answers to children's questions, color pages, and more! A popular Christian education and evangelism resource. Nonprofit, evangelical, nondenominational.

Movie Review Query Engine
http://www.mrqe.com/lookup?
Search engine to find movie reviews. Links to other movie-related sites: Internet Movie Database, Reel, TVGrid, Enews, Amazon, and Chapters.

Moviefone
http://www.moviefone.com/
Movie showtimes, previews, tickets, reviews, and more.

Official Snoopy Homepage
http://www.snoopy.com
Links for kids, adults, art aficionados, and collectors, daily comic, and tribute to Charles Schultz.

Screen It!
http://www.screenit.com
Movie reviews for parents.

Storymania

http://www.storymania.com/

A site for those who enjoy reading and writing. Find a community of creative writers and readers of all types of original works not published elsewhere. Short stories, poetry, novels, plays, and much, much more!

Upcoming Movies

http://upcomingmovies.com/

Search for movie news by date, title, genre, actors, and more.

Zap 2 It

http://www.zap2it.com

Daily TV, movies, and Internet listings with reviews.

Environment

Christ Church Environment Centre

http://www.voyager.co.nz/~envctr/

Christ Church website for natural preservation of the environment.

other sites of interest

Eddie the Eco-Dog

http://www.eddytheeco-dog.com/

Kids site that is informative and fun. Follow Eddie as he teaches children the importance of conservation.

Environmental Education Network

http://www.envirolink.org/enviroed

Acts as the clearinghouse for all environmental education information, materials and ideas on the Internet. There are resources for school students, resources for teachers, and resources for university students.

Globe

http://www.globe.gov/

Site for Global Learning and Observations to Benefit the Environment.

Government Guide
http://www.governmentguide.com/research/Environment.adp
Links, webpages, resources, and more can be found on this government-supported site for kids.

Greenpeace
http://www.greenpeace.org/
Large environmental site with news, politics, and more.

Hands on for Habitat
http://www.environment.gov.au/habitatia/
An endangered animals site with opportunities to learn about and help out with nearly extinct species.

Health and Environment Resource Center
http://www.herc.org/
Browsers will find message boards, chat rooms, and site information on this page of resources for the environment.

M.U.S.E.
http://www.musemusic.org/
Musicians United to Sustain the Environment's webpage with information, links, and more.

Rainforest, Air and Pollution
http://members.xoom.com/searcheagle/nat/air.htm
Answers questions such as "why are rain forests important?" and more.

T.R.E.E.
http://www.slac.com/~tree/
A site dedicated to Taking Responsibility for the Earth and Environment.

Family

All About Families
http://www.allaboutfamilies.org
Search engine and weekly articles taken from popular culture and biblical principles to help Christians be better husbands, wives and parents.

Christian Family Links
http://christiansunite.com/allcat.shtml
A directory of thousands of links on topics of interest to Christian families.

Christian Family Place
http://www.christianfamilyplace.com/
Comprehensive site with special kids' and teens' features. Searchable by topic.

Family Life Communications
http://www.flc.org/
Links to Family Life radio, parent talk, women of virtue, counseling, resources, and programming.

NestFamily.com
http://www.nestentertainment.com/wallen
A family site offering animated videos of Bible stories, family devotionals, American Heroes series, Keeping Kids Safe in an Unsafe World, and other tools for home, church, and school libraries.

other sites of interest

Curse Free TV (561)
http://www.familytv.org
A new invention for television that automatically filters out profanity and other offensive language. It works on television programs and video movies.

Effective Parenting
http://www.effectiveparenting.org
Committed to sharing the secrets of parenting through writing, teaching and counseling. Eager to support families with practical suggestions for effective parenting.

Family Guide Book
http://www.familyguidebook.com
Site uses traffic light approach to helping families surf the Internet. Green light means family safe, red light means questionable or unsafe, yellow means proceed with caution. Help for parents, kids, librarians, media and press.

Family Interactive Network
http://www.familyinteractive.net/
A family-oriented online community. Members enjoy filtered access to the Internet, offering a clean, family-friendly approach to the web.

Family Resources Network
http://www.familyresources.net
A resource to help families access Internet and other media safely. Site also includes help on marriage, parenting, entertainment, financial matters, and more.

Family Works
http://www.familyworks.com
Homesite for not-for-profit developer of Unity interactive, multimedia software for families.

Family-Friendly Sites
http://www.virtuocity.com/family/Index.cfm
Directory of sites that are family-friendly, membership available, add or edit sites.

Family—Activities

Domestic-Church.com
http://www.domestic-church.com/index.htm
A year's worth of family activity ideas from the online magazine for Catholic families.

Family Time
http://www.famtime.com/
Fun and easy ways to teach children Christian principles and values.

Gifts for Jesus
http://www.giftsforjesus.com/
Games, crafts and activities to include Jesus in daily family life.

Net Ministry—Christian Kids' Links
http://home.netministries.org/kids.htmls
A directory of website activities that are devotional, educational, or just plain fun.

other sites of interest

The Family Corner
http://thefamilycorner.com/
Hundreds of ideas for things the family can do together.

The Puzzle Club
http://www.puzzleclub.org/
A family activity center with games and puzzles, read along stories and parenting advice.

Family—Parenting

BiblicalParenting.com
http://www.biblicalparenting.com
A web directory of top Christian and secular resources for parents.

Christian Family Resources
http://christianfamilyforum.com
Professional counseling for the Christian family, online counseling. A network of Christian counselors, therapists, and psychologists on marriage and family issues.

Christian Parent Zone
http://www.wtss.com/parentzone
Christian parenting resources brought to you, featuring Christian parenting chat, articles, books, and advice.

Christian Parenting Resources
http://www.teensalive.org/parent.htm
Resources and information for parenting children from childhood to adolescence.

Christian Parenting Resources from Teens Alive Ministries
http://www.teensalive.org/parents.htm
Resources to help parents as child moves from childhood to adolescence.

Dads and Daughters Homepage
http://www.dadsanddaughters.org/
Tools to strengthen father-daughter relationships.

Families First: Active Christian Parenting
http://www.crossroadspella.org/xrds/ffactchr.html)
Information on parenting from a Christian perspective
for parents of children 1–4, for parents of children 5–12,
for parents of children 11–13, building school success, active Christian parenting, and other topics.

Family Time
http://www.famtime.com/
Fun and easy ways to teach children Christian principles
and values.

F

Resources for the Christian Family
http://www.christianfamresources.com
Site contains information to help your family grow stron-
ger, as well as resources on spiritual warfare, spiritual de-
liverance, and prophecy.

Single Christian Parenting
http://singlechristianparentinga.find-americansingles.com
Single Christian parenting site to arrange a date with a
Christian mate.

TVGuardian—The Foul Language Filter
http://tvguardian.com
Silences profanity and exclamatory uses of God, Jesus,
and Christ from TV, videos, and DVDs.

other sites of interest

Effective Parenting
http://www.effectiveparenting.org
Committed to sharing the secrets of parenting through
writing, teaching, and counseling. Eager to support families with practical suggestions for effective parenting.

Families, Parenting, Family Finances, Pets—4Families.com
http://www.4Families.com
Family makes the world go 'round! Family fun and resources including Fox Kids, Parent Soup, Disney, National Park Service, genealogy resources, and care for
pets.

Love at Home
http://www.loveathome.com/
An Internet resource for larger than average families, columns include: homeschooling, traditions, cooking with kids, grandparenting, pregnancy, feature articles and more. Great site!

Main Street Mom
http://www.mainstreetmom.com
Magazine site for "modern mothers with traditional values."

Making Lemonade—The Single Parents Network
http://www.makinglemonade.com/
Chat rooms and links. The single parenting place, single parents stuff, children's corner, newsletter, and more.

Momspot
http://www.momspot.com/
Message forums on a broad variety of parenting issues.

Parent Soup
http://www.parentsoup.com
Communities for pre-pregnancy, expecting parents, parents of babies, parents of toddlers, parents of school age children, and parents of teens.

Solo—A Guide for the Single Parent
http://www.soloparenting.com/
A quarterly publication created specifically to cover issues that single parents and their children are dealing with today.

Stay at Home Dads
http://www.familyinternet.com/dad/dad.htm
Site for house husbands or stay at home dads.

The Fathers Network
http://www.fathersnetwork.org
Celebrating and supporting fathers and families raising children with special health care needs and developmental disabilities.

Totalwoman.com: Family
http://www.myprimetime.com/family/center/kids/ ?p=2229&v=643
Articles, advice and discussions on a wide range of family issues.

Games and Interactives

Aboard Puzzle Depot: Trivia, Puzzles and Games for Education or Recreation!
http://www.puzzledepot.com/index.shtml
Great games for the whole family including crosswords, trivia, puzzles, and more.

AMAZING MAZES!
http://www.christiananswers.net/kids/ menumaze.html
Mazes of all types and skills.

Apple Corps
http://apple-corps.westnet.com/apple_corps.html
Design a vegetable face—pick from noses, eyes, ears, and accessories to create your own vegetable.

Apple Sauce Kids
http://home.dmv.com/~aplsauce/christfu.htm
Games and activities that teach Bible principles. Great for Sunday school, church, and family activities.

Best of the Christian Web Arcade Christian and Bible Games; Trivia
http://www.botcw.com/games/index.html
Large trivia site with games and more.

ChristFun
http://home.dmv.com/~aplsauce/christfu.htm
Activities and games based on Christian principles for Sunday school, church, and family.

Christian Connection
http://www.webzonecom.com/ccn/games/games.htm
A collection of free Christian computer games and music in zip format.

Christian Toys and Games
http://www.freelinks.com/christiantoysandgames
Toys and games with a Christian theme.

Christian Spotlight's Guide to Games
http://christiananswers.net/spotlight/games/home.html
Computer game reviews from a Christian family perspective.

Eternal Game
http://www.eternaltalk.com/egame/
The site matches your winnings with a donation to the church of your choice.

Games and Trading Cards
http://www.freelinks.com/christiantoysandgames/tradingcards.html
Links to dozens of Christian trading cards.

GCN Christian Games
http://206.132.148.20/asp/fun_home.asp
Christian games site including Bible trivia and crosswords and links to other Christian game sites.

Glenn Teitelbaum's Maze
http://home.pb.net/~tglenn/maze.htm
Interactive mazes, safe for kids.

Global Christian Network
http://206.132.148.20/asp/fun_home.asp
Christian games and Bible trivia.

Heaven's Helpers Club
http://www.geocities.com/Heartland/Park/6804/kidsheaven.html
Games, coloring pages, activities, and more.

Interactive Model Railroad
http://rr-vs.informatik.uni-ulm.de/rr/
Operate a model railroad, view the gallery, statistics, links to railroad pages, and more.

Java Arcade Games
http://thecoffeehouse.com/games
Games: asteroids, webtris, zapper, and more.

Joe's World—Lots of Free Games
http://users.50megs.com/provencial/joes_world.htm
Action games, trivia, coloring pages, and more.

Kaleidoscope Painter
http://www.bol.ucla.edu/~permadi/java/spaint/
Fun, interactive kaleidoscope painter game.

KIDiddles
http://www.kididdles.com/index.html
Musical Mouseum, trunk of tales, fun and games, today's
questune, and other links.

Kid's Quest Combo!
http://www.christiananswers.net/kids/
menu-act.html
Word search, mazes, people, sounds, et.

Net 153 Bible Puzzles Net 153 FREE Online Gameroom
http://www.net153.com/games/
Online games for a variety of browsers.

Net Fun and Games
http://www.christianity.net/fun/games/
Classic and new online games.

Puzzle Archives
http://www.nova.edu/Inter-Links/fun-games.html
Cartoons, quotes, games, etc.

Rubik's
http://www.rubiks.com
Official Rubik's (cube) website, with games, play online,
forum, information, free downloads, and links.

Tims Freeware Adventure Games
http://members.truepath.com/timshen/index.html
Text adventure games, Bible word games, jigsaw puzzles,
etc.

United Christian Network
http://www.unitedchristians.com/
A Christian resource directory with links to kids games,
toys, and other Internet resources.

other sites of interest

ARCade Room
http://www.cmurphy.com/arcade.htm
Links to online games such as Star Wars, Tetris, UFO, and more.

Idea Box
http://www.theideabox.com
Message boards, idea of the week, site of the week, activities, games, songs, and more.

The Neverending Tale
http://www.coder.com/creations/tale
A choose-your-own-adventure story online.

Official SCRABBLE® Homepage
http://www.scrabble.com/
Scrabble information and resources worldwide.

Puzzle Factory
http://www.thepuzzlefactory.com/
Jigsaw, sliders, tangrams, etc.

Sojourner—a Christian adventure game!
http://members.tripod.com/~timshen/index.html
An online adventure game.

The Theodore Tugboat Online Activity Centre
http://www.cochran.com/theodore
Activities, collectibles, home and school, big harbor, links, etc.

Who Wants to Be a Millionaire Online Game
http://abc.go.com/primetime/millionaire/
mill%5Fplay.html
Play the popular gameshow online.

Word Play
http://www.wolinskyweb.com/word.htm
Award-winning site offering links to dozens of websites that feature fun with words.

Gardening

(see also Home and Home Repair) No specifically Christian sites in this category. The following sites are provided for your convenience.

Algy's Herb Page
http://www.algy.com/herb/index.html
Directories to the potting shed, the greenhouse, and more.

Ask Earl, The Yard-Care Answer Guy
http://www.yardcare.com/
Pick a topic or ask a question at this lawn care site.

Better Homes and Gardens
http://www.bhglive.com/homeimp/docs
Home improvement encyclopedia—plumbing, wiring, carpentry, decks, masonry, and more.

Burpee Seeds and Plants
http://www.burpee.com/
Online purchasing site for seeds and other Burpee goods.

City Farmer's Urban Agriculture Notes
http://www.cityfarmer.org/
Directories to surveys, journals, and more.

Cyberlawn
http://opei.mow.org/
Virtual lawn with directories to mower maintenance, safety tips, and more.

Easy Gardening
http://www.geocities.com/Heartland/Pointe/8391/
Garden art, themes, and more in this informative site.

Family Gardening
http://www.dlcwest.com/~createdforyou/sprouts.html
Garden tips, weather information, and more. All the family gardener could ask for.

Farmer Brown's Garden Path
http://www.flinet.com/~gallus/index.html
Takes you down three paths to information on gardening and education.

From the Garden with P. Allen Smith
http://www.pallensmith.com/index.html
Hints and tips by television personality P. Allen Smith.

Garden.com
http://www.garden.com
Updated daily, this is one of the largest and most useful sites on the web, with information, an extensive search engine, and a garden planner.

GardenGuides
http://www.gardenguides.com/
Directories to garden information of all kinds.

Gardening for Kids
http://www.geocities.com/EnchantedForest/Glade/3313/
Directories to bulbs, facts, tips, and more.

Gardening Launch Pad
http://www.tpoint.net/neighbor/
Directories to flowers of all kinds, trees, and other plant life.

GardenWeb Homepage
http://www.gardenweb.com/
Site for the Internet's garden community. Contains links and other resources.

InterGarden
http://sunsite.unc.edu/london/
Articles of interest, resources, reference desk, and other links for gardeners.

Jona's Garden
http://www.totacc.com/user/jgoucher/
Useful tips, information, and links to other gardening sites.

MrGrow.com
http://www.mrgrow.com/
Mr Grow answers all your growing questions on this gardening site.

Research Central—Gardening
http://www.kalama.com/~mariner/qsergarden.htm
Gives the reader resources for a greener thumb as well as
gardening news groups.

Vegetable Garden
http://home.earthlink.net/~marcia5687/
Shop online for seeds and garden plans.

Virtually Gardening
http://www.suite101.com/topics/page.cfm/75
The Squint school of garden design, surveys, and more
on this site of gardening tips.

Genealogy

No specifically Christian sites in this category.
The following sites are provided for your convenience.

A Beginner's Guide
http://biz.ipa.net/arkresearch/guide.html
Just getting started? Try this site first.

Ancestry Genealogy Library
http://www.ancestry.com/
Extensive site, includes family tree builder, articles, information, search tips, etc.

Everton's
http://www.everton.com/
A good site for the beginner with a link to the basics in
the field as well as a search engine and reference links.

FamilySearch Internet Genealogy Service
http://www.familysearch.org
Ancestor search, keyword search, and custom search provided by the Church of Jesus Christ of Latter Day
Saints.

Genealogy Family Tree
http://www.ancestrycom.com/
Search for ancestors by locality or surname.

Genealogy Homepage
http://www.genhomepage.com/
Links to other sites, with frequent updates.

Kindred Konnections Genealogy and Family History
http://209.140.72.162/cgi-bin/genealogy/
surname?-1+0+0+English
Search over 48,000,000 ancestral archive names, and
more.

RootsWeb
http://www.rootsweb.com/
One of the largest sites on the web, with extensive search
engine and tips for beginners.

Social Security Death Index
http://www.ancestry.com/ssdi/advanced.htm
Census, church, and military records.

Gifts, Goods, and Merchandise

Cards4Christians
http://www.cards4christians.com/
Leading Internet wholesaler for Christian greeting cards
and giftwrap.

CTAInc.
http://www.ctainc.com/
Broad selection of gifts for church and school students.

Faith and Grace
http://www.faithandgrace.com/
The finest selection of Christian gifts, books, music,
clothing and more.

Inspirations
http://www.inspirations.org
Offers gift ideas, gifts for various occasions, and a free,
inspirational newsletter.

Purchase Power by 4Hisglory and
Aunt Hagar's Children's Place
http://www.homestead.com/prayze2him
Spend your money wisely. Great deals at great shops.
Links to other sites too. Site is always being updated.

Scrolls Unlimited
http://www.scrollsunlimited.com/
Inspirational and seasonal wallhangings.

Spiritual Beauty
http://www.spiritualbeauty.com/
Inspiring Christian books, music and beautiful gift baskets.

The KHG Collection
http://www.kakarigi.net/khg/
A full line of products to encourage people to read and remember the Word of God.

other sites of interest

BabyCenter.com
http://www.babycenter.com
Select products and services for new and expectant parents. Providing reliable information backed by medical professionals and consumer health.

Buy.com
http://www.buy.com
Sells through seven speciality sites for books, computers, videos, DVD, music, games, software and an outlet for serious bargain hunting.

Deal of Day
http://www.dealofday.com/
A daily listing of links to bargains and discounts on personal and household needs, entertainment, pets, and more.

Free Stuff
http://www.free-stuff.com
A variety of free offers on merchandise, software, travel, discount cards, and more.

Gift in a Basket
http://www.giftinabasket.com
Online gifts for friends or relatives. All in a handy basket.

Super Discount on the Internet
http://www.discountmarketplace.com/109.asp
Super discounts on the Internet all year long, including books on mail order, business opportunities, etc.

Surprise.com
http://www.surprise.com/
Search for gift ideas by person, occasion, and hobbies.

Government

A Christian View of Government and Law
http://www.leaderu.com/orgs/probe/docs/xian-pol.html
Man's obligations to God and the State, from Leadership U.

Christian Leadership and Government
http://www.tentmaker.org/topics/christianleadershipandgovernment.html
Articles on the qualifications for Christian leadership and the balancing of obligations to God and Man.

other sites of interest

Bureau of Governmental Research
http://www.bgr.org
Activities and information for American citizens to obtain online.

CapitolHearings.org
http://www.capitolhearings.org/
Online streaming audio from live Senate hearings.

Executive Branch—U.S. Government
http://lcweb.loc.gov/global/executive/fed.html
Includes links to the executive branch of U.S. government, including White House, National Drug Control Policy, Departments of Agriculture, Commerce, Defense, Education, HUD, and other cabinets.

Federal Bureau of Investigation
http://www.fbi.gov/
Links to contact the FBI, view the most wanted list, pressroom, employment, programs, kids room, and much more.

Great American Website
   http://www.uncle-sam.com/
   Links to the executive, legislative, and judicial branches
   of government, executive department, independent agencies, and other links.

IRS The Digital Daily
   http://www.irs.ustreas.gov
   Webpage dedicated to the IRS includes job and filing information.

Library of Congress
   http://www.loc.gov/
   Links to Thomas, copyright office, American memory, exhibitions, library today, and more.

G

Social Security Online
   http://www.uscourts.gov/
   The official site of the Social Security Administration.
   News, advice and forms.

The Federal Judiciary Homepage
   http://www.uscourts.gov/
   News, publications, information and links on the Federal
   court system.

Thomas
   http://thomas.loc.gov
   Search engine for congress. Includes congressional legislation, records, and committee information, the Thomas
   Jefferson papers, senate committees hearing schedules,
   and much more.

U.S. Census Bureau
   http://www.census.gov/
   Extensive resources on all sorts of census data and news.

United States House of Representatives
   http://www.house.gov/
   Directories to House operations, committee operations,
   and more.

Your Link to Congress
http://www.congress.org/
Links on voter registration, finding your representative, capital directory, legislation, and more.

Health and Fitness

A Christian Health and Lifestyle Center
http://www.galaxymall.com/market/chlc.html
Dedicated to providing truthful health and disease information.

Bodies in Christ Health and Nutrition
http://www.freeyellow.com/members3/bodinchr
Specializes in weight loss through biblically based teachings and nutritional products.

Christian Aerobics
http://sportsmusic.com/chris1.htm
Christian aerobics videos available for purchase online.

Christian Fitness
http://www.hfeonline.com/christian.htm
Include your spirit in your exercize program. Here's how.

Christian Health Zone
http://www.christianhealthzone.bigstep.com/
Diet and fitness advice to help you break free of the worldly trends of sickness and spiritual stagnation.

Christian Sports and Fitness Division
http://www.christianteam.org/page5.html
Use your personal sports or recreational interest to start a ministry in a CSF chapter.

other sites of interest

Bicycling
http://bicycling.about.com/health/bicycling/mbody.htm
Links to information about bicycling as a form of fitness.

Desktop Yoga
> *http://www.will-harris.com/yoga/*
> Yoga postures that can be performed at your desk to alleviate the strain of working at a computer.

Digestion Information
> *http://www.digestioninfo.com*
> Helpful information on digestive problems.

Dr. Greene's House Calls
> *http://www.drgreene.com/*
> Online pediatric news and advice with a great search feature to find what you want to know.

eFit
> *http://www.efit.com/*
> Tools, diet program, exercise program, eFitTV, basics, and more.

Family Gentle Dental Care
> *http://www.dentalgentlecare.com*
> Information about dentistry, procedures, home care, post-op care, techniques available, preventing tooth decay, nutrition, and what to do in dental emergencies.

Fat Free
> *http://www.fatfree.com/*
> An archive of over 4,000 low-fat, vegetarian recipes. Includes links for other fitness sites.

Feel 21 Fitness
> *http://www.feel21.net/fitness-nutrition.html*
> Links to women's health, fitness nutrition, men's health, prevention and wellness, herbals, and more.

Global Health and Fitness
> *http://global-fitness.com/calorie.shtml*
> Find out how many calories your body "burns" (used or expended) for more than 70 different exercises/activities.

GymAmerica
> *http://www.gymamerica.com*
> Offers guide to personal workouts. Customized for each user by top fitness experts.

H

Health A to Z
http://www.healthatoz.com/
Links to family health, condition forums, community, wellness centers, lifestyle, resources, experts, and more.

Health and Fitness Tips
http://www.health-fitness-tips.com/
Offering information and a free e-bulletin on topics including fitness, weight loss, diet, and nutrition.

Healthfinder
http://www.healthfinder.gov/
Health information, news, and more, from the U.S. Dept. of Health and Human Services.

Kids Health
http://kidshealth.org
Health topics and information for parents, kids, and teens.

Mayo Health O@sis
http://www.mayohealth.org/mato/common/htm/index.htm
Homepage of the Mayo Clinics, with news, information, research, etc.

Men and Women's Health
http://www.chetday.com/
Articles and newsletters on health and fitness with free exercise and diet programs, too.

Men's Fitness
http://www.mensfitness.com/
Webpage for Men's Fitness magazine, featuring articles, a message board, health tips, etc.

Quackwatch
http://www.quackwatch.com/
How to avoid health frauds, scams and medical quackery.

Strength Coach
http://www.strengthcoach.com/
Consult a strength coach, interactive games, and more.

Tae-Bo —The Future of Fitness
http://www.taebo.com/home.html
The official homepage of Billy Blanks and the tae-bo phe-nomenon.

Take Wellness to Heart
http://www.women.americanheart.org/
Information on heart disease and strokes in women.

Women's Cancer Network
http://www.wcn.org/
News and information on cancer in women, specifically reproductive and breast cancers.

H

Women's Health Hot Line
http://www.libov.com/
A newsletter providing general medical information con-cerning women.

Worldguide
http://www.worldguide.com/Fitness/hf.html
Advice and tips for strength training, stretching, aerobic exercise and nutrition.

Yogaahhh!
http://www2.gdi.net/~mjm/
Resources and practices of hatha yoga, search engine, rec-ommended sites, shopping, and more.

History

Amazing Discoveries in Bible Archaeology
http://www.concentric.net/~extraord/archaeology.htm
Discoveries are being made daily which prove that the Bible is the inspired Word of God.

Ask Christian History
http://www.christianitytoday.com/history/features/askch.html
Put a question to the experts and see your answer here.

Bible Atlas Maps v2.3
*http://www.zdnet.com/downloads/stories/info/
0,,0012NS,.html*
40 free downloadable maps of the Holy Land and other
Bible locations in PowerPoint format.

Biblelands—Picture Tour of the Holyland
http://www.mustardseed.net
A virtual tour of the people, places and things of the
Bible. This site features hundreds of pictures plus full
360-degree interactive pictures where you control what
you see.

Biblical Timelines
http://gbgm-umc.org/umw/bible/timeline.stm
Biblical and world events before Christ's birth, after His
birth, church history timeline from Jesus to Constantine,
and other links of interest.

Cascoly History and Bible Timelines
http://cascoly.com/history.htm
What biblical leaders were alive during the first Olympic
games? CHRONOS and Bible Timeline let you inter-
actively explore history.

Christian Biography
*http://www.geocities.com/Heartland/Ranch/6391/
bio.htm*
A timeline of Christian history with links to biographies
of many of the leading figures.

Christian Books: Life of Jesus Christ
http://www.reflectionpublishing.com
Divine Invasion helps readers to experience the person
of Jesus Christ in the same way that *This Present Dark-
ness* helped them to experience the power of prayer.

Christian History
http://www.religioustolerance.org/chr_ch.htm
History of the Christian church.

Christian History Links
http://www.tbm.org/History.htm
Christian history links.

Christian History Made Easy Learning Resources
http://pages.whowhere.com/community/christianhistory/chapterlist.html
Just click on the era you are interested in.

Christian History Timeline
http://agards-bible-timeline.com
See 6,000 years of Christian Bible and world history at a glance, from Adam to modern times.

Church History
http://www.catholicgoldmine.com/
Catholic church history; a list of popes from St. Peter to John Paul II, *The Catholic Encyclopedia,* and more.

Church History Index
http://pages.preferred.com/~mdepew/chhindex.html
An index to church history resources and links, including an outline to an introductory Survey of Church History class.

Church History Timeline Index
http://home.talkcity.com/AcademyDr/eusebius/chronindex.htm
A timeline of church history, with emphasis on the first several centuries.

Dead Sea Scrolls
http://sunsite.unc.edu/expo/deadsea.scrolls.exhibit/intro.html
The Ancient Library of Qumran and Modern Scholarship: an exhibit at the Library of Congress, Washington, D.C.

Divining America: Religion and the National Culture
http://www.nhc.rtp.nc.us:8080/tserve/divam.htm
Essays on the role of religion in American history from colonial days to the present.

Early Sources of Christianity
http://www.azstarnet.com/~rgrogan/ce.htm
An introduction to the origins of Christianity with links to source material.

EarlyChurch.com

http://www.earlychurch.com

Primary sources and a catalog of early church writings.

High Profile Maps

http://mz.media3.net/highprofilemaps/

3-D maps of the Holy Land, Roman roads, towns and villages of Jesus' time, and tabletop resource for small groups and Bible classes. Raised relief shows mountains and valleys in true scale.

Institute for the Study of American Evangelicals

http://www.christianitytoday.com/history/

Designed to help Evangelicals and others understand their historic contributions and current roles.

Internet Theology Resources: Church History and Historical Theology

http://www.csbsju.edu/library/internet/theochht.html

Annotated directory of Internet resources for the study of church history and historical theology, from the College of St. Benedict and St. John's University.

LDSWorld—Church History

http://www.ldsworld.com/churchhistory/ 0,3020,60,00.html

History, LDS links, product registration, church history, Mormon Pioneer Trail, a clickable map, and detailed day-by-day history.

Lutherans.Net

http://www.lutherans.net

Comprehensive Lutheran resources.

Martin Luther's 95 Theses

http://www.monastereo.com/reference/protestant/ 95theses.html

The major theological work leading to the start of Protestantism.

Mennonite.net: Wiring the Mennonite World

http://www.mennonite.net/

A comprehensive gathering of information on Mennonite churches, conferences, organizations, and educational institutions.

Museum of Pilgrims
http://members.nbci.com/rarebook/foyer.htm
A history of reformed theology since the Reformation in
tracts, pictures, articles and sermons.

Quaker Tour of England
http://members.xoom.com/wsamuel/quaktour.html
Virtual tour with photos and text. Places, events, people,
and ideas important in the history of the Religious Society of Friends.

Religion and the Founding of the American Republic
http://lcweb.loc.gov/exhibits/religion/
The Library of Congress exhibit exploring the religious
convictions of the early settlers.

Restoration Movement
http://www.mun.ca/rels/restmov/restmov.html
Texts, pictures, and studies about the history of the Christian churches, Churches of Christ, and Disciples of Christ.

Scrolls from the Dead Sea
http://www.lcweb.loc.gov/exhibits/scrolls/
The Library of Congress exhibit on the writing, contents
and discovery of the Dead Sea Scrolls.

Story of Oscar Schindler
http://home8.inet.tele.dk/aaaa/Schindler2.htm
A brief biography of one of the more humane figures of
the Holocaust. Contains graphic Holocost imagery.

The American Religious Experience
http://are.as.wvu.edu/
Scholarly articles and exhibits on the history of religion
in America. Online courses, too.

The Spanish Missions of California
http://library.thinkquest.org/3615/
Take a virtual tour of the old missions. Extensive background information, too.

Vatican Library and Exhibition
http://www.vatican.net
A description of some of the Vatican's extensive literary
and artistic holdings.

Worlds of Late Antiquity
http://ccat.sas.upenn.edu/jod/wola.html
Scholarly links focusing on the early days of Christianity.

other sites of interest

A Medieval Atlas
http://www.historymedren.about.com/library/weekly/aa071000a.htm
The world as it looked in the Middle Ages.

Academic Info: Modern European History
http://www.academicinfo.net/histeuro.html
Links to many resources.

African-American Journey
http://www.otterbein.edu/learning/libpages/blackhis.htm
World Book's look at African-American history with excerpts from their multimedia encyclopedia.

African History on the Web
http://web.uccs.edu/~history/index/africa.html
Many links to sites on African history.

Ancient Atlas
http://ancienthistory.about.com/library/bl/bl_maps_index.htm
Graphic representations of the world in ancient times.

Ancient/Classical History
http://ancienthistory.about.com/homework/ancienthistory/
Links to hundreds of sites on Greece, Rome and many other subjects.

Chinese History
http://web.uccs.edu/~history/index/china.html
Chinese history and cultural sites.

European History
http://www.geocities.com/Athens/Forum/9061/europe/europe.html
Many links sorted by country and subject.

European History Links
http://hecate.acofi.edu/history/pages/europe.html
Links to broad areas of European history.

Eye Witness
http://www.ibiscom.com/
First-hand accounts of events from ancient times to the present. Sound files, too.

Historical Atlas of the 20th Century
http://users.erols.com/mwhite28/20centry.htm
Dozens of beautiful and informative interactive maps showing world event and trends.

History Channel
http://www.thehistorychannel.com
Cable history channel website with "This Day in History," historical facts, and more.

History of Asia
http://web.uccs.edu/~history/index/generalasia.html
Links and articles on Asian history.

History of the World
http://www.historyoftheworld.com/
A gigantic directory of links on the history, culture and people of all nations.

Homework Center—European History
*http://www.multnomah.lib.or.us/lib/homework/
eurohist.html*
Comprehensive links to many areas of interest.

Labyrinth
*http://www.georgetown.edu/labyrinth/
labyrinth-home.html*
Resources for medieval studies.

Making of America
http://www.umdl.umich.edu/moa/
Library of primary sources in American social history from the antebellum period through reconstruction. Education, psychology, American history, sociology, religion, and science and technology.

Medieval World on the Web
http://web.uccs.edu/~history/index/medieval.html
Comprehensive site on many subjects.

Modern European History Links
http://www.nyu.edu/gsas/dept/history/internet/
geograph/europe/modern.html
Links, including European news services.

National Museum of the American Indian
http://www.si.edu/nmai/
Dedicated to the preservation, study, and exhibition of
the life, languages, literature, history, and arts of Native
Americans.

Net Serf
http://netserf.org
The Internet connection for medieval resources. Arranged by topics.

OSSHE Historical and Cultural Atlas Resource
http://www.uoregon.edu/~atlas/europe/maps.html
A beautiful selection of modern interactive maps of the
ancient and medieval world.

Renassiance History on the Web
http://web.uccs.edu/~history/index/renaissance.html
Links, photos, and articles on many subjects.

The Ancient Vine
http://www.ancientsites.com/
Extensive directory of links, articles and discussion
boards on Rome, Greece, Babylon and the ancient world.

This Week in Christian History
http://www.christianitytoday.com/history/features/
week.html
A week-by-week review of events and personalities in
Christian history.

Timelines and Charts
http://www.bible-history.com/resource/tc_gen.htm
Timelines and charts for many eras of history including
biblical, Egyptian, Greek, East Asian, and more.

World History Compass
http://www.worldhistorycompass.com/
A great place to start searching history subjects on the web. Basic information and numerous links.

World History Maps
http://www.worldhistorymaps.com/
Offers historical maps, showing countries of the world for every year in recorded history.

Hobbies and Collectibles

Christian Friendship Directory
http://friendship.crossdaily.com/
Thousands of discussion groups centered on hobbies and other interests.

Christian Gaming
http://www.christiangaming.com/
Information on Christian games, reviews, news, resources, and links.

Fellowship of Christian Magicians
http://www.gospelcom.net/fcm/
How to use visual illustrations and develop talent for gospel presentations.

Virtual Christian Center—Hobby and Craft Center
http://www.virtualchristiancenter.com/handc.htm
Links to family-friendly hobby and craft sites on the web.

other sites of interest

Antique and Collectible Malls
http://www.tias.com/
Advanced auction site featuring news, collectible information, and links to online and offline auction vendors.

Antique Talk
http://www.antiquetalk.com
Directories to online auctions, appraisals, and more. Lots of links to other antique sites.

Birdwatching.com
http://www.birdwatching.com/
Tips on getting started and learning more about this popular family activity.

Car Collector Magazine
http://www.carcollector.com/
Online magazine for the car collector and enthusiast. Classics, sports and muscle cars.

Civil War Art and Collectibles
http://www.blackcamisards.com/
Publishes and sells Civil War era limited edition fine arts, figurines, and other collectibles commemorating United States colored troops.

Collecting Channel
http://www.collectingchannel.com/
Search over 800,000 entries for collectible objects.

CollectPaperMoney.com
http://www.collectpapermoney.com/
How to get started in this fascinating hobby. Currency identifiers, collector's tips and other resources, too.

collectSPACE
http://www.collectspace.com
Dedicated to collecting space memorabilia. Includes personal collections, space news and information, directory of resources, and events.

Curioscape Antique Resource Locator
http://www.curioscape.com
A massive search engine, which helps the user find vendors for more than 50 categories of antiques.

Focus on Photography
http://www.fodors.com/focus/
100 tips with photos on how to take great travel shots.

Great Outdoor Recreation Pages—Fishing
http://www.gorp.com/gorp/activity/fishing.htm
Links to fishing information: where to go, what to fish for, how to fish, species information, and more.

Hobbies at Geoff's World
*http://www.geocities.com/Heartland/Forest/9397/
hobbies.html*
Links to all types of hobbies and collecting sites.

Hobby Car Models
http://www.hobby-carmodel.com/
Online mail-order store specializing in car models 1/8x
to 1/43x for European, Japanese, and American plastics
and resin kits.

Key, Lock and Lantern Inc.
http://members.aol.com/klnlsite
Nonprofit membership corporation for collectors of railroad memorabilia.

Learn About Antiques and Collectibles
http://www.antiques-oronoco.com
Antique furniture, glassware, magazines, postcards, toys,
jewelry, china, and much more are explained for the beginning collector.

My Dolls Collectibles
http://www.mydollscollectibles.com/
Beanie Babies, Puffkins, Barbie dolls, Hot Wheels, and
other collectibles.

Resources for Hobbies
http://www.nanana.com/hobbies.html
A wide selection of links for specific hobby sites and information.

Rick's Gameroom Collectibles
http://zany-pix.com/rix.htm
Collecting and restoring antique coin-operated arcade
machines, jukeboxes, and other American nostalgic
items.

ScrapNetwork
http://www.scrapbookideas.com/
Information for beginning scrapbookers. Links, chat site,
and weekly contests.

H

Signalfan
http://www.signalfan.com
Old traffic signals and road signs. Also for those interested in the preservation of old signals and signs for their historical value.

Snoop-2-Nuts
http://www.snoop2nuts.com/
Snoopy and Peanuts collectibles, T-shirts, leather jackets, and more.

Trains and Things
http://www.catotrains.com
Specializes in collectible engines and cars. Also offers parts and supplies.

Weird Hobby Hall of Fame
http://www.christianityonline.com/campuslife/2000/001/9.58.html
Unusual hobbies, hobbyists, and their wacky pursuits.

Wood Zone
http://www.woodzone.com/
The premier online site for new and experienced woodworkers with tips, tricks, articles, and how-to.

Holidays

Articles About Christian Holidays
http://www.wcg.org/lit/church/holidays/default.htm
Holiday information and history from the Worldwide Church of God.

Family Guide to the Biblical Holidays
http://biblicalholidays.com/feasts.htm
A site dedicated to the many holidays of Christian tradition. Read about the history of Christmas, Easter, and more.

Holiday Celebrations
http://www.faithwebbin.net/holidays
Site on the Faithwebbin network dedicated to holidays.

Holiday Page
http://wilstar.com/holidays
Site contains links to information about the most popular Christian and secular holidays celebrated in the U.S.

The Origins of Various Christian Holidays
http://www.pchelplocator.com/agape/moreissues/holidays/holidays.htm
An examination of the historical and Biblical bases for Christian celebrations.

other sites of interest

Federal Holidays
http://www.opm.gov/fedhol
United States Office of Personnel Management listing of federal holidays over a six-year period.

Holidays Homepage
http://holidays.bfn.org
Egreetings for a variety of national and religious holidays.

The Worldwide Holiday and Festival Site
http://www.holidayfestival.com/
Someone is celebrating something today. Find out where, what and why!

Web Holidays
http://www.web-holidays.com
A collection of recipes, crafts, stories, and games, for a number of holidays.

Holiday—Christmas

A Holy Christmas
http://www.rockies.net/~spirit/sermons/christmaspage1.html
Links to hundreds of Christmas sites. Music, clipart, poetry and much, much more.

A Religious Christmas in Art
http://www.execpc.com/~tmuth/st_john/xmas/art.htm
An extensive collections of fine art depictions of the Nativity and related themes.

Amazing Animated Advent Calendar
http://christmas.faithweb.com
Count down the days until Christmas. A new animation added to the Christmas tree-shaped calendar for each day in December.

Christmas Music and Stories
http://www.testimony.org/christmas/music.html
Features free stories with Christmas carols.

Saviour Is Born
http://members.tripod.com/~C_Verge/Christmas/glory.html
Site contains the Christmas story, and activities for kids, games, recipes, music, graphics, and more.

other sites of interest

Christmas.com
http://www.christmas.com/
A portal site with links to hundreds of Christmas sites on the Internet.

Christmas Wonderland
http://holidays.bfn.org/xmas
Dozens of links to celebration ideas, cooking, decorations, and more.

Happy Christmas
http://www.happychristmas.com
Laughs, jokes and real-life stories about Christmas catastrophes. An interactive site where users can swap gift ideas, electronic Christmas cards, and Christmas horror stories, as well as advice on holiday planning and book/music reviews.

Merry-Christmas.com
http://www.merry-christmas.com
Site features music, movies, recipes, games, email to Santa, interactive story book, kids' zone, and more.

Santa Claus.com
http://www.santaclaus.com
Site features book recommendations, virtual Christmas cards, links to Christmas around the world, Santa's favorite recipes, email to Santa and more.

The Ultimate Christmas Site
http://members.tripod.com/~newyearseve/
Music, games, clipart, stories and more!

Holiday—Easter

A Holy Easter
http://www.rockies.net/~spirit/sermons/easterpage.html
Links to hundreds of religious sites on Easter.

Easter Collage
http://www.execpc.com/~tmuth/easter/main.htm
Links to Easter-related sites, including music, Scripture, sermon prose, art, Lent, and more.

Easter Dating Method
http://www.assa.org.au/edm.html
Site details how Easter date is determined, offers a simplified method for calculating Easter, and gives Easter dates until A.D. 2299.

Easter on the Net
http://www.holidays.net/easter/
Comprehensive site on the religious and secular celebration of Easter.

Easter Page
http://www.execpc.com/~tmuth/easter/
Journey through Scripture, art, music, and other materials which reflect the mystery and miracle of the death and resurrection of Jesus Christ.

other sites of interest

4Easter.com
http://4easter.4anything.com
Site offers links to over two dozen Easter-related sites, including food, eggs, traditions, religion, baskets, and more.

Bunny Hutch
http://kidexchange.about.com/kids/kidexchange/library/bleaster.htm
Links to Easter-related sites and information.

Easter Pages
http://www.happy-easter.com/
Site features special online greetings and messages, electronic Easter postcards, prize contests, a virtual Easter egg hunt, and more.

Holiday—Thanksgiving

Not Just for Kids! The First Thanksgiving
http://www.night.net/thanksgiving/first.html-ssi
The history of the holiday, with special graces and psalms.

Thanksgiving Grace
http://www.night.net/thanksgiving/grace.html-ssi
A broad selection of favorite graces for the holiday meal.

Thanksgiving Stories
http://www.joyfulheart.com/holiday/thanksgiving.htm
A collection of inspirational pieces from Dr. Ralph A. Wilson.

other sites of interest

About Thanksgiving
http://www.rats2u.com/thanksgiving/
thanksgiving_index.htm
WWW guide to Thanksgiving animations, clipart, virtual cards, Thanksgiving history, travel, recipes, events, links, and more.

Caleb Johnson's Mayflower Webpage
http://members.aol.com/calebj/mayflower.html
A beautiful and comprehensive collection of information about the first Pilgrim colony.

Kids Domain Thanksgiving
http://www.kidsdomain.com/holiday/thanks
Links to games, crafts, recipes, puzzles, tales, other Thanksgiving sites, and more.

Thanksgiving on the Net
http://www.holidays.net/thanksgiving
Links to sites related to the Thanksgiving holiday.

Thanksgiving on the Web
http://holidays.bfn.org/thanksgiving
Links to dozens of Thanksgiving sites related to history, recipes, kids, celebrations, and more.

Home and Home Repair

Sunny Homemaker
http://pages.ivillage.com/sunny_homemaker/
A site to inspire Christian homemakers, moms and women.

The 21st Century Homekeeper
http://www.geocities.com/Heartland/Hills/9684/home.html
Encouragment, instruction and help for the Christian homemaker.

other sites of interest

20 Uses
www.geocities.com/promiserani/20uses/
Don't throw anything away until you check here to see how you could use it!

Ask the Builder
http://www.askbuild.com/
Practical advice from Tim Carter, nationally syndicated columnist.

BathWeb.com
http://www.bathweb.com/
Features a bathroom planner and a forum for questions.

Better Homes and Gardens
http://www.bhglive.com/homeimp
Home improvement encyclopedia—plumbing, wiring, carpentry, decks, masonry, and more.

Bob Vila's American Home
http://homearts.com/bvah/00bvahc1.htm
Get help when making important decisions about improving and redesigning your home.

Do-It-Yourself Appliance Repair
http://www.appliancerepair.net/
A troubleshooting guide for major appliances, with links to parts suppliers and service agencies.

Do-It-Yourself.com
http://doityourself.com/
More than 36 topics, covering everything from appliances, energy saving, and concrete, to woodworking.

Do-It-Yourself Pest Control Solution
http://doyourownpestcontrol.com/
Information, tips, and remedies for major pest infestations.

Fixit Homepage
http://begin.com/fixit/
Suggestions and ideas for home improvements. Look them up by room, type of job, or quick tip.

Hints from Heloise
http://www.heloise.com
The newspaper columnist online, with tips, archives, books, pamphlets, videos, etc.

Home Central
http://homecentral.com/
Extensive index of the how-to's on home repair.

Home Depot
http://homedepot.com
Illustrated step-by-step home improvement instructions.

Home Improvement Encyclopedia
http://www.bhglive.com/homeimp/
Extensive tips and information from *Better Homes and Gardens* Online.

Home Improvement Net Tips
http://www.nettips.com/homepage.html
Discover ideas and products that help maintain and upgrade the value of a home.

Home Maintenance and Repair
http://www.msue.msu.edu/msue/imp/mod02/
master02.html
Michigan State University Extension Services database
of hundreds of tips on caring for your home and the stuff
you put in it. You can find tips on everything from stain
removal to controlling carpenter bees to fixing a plugged
drain.

Hometime
http://pbs.org/hometime/pc1.htm
Welcome to Hometime's How-To Center where you will
find step-by-step instructions on over 25 different home
improvement and repair topics.

Lowe's Home Improvement Warehouse
http://www.lowes.com/Lowes/howto/
howtosection.asp?CATALOGID=20
Step-by-step guidelines to popular projects for home improvements, with a section on choosing the right
houseplan.

Martha Stewart Living
http://www.marthastewart.com
Site includes helpful information on holidays, shopping,
cooking, weddings, crafts, gardening, home, and more.

Mrs. Survival
http://www.mrssurvival.com/
Homemaking tips, advice and discussions.

Natural Handyman, The
http://www.naturalhandyman.com
A feast of home repair help, information, humor, and encouragement.

Paint It Yourself
http://www.commercial-directory.com/faux/
Help with the design and email instructions to paint
your own faux finish. Site has FAQs, photos, and examples.

H

Plumbnet
http://www.plumbnet.com/
The interactive plumbing network with lots of advice for the homeowner.

Reader's Digest
http://www.thefamilyhandyman.com/
The Family Handyman.

Remodel Online
http://www.remodelonline.com/
Over a half million pages of remodeling and repair advice!

Remodeling Online
http://www.remodeling.hw.net/
Where the smart remodelers turn for how-to, design, and business advice.

RepairClinic.com
http://www.repairclinic.com/
Making it easier to repair your own appliances.

Tipking
http://tipking.com/
Timeless household tips for an easier, cheaper and safer future.

Today's Homeowner
http://www.Todayshomeowner.com
Site featuring information on plumbing, repair, baths, and more.

Toiletology 101
http://www.toiletology.com/index.shtml
Everything you need to know to repair or replace a toilet!

WoodNet
http://www.woodnet.net
Site includes tool reviews, links to other woodworking sites, and the heart of the site: 101 woodworking tips and techniques.

Homeschooling

Bible Memory Plan for Memorizing Scripture
http://www.scripturememory.com
Bible memory plan offered by Scripture Memory Fellowship.

Center for Catholic Home Educators
http://www.geocities.com/Heartland/Village/6599/
Links to hundreds of sites helping all homeschoolers.

Christian Books—Eclectic Homeschool Bookstore
http://eho.org/Bookstore/chbookst.htm
Classics, history, Bible study tools and more.

Christian Curriculum Cellar
http://www.christiancurriculumcellar.com/
These pages make used homeschooling materials available. The curriculum is Christian-based, provided by a Christian family to help homeschoolers.

Christian Homeschool Fellowship
http://www.chfweb.com/
Searches, bookstore, articles, recommendations, recipes, statement of faith, and more.

Christian Homeschool Forum
http://www.gocin.com/homeschool/index.htm
Articles to encourage Christian homeschoolers. Links to discussions, conferences, books, magazines, reviews, and more.

Christian Homeschool Resource Center
http://www.christianhomeschoolers.com/
Information on Christianity, homeschooling, parenting, military families, Filipino-Americans, shopping, and more.

Christian Light Education
http://www.anabaptists.org/clp/
Offers a full line of educational materials for grades 1–12. These were developed for individualized homeschool settings, but are also being used extensively by schools.

Core Curriculum of America
http://members.xoom.com/CoreCurric/
Customized curriculum for homeschoolers. With input from student and parent, customize a curriculum exclusively for you.

Covenant Home Curriculum
http://covenanthome.com/
A full-service, K-12, classical, Christian homeschool curriculum provider for home educators.

Homeschool House
http://www.perkinsfamily.com/page54.html
Christian homeschooling site with curriculum ideas, Bible studies for children, and "Daring Devotions." Study the holidays with a biblical perspective.

Homeschool Discount Store
http://www.homeschooldiscount.com
Save up to 40% on educational software, homeschool curriculum, Bible software, science kits, educational games, and more.

Homeschool Publishing House
http://www.bravewc.com/hph/
Carries products for the Christian home educator. Lists new and used curriculum, as well as helps for the homeschooling family.

Homeschooling for Jesus Christ
http://members.aol.com/Dansndoll/homepage.htm
A homeschooling resource that contains tons of links and information about the Christian homeschool. Links for all subjects, and craft ideas, as well as links for many concerns of the Christian.

Homeschooling Resources
http://www.entourages.com/barbs/homeschool.htm
Christian site with links to homeschooling resources, homeschool websites, magazines, books, maps, disability sites, and more.

HSPlace
http://www.hsmom@hsplace.com/
A comprehensive site for the Christian homeschooler.

Lord's Harvest
http://members.home.net/thelordsharvest/
Christian homeschooling site—very informative and help-ful, well-constructed with great links. A must for anyone contemplating homeschooling.

Safe Kids Christian Links and Homeschool Links
http://www.christian-internet.com/homeschool
Safe, clean site for homeschoolers, parents, with fun links, activity links, curriculum, and more.

The Christian Homeschool Journal
http://members.nbci.com/hmschooljrnl/page8.html
Practical advice to making homeschooling effective. Full of fun and ready-to-use ideas.

other sites of interest

Apricot
http://www.apricotpie.com/
A haven, or living room, for homeschoolers. Homeschool-ing families can enjoy polls, essays, profiles, stories, newsletter, chatroom, and message boards.

Bookmobile—Homeschool Books
http://homeschool.itgo.com/
Buy and sell used and new homeschool books and materi-als. Since 1989 over 100,000 homeschool families have bought or sold their materials at the Bookmobile. Now you can do it online.

Books4Homeschool
http://www.books4homeschool.com/links.htm
Links to over 250 homeschool sites.

Coyle's Where in the Web and Other Homeschool and Educational Stuff
http://www.geocities.com/Athens/Aegean/3446/
Veteran homeschool Mom (11+ years) shares tips on homeschooling and educational curriculum Internet links with commentary.

Eclectic Homeschool Online
http://eho.org
A complete homeschool magazine online for creative homeschoolers. You'll find feature articles, resources, reviews, topical weblink index, bookstore, departments with articles and resources for all academic areas, homeschool advice column, state legal and support resources, discussion boards, and a chat room.

Harris Homeschool Planner
http://www.agate.net/~imec
A set of reproducible master forms that are used to create a teacher's planner and/or student planner.

Home Crusaders
http://members.aol.com/usteach/index.html
A homeschooling resource site that also has a newsletter and a branch for homeschool kids.

Home Education Magazine
http://www.geocities.com/Heartland/Acres/9395/schedules.html
One of the oldest, most respected and informative magazines on homeschooling.

Homeschooling Dads
http://www.geocities.com/Athens/5118/
This site is devoted to dads who homeschool.

Homeschools and Schoolwork
http://www.useekufind.com/pschoolw.htm
Links for homeschoolers, for the students, and for the teacher.

Home Sweet Homeschool
http://www.lauraloft.f2s.com/resource/school.htm
Extensive directory of links on homeschooling advice and resources.

HomeEducator.com
http://www.homeeducator.com/
Includes pages for *Home Educator's Family Times,* a free publication for families interested in homeschooling; the Homeschool Support Network; and more.

Home's Cool . . . Homeschool
http://www.vvm.com/~birons/homecool.htm
An easy and comprehensive connection to various home-school resources and information.

Homeschool Books
http://homeschool.itgo.com/
Bestselling and popular homeschool books.

Homeschool Headquarters
http://www.kynd.com/~homeskol/homeskol.htm
You will find over 890(and still growing) educational links covering subjects from Art to Zoo.

Homeschool Internet Yellow Pages
http://www.homeschoolyellowpages.com/
Provides one-stop place for homeschoolers to find information about vendors/suppliers of homeschool products and curriculum.

H

Homeschool Quest
http://www.useekufind.com/homeschools.htm
Curricula and lesson plans for all ages and all subjects.

Homeschool World
http://www.home-school.com/
A world of homeschool resources at your fingertips.

Homeschoolers for Christ
http://talbotbible.org/homeschool
An online support group for homeschoolers. Site includes encouragement from fellow homeschoolers, articles, chat, message boards, postcards, contact center, devotionals, email, links, and more.

Homeschool's Cool
http://www.clifhanger.com/homeschooling
How to homeschool packets with information designed to help you with everything you need to begin homeschooling.

Kids Love . . . Professor Pockets
http://www.albertweb.com/
Kids site full of colorful graphics, uplifting music, and lots to do! Online games, fun characters, science experi-

ments, educational links, stories, and an International
Kids Club to join!

Organizing Your Homeschooling Day
http://childfun.com/home/hs.shtml
Great tips for the beginning homeschooler, and the experienced one, too.

Practical Homeschooling Magazine
http://www.home-school.com/
Analyzes and compares what's available to help with difficult purchasing decisions. Special features.

Randi's Reruns
http://www.rerunbooks.com/
New and used homeschool books and curriculum, games, tapes, etc. A free contest with prizes for homeschool children. Features a page of inspirational books for adults too!

Teach Children About Money
http://www.allaboutmymoney.com/index.html?169,49
Resources for homeschoolers on teaching children the basics of finance.

Homeschool Message Boards

The following sites are message boards where you can discuss homeschooling issues online!

Christian Homeschool Forum
http://www.gocin.com/homeschool/
Encouragement, practical advice and resources for the Christian homeschooler.

Homeschooling/Unschooling Message Board
http://boardserver.mycomputer.com/
list.html?u=unschooler&f=1
Ask for advice, or share some tips with other Christian homeschoolers.

other sites of interest

2 Cool 4 School
http://www.InsideTheWeb.com/messageboard/mbs.cgi/
mb23518

Homeschool Message Board
*http://www.ilovejesus.com/cgi-bin/ubb//
forumdisplay.cgi?action=topics&forum=
Homeschooling&number=13&DaysPrune=10&*

Homeschoolers Networking Together
http://www.its-a-living.com/wwwboard/

Homeschool Fun
http://www.homeschoolfun.com/hspeak.html

Homeschool Message Board
*http://www.insidetheweb.com/messageboard/mbs.cgi/
mb55369*

Independent Study High School Message Board
http://www.paradise-web.com/plus/plus.mirage?who=jlg

H

Humor

AccordingToWho?!
http://www.AccordingToWho.com/
The college devotional with a sense of humor. Eight
o'clock classes and other life-threatening situations.
Visit the website of author and Christian communicator
Juanita Thouin.

Catholic Humor
http://www.justcatholic.org/cathhumor/
A directory of humor from Catholic websites around the
world.

Christian Cartoons
http://www.ChristianCartoons.com
The Christian cartoons/comics showcase and resource
center.

Christian Chuckles
http://www.biblenet.net/niteclub/jokes.html
A vast selection of jokes on church and Biblical topics.

Christian Comics International
http://members.aol.com/ChriCom/
Links to Christian comics and organizations.

Christian Depot
http://www.edepot.com/cath.html

Christian discussion forum, live chat, mailing list, art gallery, online bookstore, Jesus quotes of the moment, streaming audio about the life of Jesus, Christian Savior ring, Christian humor, and good introductions.

Christian Humor
http://www.agapefest.com/~rsanders/humor.htm

The best of Christian humor and good clean jokes.

Christian Humor Archive
http://www.angelsonline.net/humorarchive.htm

A broad selection of funny stories and jokes organized by subject.

Church Humor
http://www.flash.net/~go4crown/chhumor.htm

Designed to allow us to laugh (sometimes at ourselves and mistakes) and enjoy that which is good like a medicine. Features humorous "Church Bulletin Mistakes."

CrossWalk Ministries
*http://www.worldvillage.com/wv/square/chapel/xwalk/
html/xwalk.htm*

Well-known Christian author and humorist Mary Lawrence shares her wit and wisdom in CrossWalk. You'll be inspired, encouraged, and tickled, as her real-life experiences open your eyes to spiritual truths.

Ecunet's Eculaugh
http://ww1.ecunet.org/ecunet.html

Good clean religious humor.

GLAD—Christian Humor Magazine
http://www.wordcentered.com

Uses cartoons and humor to teach the Bible and biblical principles.

HooRay
http://www.hooray2u.com

About Jesus and His message—comment in "Punchline Pictures"; communicates with humor, graphics, and Bible insight.

Humor
http://www.jr.co.il/hotsites/humor.htm
A directory of the best clean humor sites on the web.

Humor Archive
http://www.bible-reading.com/humor.html
Links to dozens of Christian jokes.

Pastor Tim's CleanLaugh Site
http://www.cybersalt.org/cleanlaugh/index.html
Daily laughs and clean humor. Site offers free daily joke
via email and joke archives.

Penn's Ink Christian Cartoons
http://www.word-of-grace.com
Some Christian cartoons by featured leadership cartoon-
ist Penn Clark.

Reverend Fun
http://www.gospelcom.net/rev-fun/rf.php3
Site features daily cartoon, as well as archives. Cartoons
are also available for bulletin and newsletter publication.

Sidestream Christian Cartoons and Clipart
http://www.sidestream.com
Christian cartoons updated daily, free clipart.

Smiling Angels
http://joyous.faithweb.com/
Thrice weekly email with clean jokes, Bible verses and inspirational quotes. Extensive archives online.

The Catholic Humor Pages
http://www.cpats.org/catholichumor.cfm
Jokes and stories designed to show that humor is an important part of faith sharing.

The Christian Humor Hotline
http://www.angelfire.com/ca4/HumorHotline/
Long jokes, short jokes, bulletin bloopers and more.

The Christian Humor Start Page
http://www.inhis.com/
Hundreds of jokes organized by subject, with new additions regularly.

H

Time to Laugh
http://members.xoom.com/legomai/index.htm
A collection of essays, humor, and movie reviews with an
evangelical, Christian perspective.

Top 100 Inspirational Stories and Anecdotes
http://www.bizmove.com/stories/index.htm
Collection of inspiring, amusing, eye-opening, and
spirit-soothing stories and anecdotes that will inspire
and motivate.

Winsome Wit
http://www.winsomewit.com/
An online ezine to promote well-written, thoughtful
Christian writing using wit, parody, satire, and humor.
The goal is to engage the secular mind with Christian
truth from an oblique angle.

other sites of interest

Best Jokes
http://www.thebestfreesite.com/jokes/humor.html
Site contains over 1000 of the best clean jokes!

Cartoon Corner
http://www.cartooncorner.com
Art studio, puzzles, stories, funny pages, and more.

Chet Meek's Page of Puns
http://internet.ocii.com/~cmeek/puns.htm
Puns, word plays, other nonsense and foolishness, humor,
jokes, and just good, clean fun.

Clean Humor Information
http://submitpages.com/h/clean_humor.htm
Clean humor pictures, information, and links.

Clean Jokes-Humor
http://www.surfccc.com/humor/
Great site with stories, cartoons, jokes, and more. For
children or adults.

Comics.com
http://www.unitedmedia.com/
Site that links to many daily comic websites including
Peanuts, Garfield, and more.

Droodles
http://www.droodles.com/
Hundreds of funny drawings for families to figure out the riddle. New ones weekly.

Funny Bone
http://www.funnybone.ws
Contains material that is hazardous to your funny bone.

Good Clean Fun
http://www.slonet.org/~tellswor/
A large family humor archive. Jokes, stories, and more.

Good Clean Funnies List
http://www.gcfl.net/
Get a good laugh in the morning, before or at the start of your work day.

Great Clean Humor
http://www.premiumhealth.com/laughlift/laugh.html
Get ready to laugh! You've entered the "Laugh" portion of the Laugh and Lift site. Here's some of the best clean humor on the net!

Harold's Jokes
http://www.provide.net/~harolds1/
This site contains only material suitable for the entire family, including clean jokes and inspirational stories.

Joke a Day
http://ajokeaday.com/
Your number-one source for jokes, humor, and entertainment, via email.

Jokes and Quotes
http://www.fortunecity.com/millennium/rintintin/144/jokes.html
Clean, moral-based jokes and famous, funny quotes.

Jokes in a Box
http://vtliving.com/jokes/
Click on boxes to discover jokes on this fun, humor website.

King Features Comics
http://www.kingfeatures.com/comics/index.htm
Large comic link site filled with many wellknown dailies.

Laugh Lines
http://www.laugh-lines.com/index.shtml
A weekly free and clean humor website and e-bulletin!

Laugh of the Day
http://www.laugh-of-the-day.com/
The mission is to make you laugh each and every day. A totally free site; stop by and have a laugh before you head off to work or school.

Limericks
http://www.webcom.com/texasred/garden.html
Features original, clean limericks based on Galileo's drawings of sunspot observations, dated May 3, 1612. On a parchment background.

New Life Network
http://www.nlnnet.com/subscribe_humor.html
Weekly clean humor by email.

Official Peanuts Website
http://www.peanuts.com/
Large site with Peanuts news and information. Great fan site with cartoons and links.

One-liners and Proverbs
http://www.oneliners-and-proverbs.com/
Serving the world with good quotes, one-liners and proverbs.

Scatty.com
http://www.scatty.com/
Humor for kids and family.

Story Palace
http://storypalace.ourfamily.com/main2.html
Enjoy hundreds of selected clean jokes here.

Stupid Page, The
http://www.sebourn.com/
Clean jokes and funny stories about stupid people, signs, and product warnings!

T-Bone's Corner
http://hometown.aol.com/TBONELAFS/
Humorous, clean and original stories written each week.

Today's Cartoon
http://www.glasbergen.com/
Cartoons by Randy Glasbergen. Financial, business, family humor, and more.

Latino and Spanish Speaking Sites

Alianza Evangélica Española (AEE)
http://www.lander.es/~aee/
Christian portal for Spanish-speaking believers.

AtRe VeTe Ministries
http://atrevete.com/
One of the best Christian sites in Spanish, featuring devotionals, chat, guidance, games, the Bible, and much more.

Bible Studies/Estudios Bíblicos
http://members.tripod.com/~Carlosrc_2/
Free Bible studies in both English and Spanish.

Cry of The Heart
http://www.heart-cry.com/
Steps to achieve a real and vital relationship with God. Spanish version, too.

Cristiani in Azione
http://www.cristiani-in-azione.ch
Bible study, articles, news of Israel, daily bread, chat, forum, and more.

Editorial Caribe
http://www.gospelcom.net/caribe/
The Spanish division of Thomas Nelson Publishers, offering Spanish editions of Nelson's books and Bibles, devotionals, etc.

Idportodoelmundo.com—Spanish Christian evangelism resources
http://www.idportodoelmundo.com
Links to worldwide missions and information about missionaries.

La Musica de Cross
http://www.crossproductions.net
Latin Christian music on the web. A ministry of Christian music production, representation and distribution.

Mente Abierta
http://www.menteabierta.org
Christian answer for agnostic beliefs.

Publicaciones Voz de Gracia—Publications
http://publicacionesvozdegracia.com
The Voice of Grace publishes Christian literature to spread the Word of God.

Pueblos
http://www.pueblos.org/
World Missions site with courses, information and aids for missionaries and local church.

Sonido De Alabanza
http://sonidodealabanza.iuma.com
Page of Sonido De Alabanza worship team. A Spanish Christian ministry.

TransWorld Radio
http://www.gospelcom.net/twr/rtm//
Worldwide radio ministry that broadcasts more than 1,400 hours of Christian programming each week.

Vida Cristiana
http://www.vidacristiana.com/
Homesite for the Spanish-language Christian magazine.

Law and Legal Services

Christian Administrative Service
http://www.churchadministration.com/
Pastor Joseph, an attorney and administrator, is now making available his experience in administration. In-

cludes staff organization, record keeping, fundraising procedures, legal consultants, and more.

Christian Law Association
http://www.christianlaw.org/
A ministry of helps to Bible-believing Christians, churches and ministries. Providing free legal services since 1969.

Christian Legal Society
http://www.christianlegalsociety.org/
A network of nearly 4,500 attorneys, judges, law professors and law students.

Cops For Christ
http://www.geocities.com/Heartland/Meadows/3192/ links.html
Links to sites for organizations for Christians in law enforcement.

other sites of interest

Ask a Cop
http://users.firstva.com/askacop/
Tips on home security, personal safety, and driving. General law enforcement information.

AttorneyFind
http://www.attorneyfind.com/
Search in over 70 categories for a specialist near you.

Child Custody and Divorce: Free Legal Advice
http://www.childcustody.net/
An easy to read examination on many of the basic questions about divorce and custody.

ClassAction.com
http://www.classaction.com/
News, basic information, and resources on class action lawsuits around the country.

Constitutions, Statutes and Codes
http://www.law.cornell.edu/statutes.html
U.S. Constitution, state statutes by topic, full U.S. Code, Bills and other legislative information, etc.

Cop Link
http://www.geocities.com/CapitolHill/4545
Wanted persons, missing persons, news, and products.
Local, national, and international agencies.

Crime & Clues
http://www.crimeandclues.com/
Information on the art and science of criminal investigation.

Divorce Net: Family Law Advice on Divorce
http://www.divorcenet.com/
General information on divorce and family law with
links to state information.

Find Forms
http://www.findforms.com/
Search engine to find free legal forms.

Find Law
http://www.findlaw.com
A legal research and resource library with over 15,000
publications. Also includes information on law schools,
lawyers and firms, directories, professional development,
and government resources.

FreeLegal Advice and Law Information
http://freeadvice.com/
Basic advice on many areas of law.

Internet Legal Resource Guide
http://www.ilrg.com/
Links to many sites on legal subjects.

Katsuey's Legal Resource Links
http://www.katsuey.com/
Links to legal resources online.

Law Libraries—LibrarySpot
http://www.libraryspot.com/lawlibraries.htm
Links to many available online resources.

Law on the Net
http://www.bucks.edu/library/lib_resource/
lawonnet.htm
Links to legal resources online.

LAWS.com
  http://www.laws.com/resource.html
  A directory of links to U.S. and international legal resources on the web.

LegalDocs
  http://legaldocs.com/
  This site allows you to prepare customized legal documents directly online.

Police Headquarters
  http://www.firstcop.com/
  Where cops meet to chat, share information on police tactics, community and traditional policing, and terrorism; find police resources, helps, books, publications as well as lists of officers and agencies.

U.S. Code (searchable)—Law Revision Counsel—U.S. House of Representatives
  http://uscode.house.gov/usc.htm
  Up to date Federal statutes.

United States Code—Cornell
  http://www.law.cornell.edu/uscode/
  Current Federal laws, searchable by subject.

Welcome to Court TV Online
  http://www.courttv.com/
  Site for the popular cable TV channel; news on current trials and legal issues.

Libraries and Research

Bible Research Site
  http://www.research.faithweb.com
  Information on language and texts, biblical studies, theological studies, history, software, music, religion news, articles.

Heroes of History
  http://www.heroesofhistory.com
  Facts and biographical information on historic and contemporary heroes, from C.S. Lewis to Florence Nightin-

gale to T.D. Jakes to Corrie ten Boom. Site also contains links to classic texts, museums and bibliographies, as well as a select reading list.

other sites of interest

Awesome Library
http://www.awesomelibrary.org/student.html#home
Links to school subjects, games, fun, and more! Also available in Spanish.

Bodleian Library
http://rsl.ox.ac.uk/
Information about the library, digital projects, library catalog, shopping, exhibits, and more.

British Library
http://www.bl.uk/
Homepage for the famous institution.

California Digital Library
http://www.cdlib.org/
Collections (including newspaper archives) and links.

Digital Library—The New York Public Library
http://digital.nypl.org/
Exhibits, collections, books and many links.

Digital Research Store
http://digital.library.pitt.edu/
Literature and historical collections.

Library of Congress
http://www.loc.gov/
Links to Thomas, copyright office, American memory, exhibitions, the library today, and more.

LibrarySpot
http://www.libraryspot.com
Encyclopedias, maps, libraries and more.

New York Public Library
http://www.nypl.org/
Exhibits, collections, digital resources links.

Perseus Project Homepage
  http://www.perseus.tufts.edu/
  Digital resources on art and archaeology.

The ThinkQuest Library
  http://www.thinkquest.org/library/
  Research aids grouped by topics for students of all ages.

U.S. National Library of Medicine—Homepage
  http://www.nlm.nih.gov/
  Health information, news and links.

UNESCO/IFLA Directory of Digitized Collections
  http://thoth.bl.uk/
  Central site for searching digital collections around the world.

Virtual Library—Energy, Science, and Technology
  http://www.osti.gov/virtual.html
  Links to many technical and scientific resources.

Literature and Literary Resources

A Guide to Christian Literature on the Internet
  http://www.iclnet.org/pub/resources/christian-books.html
  An extensive list of books available in electronic form covering many topics.

Abundant Life . . . Our Destiny Is Glory
  http://home.infospace.com/bigheart1
  Encouragement through Christian poems, songs, allegories and meditations.

Afterhours Inspirational Christian Stories
  http://inspirationalstories.com/2_chr.html
  Stories to maintain your faith and transform your life.

Ancient Paths: A Journal of Christian Art and Literature
  http://mypage.goplay.com/ancientpaths/
  Site contains prizewinning literature, submission guidelines, contest information, resources for writers, Bible trivia, and much more.

Bible Reading Fellowship
http://www.biblereading.org/
Founded in England in 1922 with the primary purpose of
bringing people into a greater knowledge of God
through systematic reading of the Bible.

Biblical Viewpoints Publications
http://www.mich.com/~lhaines
A Mennonite-Anabaptist witness to Bible teachings.

Bloodstone Reformed Links and Literature
http://members.aol.com/blstone77/index.html
Reformed Christian literature, Bible studies, references,
links, and eschatology.

CFC Literature
http://home.rica.net/cfcliterature
Christian books written for those pursuing New Testament church life. Major focus—spiritual survival, what
will keep God's people safe and sound in the faith, etc.

Christian Gazette
http://w3.one.net/~dovesnst
Inspirational site to uplift and inspire through the works
of Christian writers, Bible verses, and songs, literature.

Christian Literature World, Inc.
http://www.chrlitworld.com/index.htm
Its purpose is to glorify God and to make Him known
through the distribution of Bibles, Christian books,
Christian software and Internet tools.

Christian Poems
*http://www.bfree.on.ca/comdir/churches/hoperc/
poems.htm*
Collection of beautiful, uplifting, inspiring and thought-
provoking religious poems.

Christian Poetry
http://www.eskimo.com/~telical/chrspoet.html
Collection by Robert Pearson, with links to an explanation of emotive virtuism.

Christian Poetry Gallery
http://www.geocities.com/Athens/Troy/4986/
Collection of poetry from Christians around the world.

Christian Poetry: Moments
http://www.Reflect-A-Moment.com/
Reflections in the Spirit that exhort and encourage
through prophetic and inspirational poems, psalms of
praise, and poetry readings.

Christian Poets Corner
http://www.comnet.ca/~ch-poets
Christian inspirational poetry of the world where Christian poets can share their God-given poetic gift of godly
wisdom and truth.

Classical Christian Poetry
http://www.geocities.com/Athens/Troy/1787/
The poetry of over 40 major English and American poets
from Elizabethan period to present, alongside artwork
from the Italian Renaissance.

Classics Ethereal Library
http://www.ccel.org/
One of the largest collections of Christian classics online.

Club of Queer Trades
*http://www.ccel.org/chesterton/queertrades/
queertrades.html*
Chesterton's wit-filled collection of mysteries.

Cross Way Publications
http://www.ChristianPoetry.org
Spreading the gospel through the medium of poetry.

FEBC Bookroom
http://www.lifefebc.com/febcbkrm/
Offers reformed, premillennial, and fundamental books
and literature authored by the faculty of Far Eastern
Bible College.

Free Christian Poetry
http://www.angelfire.com/mo/freepoetry/index.html
Free poetry for your bulletins or newsletter.

Grace Online Library
http://www.graceonlinelibrary.org/
Dedicated to the free distribution of sound Christian literature on the web.

Graham's Homepage for Quotes
http://www.weeks-g.dircon.co.uk/
A site with hundreds of quotes, Christian and secular, arranged by topic, with plenty of wit and humor from all over the world.

Guide to Christian Literature
http://www.iclnet.org/pub/resources/
christian-books.html
An extensive list of online resources for Christians.

Heart Alive
http://www.heartalive.cjb.net
Animated e-poems to glorify God and show both Christians and non-Christians God's love, joy, peace, and hope.

Innocence of Father Brown
http://www.ccel.org/chesterton/innocence/
title.html
Chesterton's timeless novel.

Inspirational Christian Stories and Poems
http://www.getfed.com
Inspirational Christian stories, poems, thoughts, essays, and song lyrics.

Inspirations of God
http://www.geocities.com/Paris/Gallery/6930/
150 poems to thank God for a life-saving miracle, they are designed to help us find our way home.

JCFaith's Poetry Corner
http://www.geocities.com/jcfaith
Visitors are invited to read Christian poetry and submit their own to be reviewed for publication on the site.

John Donne
http://www.sonnets.org/donne.htm
The sonnets of John Donne online.

Jonathan Edwards
http://WWW.JonathanEdwards.com/
The world's largest Edwards site. Works, sermons, and
other resources. Gallery, bibliography, and other links.

Library of Online Evangelical Christian Books
http://members.aol.com/XianBooks/library.html
Over thirty volumes available for reading online.

Light Princess
http://www.ccel.org/macdonald/princess/title.html
Full text of George MacDonald's novel.

Literary Resources—Classical and Biblical
http://andromeda.rutgers.edu/~jlynch/Lit/classic.html
Links to dozens of websites on the Bible, and Greek and
Latin texts.

Locust and Honey: A Review of Christian Poetry
http://www.locustandhoney.com
Quarterly review of Christian poetry to the glory of God
offering online poetry lexicon.

Logos Maranatha
http://www.logosmaranatha.com/
Christian literature—includes works by Matthew Henry
and Jonathan Edwards.

Man Who Was Thursday
http://www.ccel.org/chesterton/thursday/thursday.html
Chesterton's timeless novel.

Necessity of Prayer
http://www.ccel.org/bounds/necessity/necessity.html
Edward Bounds's immortal book on building a life of
prayer.

New Amplified Pilgrim's Progress
http://www.orionsgate.org
Family-centered site specializing in the modernization
and dramatization of old Christian Classics such as "The
Pilgrim's Progress" books, audiobooks, videos.

On the Christian Life

http://www.ccel.org/calvin/christian_life/
christian_life.html

John Calvin's examination of the principles of living a Christian life.

Original Christian Writings

http://members.aol.com/ggbwriting/home

Thought-provoking, creative, and unusual perspectives on the Bible and everyday Christian living. Regularly updated with new stories.

Orthodoxy

http://www.ccel.org/chesterton/orthodoxy/
orthodoxy.html

Chesterton's autobiographical look at his growing Christian faith.

Paradise Lost

http://www.ccel.org/milton/paradise_lost/
paradise_lost.txt

The online text of Milton's work.

Paradise Regained

http://www.ccel.org/milton/paradise_regained/
paradise_regained.txt

The online text of Milton's work.

Pilgrim's Progress

http://www.ccel.org/bunyan/pilgrims_progress/title.html

John Bunyan's best known work.

Practice of the Presence of God

http://www.ccel.org/bro_lawrence/practice/practice.html

Brother Lawrence's immortal work on living the Christian life.

Religious Affections

http://www.ccel.org/edwards/religious_affections/
religious_affections.html

Jonathan Edwards's treatise.

Selected Works of Martin Luther
http://www.iclnet.org/pub/resources/text/
wittenberg/wittenberg-luther.html
The online texts of much of Luther's writings.

Sharman Farm Christian Ebooks
http://www.vision.net.au/~msharman/
Download great new and old Christian titles for free.

Sinners in the Hands of an Angry God
http://www.ccel.org/edwards/sinners/sinners.html
The text of Jonathan Edwards's best known sermon.

Songs and Poetry of Joan Caldwell
http://www.europa.com/~tarie/cgsongs.html
Includes some of over 25 years of published music by various artists.

Soothing Poetic Pages
http://www.geocities.com/Athens/Acropolis/3634/
hisarms.html
Christian inspired poems, prayers and inspirationals
which are encouraging, uplifting and soothing.

Till He Come
http://www.ccel.org/spurgeon/till_he_come/
title.html
The online text of Spurgeon's work.

Tyndale House Publishers
http://www.tyndale.com/
Ministering to the spiritual needs of people primarily
through literature consistent with biblical principles.

Walking with God
http://members.home.net/thorz/wwgod.html
Original fiction, sci-fi, articles and other writings geared
to the Christian web surfer as well as Bible search and
reference.

Way of Life Literature
http://wayoflife.org/~dcloud
Fundamental Baptist Bible studies, apologetics, and
more.

Way of Perfection
http://www.ccel.org/teresa/way/main.html
The story of St. Teresa of Avila.

Wellspring: A Journal of Christian Poetry
http://www.angelfire.com/wa2/wellspring
Features quality Christian poetry by a variety of authors.

Wesley, John: Sermons
http://www.ccel.org/wesley/sermons/sermons.html
The online text of John Wesley's sermons.

Wisdom of Father Brown
http://www.ccel.org/chesterton/wisdom/title.html
The text of Chesterton's novel.

Writings from the Ministry of George H. Warnock
http://www.meatindueseason.org
Twelve Publications for online viewing or download, free teaching volumes expounding types and shadows of O.T.

other sites of interest

23 Tales by Leo Tolstoy
http://www.ccel.org/tolstoy/23_tales/23_tales.html
A selection of Tolstoy's works, including Ivan the Fool, and several fairy tales.

Ancient Greek
http://kenwoodward.ne.mediaone.net/greek/template/xample13.htm
Enchridion—a user friendly guide for reading ancient Greek.

Andrew Crumey's "Literary Links"
http://www.users.globalnet.co.uk/~crumey/links.html
Extensive links to literature sites.

Authorlink
http://www.authorlink.com/
Resources for writers, editors, etc.

Bartleby.com: Great Books Online
http://www.bartleby.com/
Literature, poetry, and reference works online.

Bibliomania: Best Online Literature and Reference Books
http://www.bibliomania.com/
Broad list of online texts.

Book Reviews, Authors, Fiction, and Bestsellers on Bookreporter.com
http://www.thebookreport.com/
Reviews, articles, news, and bestseller lists.

BookReview.com—Your Resource for Literary Reviews, News and Events
http://www.bookreview.com/
Extensive reviews of new and classic books.

Books, Books, Books
http://www3.ns.sympatico.ca/allegrow/books.htm
Links and articles on books and literature.

BookSpot: Book Reviews, Book Awards and Much More
http://www.bookspot.com/
Articles and links to many literary sites.

Bookwire Electronic Children's Book Index
http://www.bookwire.com/links/readingroom/echildbooks.html
Online texts of classic children's books.

Celebration of Women Writers
http://digital.library.upenn.edu/women/
Electronic texts, biographies, bibliographies.

Children's Literature
http://www.childrenslit.com/
Reviews, news, recommendations and author/illustrator interviews.

Children's Literature Web Guide
http://www.acs.ucalgary.ca/~dkbrown
Features, discussion boards, quick reference, links, and more Internet resources related to books for children.

Children's Literature—Resource for Parents
http://www.acs.ucalgary.ca/~dkbrown/rparent.html
A broad list of links to resources for children.

L

Complete Works of William Shakespeare
http://tech-two.mit.edu/Shakespeare/works.html
Full text files, as well as search capabilities, and FAQs.

CVCO—Overbooked Table of Contents
http://freenet.vcu.edu/education/literature/bklink.html
Links to many literary websites.

EagerReaders.com
http://www.eagerreaders.com/
A highly-selective list of 700+ parent-screened books, appropriate for both eager and reluctant readers.

Electronic Literature Foundation Library
http://elf.chaoscafe.com/elf_by_Author.htm
Classic books online.

Electronic Reader's Advisor
http://www.nypl.org/branch/services/oas/ra.html
Links to many sites from the New York Public Library.

Electronic Text Center—University of Virginia
http://etext.lib.virginia.edu/
Homepage for over 50,000 e-books.

English Server
http://english-server.hss.cmu.edu/
29,000 e-books organized by subject; search engine for the collection.

Great Books Index
http://www.mirror.org/books/gb.home.html
Online editions of many classic books.

Homer on the Internet
http://www.rmc.edu/academics/departments/clas/ hlinks.html
Texts and translations, general information, Perseus links, and other stuff.

Internet Book Review Resource List
http://www.sfsite.com/fi/fibrsi/index.htm
A collection of reviews sorted by author.

Internet Classics Archive
http://classics.mit.edu/index.html
Read 441 classic works in multiple translations, purchase works, help pages, other links, and trivia.

IPL Online Texts Collection
http://www.ipl.org/reading/books/
13,000 electronic text titles.

Kids Web—Literature
http://www.kidsvista.com/Arts/literature.html
Extensive links to children's literature sites.

Literary Guide to Classic Literature
http://www.geocities.com/Wellesley/Garden/1092/
Links to sites on selected English authors.

Literary Leaps—1000s of Publishing, Publisher, Author and Book Links
http://www.literaryleaps.com/
Search engine and links to many literary sites.

L

Literature Resources
http://www.teleport.com/~mgroves/
Literature links for the high school student.

LitLinks
http://www.ualberta.ca/~amactavi/litlinks.htm
Many links to literature sites and texts.

OnLine Books Page
http://digital.library.upenn.edu/books/
Over 10,000 titles online.

Online Literature Library—Classics at the Online Literature Library
http://www.literature.org/authors/
A collection of electronic texts.

Poets.org
http://www.poets.org/index.cfm
Find a poet, find a poem, listening booth, discussion forums, events, literary links, search, and more.

Project Gutenberg
http://promo.net/pg/
Large library of electronic texts.

Representative Poetry Online
http://www.library.utoronto.ca/utel/rp/intro.html
Poetry indices by last name, title, first line, as well as
timelines, glossary, and essays.

The Pulitzer Prizes
http://www.pulitzer.org/
Homesite for the prestigious literature awards, with an
extensive archive of past winners.

Voice of the Shuttle
http://vos.ucsb.edu/
Extensive links to literature sites.

Writers and Readers Search Engine
http://www.fictionsearch.com/
Search engine for literary subjects. Christian poetry and
music, also Christian environmental novels and mystery
novels.

Maps

Bible Atlas Maps v2.3
*http://www.zdnet.com/downloads/stories/info/
0,,0012NS,.html*
40 free downloadable maps of the Holy Land and other
Bible locations in PowerPoint format.

Charts4Christ
http://www.charts4christ.com/
Maps, charts and other graphic information for all students of the Bible.

other sites of interest

4 Maps
http://4maps.4anything.com/
Street maps, wall maps, historical maps, and more.

Arc Data Online
http://www.esri.com/data/online/index.html
Create your own U.S. and world maps using the data
you select.

Boundaries of the United States
*http://4maps.4anything.com/network-frame/
0,1855,4738-20519,00.html*
Map shows changing boundaries in the United States as
year changes.

Funk and Wagnalls—World Atlas
http://www.funkandwagnalls.com/atlas/
Click and go to any spot in the world. Links to other basic resources and reference works, too.

Graphic Maps' World Atlas
http://www.graphicmaps.com/aatlas/world.htm
Maps, geography info, travel guides, quizzes and more.

Historical Atlas of the 20th Century
http://users.erols.com/mwhite28/20centry.htm
Dozens of beautiful and informative interactive maps
showing world event and trends.

Historical Maps of Europe
http://www.salve.edu/~romanemp/Bigcart.htm
Maps of European geographic and political divisions
from A.D. 100 to 1500.

Map Machine @ Nationalgeographic.com
http://plasma.nationalgeographic.com/mapmachine/
Give the location, and this interactive site will show it to
you on a variety of maps.

Maps on Us
http://www.mapsonus.com
Site dedicated to making maps for travelers or researchers.

MapBlast
http://www.mapblast.com
An atlas site that promises to find anything. Includes
maps and directions.

M

MapQuest
http://www.mapquest.com
Driving directions, maps, and more can be found on this
atlas site that even includes live traffic reports.

Maps.com
http://www.maps.com/
Shop, travel resources, atlas, driving directions, topo-
graphic maps, and much more.

Panoramic Maps
*http://4maps.4anything.com/network-frame/
0,1855,4738-13513,00.html*
Panoramic maps brought to you by the Geography and
Map division of the Library of Congress.

Yahoo! Maps and Driving Directions
http://maps.yahoo.com/py/maps.py
Enter an address to get a map or driving directions.

Medical Information

Beracah-Needs Share Program
for Christian's Medical Needs
http://www.beracah.org
Beracah Ministries needs share program is a scripturally
based not-for-profit Christian ministry of voluntary mutual giving.

Christian Medical Fellowship
http://www.cmf.org.uk
Homesite of the Christian Medical Fellowship.

Christian Medical Foundation
http://www.wwmedical.com/cmf
An interdenominational organization based on following
ethical practices and recognition of the spirit of God in
healing.

Christians in Healthcare—Overseas
http://www.christian-healthcare.org.uk/c-hc/ovrseas.htm
Christians in Healthcare offers advice and guidance on
job opportunities for those wanting to serve the Lord
overseas, especially in Middle Eastern countries.

Christian-Search.Net: Business/Medical
http://christian-search.net/Business/Medical
Medical section of Christian-Search.Net

Heal the Nations: Christian Medical Missions
http://www.healnation.org
Homesite of a Christian medical missions organization
whose vision is to improve our world's health one village
at a time.

HMT International
http://www.galaxymall.com/medical/missions
Short-term (two week) Christian medical missions to
Guatemala, Dominican Republic and Haiti. Medical, dental and non-medical personnel needed.

Hospital Christian Fellowship International
http://www.hcfusa.com
Fellowship offers education, Bible study, and guidance
for Christian healthcare professionals.

Institute of Christian Growth
http://www.instchristiangrowth.org
Institute offers a program for the study of Christianity in
medicine, with audio and video tapes available for study.

Medicine and the Christian Mind
http://www.cmf.org.uk/pubs/nucleus/nucjan00/mind.htm
Site information from the perspective that being a Christian should shape one's understanding and practice of
medicine.

other sites of interest

411-health.com-Health, Fitness and Diet
http://www.411-health.com
Information on everything health-related, from diets to
dentists, health insurance to holistic medicine, etc.

4Medicine.com
http://www.4Medicine.com
Discover the details behind your latest prescription or
over the counter medication from Pharmacia/Upjohn,
Bayer, FDA, drug interactions and online pharmacies.

M

ACHE—American Council for Headache Education
http://www.achenet.org/
An organization dedicated to advancing the treatment and understanding of headaches. Advice and discussion groups, too.

Allallergy
http://www.allallergy.net/
A comprehensive directory of allergy information on the web. Articles, organizations, publications and more.

American Heart Association National Center
http://www.americanheart.org
American Heart Association National Center.

American Medical Association Physician Select
http://www.ama-assn.org/aps/amahg.htm
An online search for the best doctors, with more than 650,000 AMA members listed.

Best Doctors
http://www.bestdoctors.com/
Extensive online search for doctors in any area, plus information on specialties, etc.

Better Homes and Gardens: Colds, Flu, and Allergies
http://www.bhglive.com/health/coldflu.html
Guides and articles written to help cure and prevent the flu.

BreastCancer.net
http://www.breastcancer.net/
News, support, treatment information and more.

Complete Home Medical Guide
http://cpmcnet.columbia.edu/texts/guide
Guide on how to make the best use of medical resources.

Depression
http://www.depression.com/
Information, advice and extensive resources on this common but misunderstood health problem.

Diabetes
   http://www.diabetes.com/
   Articles, resources, treatment and news on diabetes.

Dr. Greene's House Calls
   http://www.drgreene.com/
   Online pediatric news and advice with a great search feature to find what you want to know.

Human Anatomy Online
   http://www.innerbody.com/
   Elementary information about the human body.

Internet Mental Health
   http://www.mentalhealth.com/
   Links to disorders, diagnosis, medications, magazines, and other links.

LifeClinic.com
   http://www.bloodpressure.com/
   News, recipes and fitness tips on diabetes, heart disease, strokes and other conditions.

Male Health Center
   http://www.malehealthcenter.com/
   Information, advice and links on diet, exercize and general male health topics.

Mayo Health O@sis
   http://www.mayo.ivi.com/ivi/mayo/common/htm
   News, information on specialties, etc. Updated frequently.

MedicineNet
   http://www.medicinenet.com/
   Searchable, easy-to-read, in-depth information about medical conditions, news, etc. Physician written.

MedLine
   http://www.healthgate.com/HealthGate/MEDLINE/search.shtml
   Search engine for basic medical information.

M

Medline Plus
http://medlineplus.gov/
Information on hundreds of diseases, conditions, and wellness issues; doctors, dentists, hospitals, newsletters, and more.

Mr. Bones
http://www.lhs.berkeley.edu/shockwave/bones.html
Can you put the human skeleton together, or will you need help?

Muscular Dystrophy Association (MDA) USA Homepage
http://www.mdausa.org
Headed by national chairman Jerry Lewis, the Muscular Dystrophy Association is a major source for news and information about neuromuscular diseases, MDA research and services.

Pain.com
http://www.pain.com/
Pain management news, links and resources.

Patient's Introduction to Cancer
http://www.diet-pills.com/geninf.htm
Links to treatments, coping, rights, and more.

Prostate
http://www.prostatitis.org/prostateorg/
A wide-ranging site dealing with a major men's health concern.

Quackwatch
http://www.quackwatch.com/
How to avoid health frauds, scams and medical quackery.

Resource Directory for Older People
http://www.aoa.dhhs.gov/aoa/dir/43.html
A cooperative effort of the National Institute on Aging and the Administration on Aging.

Rx List
http://www.rxlist.com
A listing of prescription drugs and alternative medicines.

Sleepnet
http://www.sleepnet.com/
Comprehensive site for information and resources on
sleep disorders.

Virtual Hospital
http://vh.radiology.uiowa.edu/
A virtual tour through a metropolitan
hospital.

Virtual Human Project
*http://www.nlm.nih.gov/research/visible/
visible_human.html*
A project of the National Library of Medicine; features
complete, three-dimensional representations of the normal male and female human bodies.

Visible Embryo
http://www.visembryo.com
A comprehensive, educational resource of information on
human development from conception to birth, including
games, and links. Designed for both medical students
and interested lay persons.

WebMD
http://www.searchwebmd.com
The American Medical Associations comprehensive online health resource providing health information and
support needs.

WHO
http://www.who.int/
Homesite of the World Health Organization, with informative articles on health issues around the world.

Message Forums

1Christian.net World Wide Message Board
http://www.1christian.net/newWWMB/
Dedicated to the best in Christian music.

Bible Scriptures Truths Message Board
http://www.bravenet.com/forum/show.asp?userid=dv8190
A forum for the inconsistencies within the Bible and the
way science sees the Bible.

Catholic Community Forum
http://www.catholic-forum.com/
An online community for Catholics and anyone interested in the Catholic Church. Featuring chat, discussion boards, numerous described links, resources, daily inspirational newsletter, and more.

Christian Homeschool Forum
http://www.gocin.com/homeschool/
Encouragement, practical advice and resources for the Christian homeschooler.

Christian Leadership
http://www.iclnet.org/pub/resources/lf/lf.html
A forum for leaders to share ideas for ministry and help solve problems that other leaders face; to enable leaders to become more effective in their ministries.

Christian Men
http://www.botcw.com/cgi-bin/forums/
forums.cgi?az=listandforum=men
A message board for topics of interest to men.

Christian Message Board
http://www.daveandangel.com/cgi-bin/ikonboard//
ikonboard.cgi
A public forum message board for Christian topics of discussion.

Christian Music Today
http://www.bravenet.com/forum/
show.asp?userid=wf10845
A forum for the discussion of different types of Christian music.

Christian Singles Match
http://www.christiansinglesmatch.com/
A communications forum for Christians to start new relationships. Features news, markets, Christian resources, and more.

Christian Wholeness and Health Discussion Forum
http://www.delphi.com/christianhealth/
This is a discussion forum and resource site for Christian health issues.

Christian Women

http://www.botcw.com/cgi-bin/forums
/forums.cgi?az=listandforum=women

A message board for topics of interest to women.

Cornerstone Connection

http://www.slic.com/heisiam/cconnect/welcome.htm

A place where Christians and skeptics alike can get connected to Jesus Christ by participating in the discussion forum, where you can ask and answer sincere questions about Christianity.

Curriculum

http://www.botcw.com/cgi-bin/forums/
forums.cgi?az=listandforum=curriculum

A general board for the discussion of homeschool curriculums.

Fellowship Net

http://www.bham.net/fn/

A gathering place to develop relationships with a caring community. You'll find principles and truth that will help you in your life. Bible studies, prayer requests, praise, and more.

Fisherman's Net Christian Forum

http://www0.delphi.com/custom12/

Homepage of the Fisherman's Net Christian Forum on Delphi Forums—a place for Christians to meet and fellowship.

Gentle Christian Mothers Message Board

http://pub11.ezboard.com/bgentlechristianmothers

A place of encouragement and support for Christian mothers.

Homeschooling/Unschooling Message Board

http://boardserver.mycomputer.com/
list.html?u=unschooler&f=1

Ask for advice, or share some tips with other Christian homeschoolers.

M

Homeschooling with Diana Waring
http://www.botcw.com/cgi-bin/forums/forums.cgi?az=listandforum=diana
An active message board for Christian homeschoolers.

Marriage
http://www.botcw.com/cgi-bin/forums/forums.cgi?az=listandforum=Marriage
A forum for discussing what it takes to have a biblically based marriage.

Men's Message Boards
http://christianitytoday.aol.com/men/features/aolboards.html
Forums from *Christianity Today* for discussion of a wide range of men's issues.

New Christian Message Board Review Site
http://pub6.ezboard.com/fbiblediscussionandsharing recommendedwebsites.showMessage?topicID=37.topic
A guide to finding the right forum for you. Reviews updated regularly.

Sinai Christian Chat
http://www.InsideTheWeb.com/messageboard/mbs.cgi?acct=mb140310
An open forum for Christian topics of all types.

The Alpha and Omega Christian Message Board
http://www.InsideTheWeb.com/messageboard/mbs.cgi/mb18165
An open forum for Christian topics of all types.

The Christian Message Board
http://www.christianmb.com/
A place to share news, opinion, prayers and support with fellow Christians.

Where the Son Shines
http://www.wtss.com/
Chat rooms, prayer message boards and more. Connecting Christians in in local missions and compassionate outreach.

other sites of interest

Homeschool Message Boards:

Links to a variety of boards on homeschooling and related topics.

> *http://www.kaleidoscapes.com/*
> *http://www.its-a-living.com/wwwboard/*
> *http://www.homeschoolfun.com/wwwboard/*
> *wwwboard.html*
> *http://www.InsideTheWeb.com/messageboard/mbs.cgi/*
> *mb23518*

Just Moms

> *http://www.justmoms.com/jmboards/*
> Features a variety of forums, including prayer, Bible study, schools, special needs kids, etc.

Movies

(See also Entertainment; Videos)

Access Christian—Entertainment, Music, Books and News

> *http://www.accesschristian.com/*
> News and links on Christian and secular entertainment.

Christian Cinema

> *http://www.christiancinema.com/*
> The best of Christian movies available on tape. Free newsletter updates, too.

Christian Movie Theater Online

> *http://www.angelfire.com/mt/BibleTruths/*
> *MovieCenter.html*
> Using Real Audio and video player free to download, this is a fun family entertainment site.

Christian Movies Theater

> *http://www.angelfire.com/sys/*
> *popup_source.shtml?Category=*
> Free online showings of selected Christian films and cartoons.

Christian Movies.com
http://www.christianmovies.com/
A source for the best Christian videos and industry news.

Christian Spotlight on the Movies
http://www.ChristianAnswers.Net/spotlight/home.html
A movie rating review site for Christians. Contains current movie reviews and archival search by title or by "moral rating."

CrossCurrrents
http://christianity.miningco.com/library/weekly/ blmovies.htm
Short reviews of many films from a Christian perspective.

Ducky Movie Reviews
http://www.killerducky.com
Site offers Christian movie reviews.

FamilyStyle Movie Guide: Movie Reviews for Parents
http://www.familystyle.com/
Movie reviews and news for parents.

Kids in Mind
http://www.kids-in-mind.com/About.htm
Straightforward family friendly reviews.

Monthly Christian Current Events, Reviews, Updates, Movies
http://www.kingdomquest.com/joeog/monthly.htm
Previews and reviews of family films.

Movie Mom
http://www.moviemom.com/
New and classic film reviews for families.

Movie Reviews and Discussion Guides for Christian Youth Groups
http://home.pix.za/gc/gc12/movies/index.htm
Provides basic plot descriptions, ties in biblical elements, where applicable, and offers discussion questions.

NCCB/USCC—Movie Reviews
http://www.nccbuscc.org/movies/videoall.htm
Hundreds of video and film reviews from the U.S. Catholic Conference.

Ncubator.com-Christian Resource Directory
http://ncubator.com/Arts/index.htm
Movies and entertainment news and views for young Christians.

Phantom Tollbooth
http://www.tollbooth.org/
Reviews and articles on general and Christian movies and music.

Preview Family TV and Movie Reviews
http://www.gospelcom.net/preview/
Movie and TV reviews from a family and Christian standpoint.

The Big Thicket Christian Directory—Children's Videos
http://www.bigthicketdirectory.com/christian/storevideochildren.html
Popular children's Christian movies and cartoons at discounted prices.

Welcome to Hollywood Jesus
http://www.hollywoodjesus.com/
News and reviews with a Christian viewpoint.

other sites of interest

Access Place Movies
http://www.accessplace.com/movies.htm
Links to many sites on movies, reviews and stars.

AFI 100 Greatest Movies
http://www.washingtonpost.com/wp-srv/style/movies/features/afi100list.htm
Selected by a panel of industry leaders from across all aspects of filmmaking.

All Movie Guide
http://www.allmovie.com/
Extensive guide to new and classic films with search engine.

Cinema Sites
http://www.cinema-sites.com/
Broad directory to many movie sites.

E! Online—Plus—Movies
http://www.moviefinder.com/
Reviews, news, links.

Entertainment Weekly Online
http://cgi.pathfinder.com/ew/
Online edition of magazine with news, reviews and articles.

Family Films
http://www.familyfilms.com
Resource for family entertainment films.

Film.com: Movie Reviews, News, Trailers, and More.
http://www.film.com/
News, reviews, articles, theater showtimes.

Filmbug Movie and Movie Star Search.
http://www.filmbug.com/
Large search engine for film topics and stars.

Internet Movie Database (IMDb).
http://www.imdb.com/
Basic resource site for film information.

Movie Review Query Engine
http://www.mrqe.com/lookup?
Search engine to find movie reviews. Links to other movie-related sites: Internet Movie Database, Reel, TVGrid, Enews, Amazon, and Chapters.

Moviefone
http://www.moviefone.com/
Movie showtimes, previews, tickets, reviews, and more.

Mr. Movie's Movie Guide
http://198.87.149.71/paa/MrMovie/
Articles and news about film.

NothingButMovies.com—The Internet's Most Complete Movie Portal
http://www.nothingbutmovies.com/
Links to hundreds of movie sites.

Preview Family Movie and TV Review
http://www.gospelcom.net/preview/
Extensive reviews of new and recent films for families.

Reel USA—Free Offers, Trailers, Scripts and Movie Coupons
http://www.reelusa.com/
Scripts, trailers and coupons good at theaters.

Roger Ebert on Movies
http://www.suntimes.com/ebert/
Reviews from one of the industry's most respected critics.

Screen It!
http://www.screenit.com
Entertainment Reviews for Parents.

Spotlights
http://home.ipoline.com/~legends/Insatiable/Spotlights/
Links to hundreds of sites about movies, TV and the stars.

Upcoming Movies
http://upcomingmovies.com/
Search for movie news by date, title, genre, actors, and more.

Welcome to Hollywood.com!
http://www.hollywood.com/
News, reviews, articles, theater showtimes.

WOWWORKS Movies
http://www.wowworks.com/movies/
Extensive directory of movie sites

Museums

Bible Lands Museum Jerusalem
http://www.blmj.org/
Virtual tours of permanent and special exhibits from the museum's collection of ancient artifacts.

Christus Rex
http://www.christusrex.org/www1/icons/index.html
A Catholic website with extensive links to Christian art
and history.

Glencairn Museum
http://www.glencairnmuseum.org/
Religious life through the ages is presented through a re-
markable collection from many cultures.

Israel Bible Museum
http://www.israelbiblemuseum.com/
Featuring over 300 Biblical scenes pained by Philip
Ratner.

other sites of interest

American Museum of Natural History
http://www.amnh.org/
From the earth to the stars, from dinosaurs to butter-
flies, they are all here on one website.

Artcom Museum Tour
http://www.artcom.com/Museums/index.htm
Over 1,700 museum websites are collected here.

Artmuseum.net
http://www.artmuseum.net/
Free registration site with exhibits, including sound and
video clips, from many of the world's great museums.

Brooklyn Children's Museum
http://www.bchildmus.org/
Exhibits, collections, programs and "hands-on" interactive activities.

Country Music Hall of Fame
http://www.country.com/hof/hof-f.html
Discover the roots of country music.

Museumspot
http://www.museumspot.com/
A directory of museum websites with featured sites on
varied subjects worth visiting. Great calendar of events,
too.

National Air and Space Museum
http://www.nasm.si.edu/
From the Wright Brothers to the moon and beyond, all at
your fingertips.

National Museum of American History
http://americanhistory.si.edu/
See the real "Star Spangled Banner" and other great exhibits from American history.

National Museum of Health and Medicine
http://natmedmuse.afip.org/
Historic and scientific exhibits and collections.

National Museum of Women's History
http://www.nmwh.org/
Dedicated to recognizing the contribution of women to
world history and culture.

Smithsonian Online Collections
http://collections.si.edu/main.asp
Extensive and constantly changing exhibits from the
Smithsonian Institution.

The Adler Planetarium
http://www.adlerplanetarium.org/
The first planetarium in the Western Hemisphere. Check
out the galleries by webcam.

The British Museum
http://www.thebritishmuseum.ac.uk/
Explore the cultures of the world at the website of this
famous institution.

The Children's Museum of Indianapolis
http://www.childrensmuseum.org/
Science, history and adventure for the entire family at
the world's largest children's museum.

The Field Museum
http://www.fmnh.org/
Go to see Sue, the most complete Tyrannosaurus skeleton, but stay to see so much more!

The Louvre
http://www.louvre.fr/louvrea.htm
Mona Lisa, Venus de Milo, and thousands of other works of art, all online.

The Metropolitan Museum of Art
http://www.metmuseum.org/
Over 3,500 works of art online, from decorative arts to musical instruments.

The Museum of Science and Industry
http://www.msichicago.org/
Make an online visit to a submarine, or a coal mine, or a miniature castle, and much, much more.

The National Museum of the American Indian
http://www.si.edu/nmai/
Exhibits, educational programs and calendar of events.

The Natural History Museum, London, England
http://www.nhm.ac.uk/
Galleries, exhibits and hands-on exhibitions. A beautiful "diary" of changes in the wildlife garden.

The Worldwide Museum of Natural History
http://www.wmnh.com/wmhome.htm
A great online source for information on things animal, vegetable and mineral.

Music

Altered Soul
http://www.alteredsoul.tsx.org
Website for Altered Soul, a Christian rock band committed to serving Christ.

Amy Grant
http://www.amygrant.com/
Links to three of Amy's websites—A&M, Myrrh, and Friends of Amy.

Andrieux House Music Company
http://www.andrieuxhousemusic.com
Listen to the music clips, and read the story of God's healing power.

Anointed
http://www.anointed1.com/
Music, discography, tour, videos, Bible study, and more.

Audio Adrenaline
http://www.audioadrenaline.com/
Tour dates, bios, fan sites, tour photos, discography, and more.

Carman
http://carman.org/
Facts, news, prayer, concerts, and more.

Cathedrals
http://www.cathedralquartet.com
Homepage for one of the best-loved southern gospel groups.

CCM Magazine
http://www.ccmmagazine.com/
Links to news, features, reviews, and tours of contemporary Christian musicians.

CCMusic
http://www.ccmusic.org/
Christian artist lists, directory of links and discussion boards on the top artists and groups.

CeCe Winans
http://www.cecewinans.com
Tour dates, news, CeCe's vision, projects, and more.

Childguide Music
http://www.childguidemusic.com
Offers Christian music and books promoting Christian composers, authors and their ministries.

Christian Contemporary Music
http://members.infomak.com/livinloud
Site contains pop, rock, and inspirational music on CD and MP3 format. Site also features biographies, devotionals, photos, and more.

M

Christian Music Box
http://www.christianmusicbox.com
Provides professional and quality online exposure to unsigned Christian talent with web design, promotion, namebrand clothing and album sales.

Christian Music Source
http://www.christianmusicsource.com
Christian Music Source with over 3,000 CDs, tapes, videos and songbooks by all your favorite artists; links to other music sites and more.

Christian Music's Best
http://www.cmbest.com
Site offers chat, music reviews, free web space, and free email plus search engine. Check us out!

Christian Radio.com—Christian Music Artists
http://www.christianradio.com/music.asp
A search engine to find sites on your favorite Christian singers and musicians.

Christian Rock
http://christianrock.net
The best of Christian rock on the net. Request your favorite artist and learn new ones. For Christian rock enthusiasts.

DC Talk
http://www.dctalk.com/
About DC Talk, news and updates, tour information, pictures, music, and more.

FindGrace.com
http://www.findgrace.com
Offers Christian MP3 music, free Bible software, news commentary and online Bible study.

Free Praise Music Downloads
http://www.gcfc.faithweb.com
Free contemporary praise music MP3s, along with chord charts and lyrics, for downloading, and using in worship services, or for private praise.

Gloria's Southern Gospel Links
http://members.tripod.com/~gloco/GloriaHome Page2index.html
There are over 300 links to southern gospel music, media, and Christian links.

Gospel Music Association
http://www.gospelmusic.org
Homepage for the GMA, featuring news, updates, newsletter archives, membership information, etc.

Gospel Music Hall of Fame and Museum
http://www.gmhf.org
Gospel Music Hall of Fame and Museum provides information on gospel pioneers, gospel music trivia, artist profiles and facts about those who have made significant contributions to black gospel music.

Gospel Music Workshop of America
http://www.gmwa.org
Chatroom, information and events; sponsored by or related to the annual seven-day conference founded by the late Rev. James Cleveland.

History of Hymns
http://www.umr.org/UMRweb3.htm
The stories behind dozens of the most popular hymns.

Jake Hess
http://www.jakehess.com
News, information, photos, and more, about one of southern gospel's favorite singers!

Jars of Clay
http://www.jarsofclay.com/mainpage.html
Snapshots, fan club, on tour, music, and more.

Joy Music Ministry
http://members.aol.com/ptlsong
Homesite for Christian female singer and songwriter. Users can listen to the artist with the Real Player G2 or online ordering CD.

M

Kim Hill
http://www.kimhillmusic.com/
Career news, biography, music, performances, lyrics, and more.

Kirk Franklin
http://www.nunation.com/
Biography, discography, merchandising, and fan club.

ListenFirst
http://christiantunes.com
Site offers an Internet Christian music resource.

Martins
http://www.the-martins.com
Homepage for the group, with biographies, news, information, concert dates, etc.

Matthew's Christian Music Site
http://www.christianmusiclinks.com//Home/home3.html
Christian music in rock, ska, punk, swing, hard rock and alternative. List Christian radio stations and Christian music links, Christian bands.

Michael W. Smith Homepage
http://www.michaelwsmith.com/
Links to music, photos, Rocketown, Compassion International, Billy Graham Crusade, Kanakuk Camp, and more.

Ministry of Music: A Study in the Scriptures
http://www.dianedew.com/music.htm
Bible study outline tracing the history of musical instruments, singing and worship from Genesis to Revelation; the place of music in the assembly; the significance of the anointing, as well as human training and natural talent; dancing in Scripture; etc.

Point of Grace
http://www.pointofgrace.net/
Bio, music, upclose, tour, store.

Psalms in Song: Music Book and Teaching Resources
http://home.earthlink.net/~apex_ps
Songbook for children ages four to twelve and the adults
who work with them. Titled "How I Praise You: 150 Little Psalms in Song," it is a Bible memorization aid. Useful for children's choir, VBS, homeschool, Sunday
School, and youth programs.

Sandi Patty
http://www.sandipatty.com/
Sandi Patty homepage is a virtual home—browse
through the rooms and view her products.

SDA Digital Hymnal
http://www.tagnet.org/digitalhymnal
A collection of over 600 Christian hymns in MIDI and
some in MP3 format, words, and historical notes for you
to listen and download. Site also includes an interactive
hymn match game to play online.

Seniors Christian Radio
http://www.wiredseniors.com/christianradio/
home.htm
Links to radio stations with descriptions.

SoGospel.com
http://www.sogospel.com
News and information about southern gospel music.

Steven Curtis Chapman
http://www.scchapman.com/
News, music, visuals, biography, links, contact, Bible
study, the tour.

Twila Paris
http://www.twilaparis.com/
Links, discography, listen, True North, communicate,
tour, and more.

Worship Place
http://www.worshipplace.com
Specializes in worship books and music. Also offers
newsletter along with articles, worship links, classified
ads, etc.

M

other sites of interest

All About Jazz
http://www.allaboutjazz.com
News, reviews, interviews, artists, articles, festivals, gallery, topics, styles, global gig, timeline, and more.

America's Jazz Heritage
http://www.si.edu/ajazzh
Exhibitions, programs, audio/radio, publications, and links from the Smithsonian Institution.

Any Swing Goes
http://www.anyswinggoes.com/
A source for swing music, news, and culture.

Big Band and Jazz Hall of Fame
http://www.jazzhall.org
The Hall, what's new, jazzology, inductees, jazz news, jazz history, contest, and more.

CDNOWcom
http://www.cdnow.com
An online music store with a mission to find any CD now. Offers 500,000 music related items to its customers.

Charts All Over the World
http://www.lanet.lv/misc/charts/
Search through 900 webpages featuring music charts.

Classical Net
http://classical.efront.com/
Thousands of CD reviews, soundfiles and links to classical music sites on the Internet.

Country Music Hall of Fame
http://www.country.com/hof/hof-f.html
Discover the roots of country music.

Eyeneer Music Archives
http://www.eyeneer.com
Links to world music, contemporary classic, jazz, and much more.

FolkMusic.org
http://www.folkmusic.org/
The most comprehensive source for information on folk
and acoustic music on the web.

GrassrootsMusic.com
http://GrassrootsMusic.com/
Specializing in independent and label releases from folk,
folk-rock, and modern rock Christian artists. Shop se-
curely, listen to audio clips, and read exclusive artist interviews and features.

International Lyrics Server
http://www.lyrics.ch/index.htm
Search by artist, album, or song to view lyrics to more
than 62,000 songs.

Jazz Online
http://www.jazzonln.com
Fresh reviews, jazz messenger, liquid jazz, jazz 101, talk,
archives, and more.

M

Joni Mitchell Homepage
http://www.jonimitchell.com/Frames1.html
Links to writings, galleries, bio, sounds, conversations,
and more.

Louis Armstrong Online
http://www.satchmo.net/index1.html
Links to biography, the house, archives,
programs, staff listing, online exhibit, recordings, and
more.

Lyrics World
http://summer.com.br/%~pfilho/html/main_index
Search the website for the lyrics to your favorite songs.

MIDI Jukebox
*http://homepages.go.com/~thomaswinters/
midi.html*
MIDI songs from popular television shows, and more.

Oldies Music Links
http://www.oldiesmusic.com/links2.htm
Links to Oldies-related sites on the web. Search, shop, number one songs, trivia, and more.

Operabase
http://www.operabase.com
Search over 55,000 opera performances by date, composer, title, or location in multiple languages.

The Rock and Roll Hall of Fame
http://www.rockhall.com/
Exhibits, collections and sound files on the history of rock and roll.

Ultimate Band List
http://ubl.artistdirect.com/
Find music information on artists, music news, concerts, tickets, and contests.

World Wide Polka
http://www.worldwidepolka.com
A directory of Internet Polka shows but much, much more. The author believes that Polka music should serve the Lord and explains how this can be done with his theory.

Nations and Peoples of the World

(This category contains sites with information on more than one country. For sites on a specific country, you can use this category as a starting point, or check the "Travel and International Information" category.)

Adherents.com
http://www.adherents.com/
An introductory resource on the religions and beliefs of the people of the world.

Freedom of Religion or Belief
http://www.hri.ca/partners/forob/e/COUNTRY/
A country-by-country analysis of the state of freedom of religion around the world.

other sites of interest

BUBL Link/5:15
http://bubl.ac.uk/link/countries.html
An enormous directory of links to sites on individual
countries and regions of the world.

Countries
http://www.countries.com/
Well organized and easy to use resource to find information about individual countries.

Country Studies
http://lcweb2.loc.gov/frd/cs/cshome.html
Online reference works on over 100 countries from the
Library of Congress.

Countrywatch
http://www.countrywatch.com/
A great source for information on nations, including history, economy and environment.

Gheos World Atlas
http://gheos.com/atlas/
A comprehensive source of basic information on countries around the world. Travel tips, too.

Global200 Countries MetaHub
http://www.global200countries.com/ctry/defaultc.asp
Easily accessible basic country information, with travel
and business advice.

Infonation
*http://www.un.org/Pubs/CyberSchoolBus/infonation/
e_infonation.htm*
View and compare basic information on all the member
states of the United Nations. A great resource!

Mr. Dowling's Electronic Passport
http://www.mrdowling.com/
A site developed by a teacher with hundreds of entries
on countries and history.

Nations Online
http://www.nationsonline.org/
A portal site for searching the world. Geography, culture, politics, religions and more.

Regional and Country Information Resources
http://www.ipl.org/ref/RR/static/rci00.00.00.html
A directory of links to sites on countries and regions of the world from the Internet Public Library.

The CIA World Factbook
http://www.cia.gov/cia/publications/factbook/
A comprehensive research site for comparative information on many nations.

World Area Studies Internet Resources
http://www.wcsu.ctstateu.edu/socialsci/area.html
A directory of hundreds of links arranged by geographical areas of the world.

World Desk Reference
http://travel.dk.com/wdr/
5,000 illustrations, 600 maps and over 25,000 statistics about countries on one site.

World Gazetteer
http://www.gazetteer.de/
Population data on countries around the world, with hundreds of links to sites for each country.

World World
http://www.worldworld.com/
Basic information on many countries in chart form.

Your Nation
http://www.your-nation.com/
about_input.asp?firsttime=yes
Compare and rank hundreds of countries and regions on dozens of different subjects.

Native Americans

Cherokee Prayer Initiative
http://www.missioncarolina.org/cpi.html
A two year prayer effort offering prayers of healing, re-

pentance, forgiveness and blessing in the Cherokee Home-land.

Eagle's Wing Ministry
http://www.eagles-wingsmin.com/
A ministry of Native American believers reaching Native Americans and others with the good news of Jesus Christ.

Tribe of Christ—A Native American Church
http://www.tribeofchrist.com/
A fellowship of Native American followers of Jesus Christ reaching out to both native and non-native peoples.

Warriors for Christ!
*http://www.firstnationsmonday.com/
warriorsforchrist.htm*
Native American Christian mission that brings traditional dance and music to schools and community celebrations.

Wiconi International
http://www.wiconi.com/
A ministry by Native people to help Native people find faith and life in Jesus Christ.

other sites of interest

Bill's Aboriginal Links: Canada and US
http://www.bloorstreet.com/300block/aborcan.htm
Links to hundreds of sites on Canadian and American Native Americans.

Canku Ota
http://www.turtletrack.org/
An online newsletter celebrating Native American culture. Great kid's page, too.

Internet Resources in Native American Studies
http://www.library.pima.edu/native.htm
Links to many Native American sites.

Musical Instruments
*http://www.civilization.ca/membrs/fph/stones/instru/
inmenu.htm*
Examples of the wide variety of musical instruments
used by Canadian Native American cultures.

Native American Books
http://indy4.fdl.cc.mn.us/isk/books/bookmenu.html
A bibliography for students and adults as well as links
to many other sites (Please check for bad links, there are
lots).

Native American Home—Charlotte's Web
*http://www.charweb.org/neighbors/na/
na-index.htm*
Links to many Native American sites.

Native American Indian
http://indy4.fdl.cc.mn.us/%~isk
Many links to sites on Native American culture, art and
science.

Native American Sites
http://www.nativeculture.com/lisamitten/indians.html
A directory of links on Native American subjects, organized by topic.

Noah's News
http://members.aol.com/_ht_a/newsbynoah
Links to many Native American sites.

Pow Wow Dancing
http://www.powwows.com/
Descriptions, photos, crafts and links on Native American dance styles.

Sipapu—The Anasazi Emergence into the Cyber World
http://sipapu.gsu.edu/
A comprehensive site for this Southwestern U.S. tribe.

The National Museum of the American Indian
http://www.si.edu/nmai/
Exhibits, educational programs and calendar of events.

News Services

Absolute News
http://news.christiansunite.com/
World religion news of interest to Christians.

Associated Baptist Press
http://www.helwys.com/abpnews.htm
Associated Baptist Press is an independent national news service dedicated to providing credible and reliable news for and about Baptists.

Browse Worldwide Faith News
http://www.wfn.org/conferences/wfn.news/
Archive of church and religion stories of the last 30 days.

Bugler News
http://www.awwwsome.com/bugler
Site contains links to both secular and Christian newspapers. Also links to current newstories, world events, articles, inspirational stories and more.

Charisma News Service Online
http://www.charismanews.com/
CNS is a gatherer and disseminator of news for both Christian and secular media.

Christian Daily News
http://www.christiannews.org
Published by Christian Word Ministries, site features news affecting Christians from around the world; also information on missions, revivals, feature articles, world news, and archives.

Christian Family News
http://www.christianfamilynews.com/
To promote unity and true Christian fellowship in the body of Christ, and to tell people about Christ.

Christian News at Worthy News. News from a Christian View
http://www.worthynews.com/
World and national headlines, church news and commentary.

N

Family News in Focus
http://www.lightsource.com/
Stay informed with up-to-the-minute reports on pressing moral and social issues. This straight-shooting information and analysis feature comes to you in just four and one-half minutes.

Free Daily
http://www.freedaily.com/
Christian perspectives on the news.

LifeLine News
http://www.lifelinenews.net
World and national news, church news, etc.

Mission Network News
http://www.gospelcom.net/mnn/
World religious news with audio clips.

Nando Times
http://www.nandotimes.com/
General news service, frequent updates.

Religion News Links from Religion Today
http://www.religiontoday.com/NewsLinks
Christian news links and other religion news resources. Includes a directory of denominations, denominational publications, religion news services, newsletters, newspapers, magazines, and non-religious news links.

Religion News Service
http://www.religionnews.com/
News service focusing on topics of religion and morals.

Today's Daily Religion News Report
http://news.crosswalk.com/
Religious news summaries and feature stories on revival, evangelism, missions, church growth, religious persecution, ethics and society.

United News and Information Website
http://www.uninews.com/uni/home.html
Audio news reports for the Christian community.

Vanguard Magazine
http://vanguardmag.com/
Christian content in international and business news
stock indices and investment tools. Also features Accu-
Weather, newspapers, magazines, maps, Christian TV
guide, comics, free greeting cards, and a free KJV Bible
for your PC.

Worldwide Faith News
http://www.wfn.org/
A full text searchable archive of official news releases
from the offices of national and world faith groups.

other sites of interest

10,000 Newspapers on the Net
http://www.onlinenewspapers.com/
Newspapers from around the world.

4News.com
http://www.4News.com/?%3B019039a
Up to the minute world news from CNN Interactive,
ABC News, ESPN and Investors Business Daily—plus a
foreign perspective from BBC News and Le Monde.

ABCNEWS.com
http://abcnews.go.com/
Network news homepage with frequent updates.

AssignmentEditor.com—The Newsroom Homepage
http://assignmenteditor.com/
Links to hundreds of newspapers and other sources.

BBC News | WORLD
http://news.bbc.co.uk/hi/english/world/default.stm
Extensive world news coverage from the leading British
resource.

Cable News Network
http://www.cnn.com
Official site contains multimedia links, latest national
and worldwide news as well as information on a variety
of topics, including technology, health, politics, nature,
entertainment, books, travel, and much more.

CBC NEWS ONLINE—Canada's Online News Resource
http://www.cbcnews.cbc.ca/
World and Canadian news resource.

CBS News
http://www.cbsnews.com/
News headlines, links to news magazine television shows, and links to local news.

Children's Express Worldwide—News by Kids for Everybody
http://www.cenews.org/
News written by kids, ages eight to eighteen.

Christian Science Monitor
http://www.csmonitor.com
News in text and audio, searchable archives, interactive message forum, weekly news quiz, AP wire and a crossword.

CNN
http://www.cnn.com/
News magazine online. Links to world, U.S., sports, health, travel, food, arts, and more.

E&P Directory of Online Newspapers
http://www.mediainfo.com/emedia
Links to newspapers around the world.

FOXNews.com
http://www.foxnews.com/
Up-to-the-minute news with audio and video features.

Home Town News
http://www.hometownnews.com/
Over 2,000 U.S. newspapers linked

Hometown Newslinks
http://www.newscoast.com/hometown.htm
Links to newspapers from the U.S., Canada, England, Australia, Germany, Italy, and Russia.

IPL Reading Room Newspapers
http://www.ipl.org/reading/news/
Links to many world newspapers.

MSNBC Cover
http://www.msnbc.com/news/default.asp
Breaking news coverage with search feature.

New York Times on the Web
http://www.nytimes.com/
Free access to current edition articles.

NewsCentral—The Largest Newspaper Index on the Web
http://www.all-links.com/newscentral/
Thousands of links to world newspapers.

NewsDirectory: Newspapers and Media
http://www.newsdirectory.com/
Directory of world newspapers, magazines and TV sites
online.

NewspaperLinks.com,
http://www.newspaperlinks.com/content.asp
Searchable by state, city and paper.

Newspapers Online
http://www.newspapers.com/
Search engine for world and U.S. newspapers.

redOzone.com—Worldwide News Papers
http://www.redozone.addr.com/news.html
Links to many world papers in English and foreign languages.

Reuters Group PLC Home
http://www.reuters.com/
Late breaking news with search feature.

Search the Washington Post
*http://search.washingtonpost.com/wp-srv/searches/
mainsrch.htm*
Search Post news, archives, sports, entertainment, and
Newsweek magazine.

**USA Newspapers | Paperboy USA | Online Newspaper
Directory**
http://www.thepaperboy.com/usa/
Headline service and links to top U.S. newspapers.

N

USA Today
http://www.usatoday.com/
News, sports, money, life, weather. Search the site, subscribe to the newspaper, and other links.

Washingtonpost.com—News Front
http://www.washingtonpost.com
Comprehensive news and feature services.

Wire, The
http://wire.ap.org/
Breaking news from the Associated Press, organized by newspaper.

Online Communities

711 Web Cafe—Interactive Chat Community
http://www.711webcafe.net/
711 Web Cafe Chat Community is your online gathering for Christian fellowship.

Acts Christian Search
http://www.actschristian.com/
Christian search engine and directory with links to hundreds of Christian sites including chat, singles, entertainment, churches, theology, teens, music, Bible study, and more.

Agape Enterprises International
http://www.agape-net.org/
Designed to provide a place for Christians to fellowship and network while reaching out to the community. Offers help with everyday practical needs.

Ambassadors Christian Resource Center
http://borg.com/~newhope/ambassadors
An all-purpose site that seeks to minister to the whole person. As a result we offer anything from worship to weather.

Belief.net
http://www.beliefnet.com/
A large and comprehensive multi-faith e-Community.

Best Christian Links
http://www.tbcl.com/
A fast growing, professional directory of Christian and "Family Friendly" Internet sites.

Best of the Christian Web
http://www.botcw.com/
This site lists the top Christian websites on the net.

Bible InfoNet
http://www.bible-infonet.org/
The Bible InfoNet has many short and long articles, outlines and chart lessons on a large variety of Bible topics as well as a bulletin board for discussion, items for sale, and more.

Black and Christian Community
http://www.blackandchristian.com/
An inspirational and informational resource for African-American Christians and others interested in the African-American religious experience.

Christian Community Net
http://www.christiancommunity.co.uk/
Creating a friendly global community.

Christian Online Community
http://www.colc.com/
The Christian OnLine Community is a virtual meeting place that brings together Christian organizations and its supporters worldwide.

Christian Students' Netlinks
http://surf.to/netlinks
Providing links to some of the best Christian related sites on the web of interest to Christian students of all ages and families too. Also of interest to youth groups, Christian schools and colleges, etc.

Cristiani in Azione
http://www.cristiani-in-azione.ch
Site offers Bible study, articles, news of Israel, daily bread, chat, forum, and more.

Father's Business

http://www.fbonline.net/

A safe, family-friendly online service providing communication, information, and entertainment for Christians, and connecting Christian communities to advance God's message.

I Love Jesus

http://www.ilovejesus.com

A website community for Christians that would like to host your Christian website and give you an email address that makes a statement (I love Jesus)! Message boards, theme-specific areas, etc.

Isaiah 54 Woman's Homepage

http://www.geocities.com/Heartland/Valley/6175

The Isaiah 54 Woman's Homepage is designed to invite challenging discussion and provide a means by which to link with a large prayer community. Links to sites relating to family concerns, creation, etc.

JesusPeople

http://www.jesuspeople.com/jp

Get you own @JesusPeople.com email address. Also features information on music, communities, coffeehouses, ministries, tracts, worship, message board, and more.

Links to Christian Communities

http://www.jesus.org.uk/commlinx.html

A directory of websites of Christian groups and organizations.

Reality Check

http://www.angelfire.com/tx3/RealityCheck

Reality Check is a group of real people with real problems that meet once a week for fun, fellowship, and Jesus.

YouthBuilt.com

http://www.youthbuilt.com

A Christian online community and portal for Christian youth. We offer useful resources, free websites, and entertainment tools to teens, clubs, and adults.

other sites of interest

AmericanNet.com Family Safe Community
http://www.AmericanNet.com/
Family safe community, shopping stores, search engine, etc.

Apple City Mall—the Happiest Place on the Net
http://applecity.com/
A fun place for the entire family. Kid-safe site with lots
of links to other kid-safe sites. Web hosting and design.
Those desiring to join our mall must have kid-safe webpages.

Mighty Media Keypals Club
http://www.mightymedia.com/keypals/
The safest way to connect classroom to classroom, student to student, worldwide. Over 25,000 registered users
from 76 countries.

Parent Soup
http://www.parentsoup.com
Communities for pre-pregnancy, expecting parents, parents of babies, parents of toddlers, parents of school age
children, and parents of teens.

Pets

Cookie's & Cream's Bunny Webpage
http://www.geocities.com/jmasciopinto
For bunny lovers and Christians, too.

Creatures In Heaven
http://www.creatures.com/
Features, pet care tips links to online resources and inspirational stories.

other sites of interest

1,000 Tips 4 Trips—Traveling with Pets
http://www.tips4trips.com/Tips/pettips.htm
Lists user-submitted tips for traveling with pets.

21cats.org
http://www.21cats.org
Comprehensive site on cat care.

About.com—Exotic Pets
http://exoticpets.about.com/
Discusses the issues surrounding keeping non-domestic species.

Acme Pet
http://acmepet.petsmart.com/
Online community with lots of information on a variety of pets and their care.

Adopt-a-Pet
http://www.adoptapet.com/
This site features a directory of and links to pet adoption agencies and humane societies.

AKC—American Kennel Club
http://www.akc.org
Homesite for purebred dog organization; information, advice and photos

All About Cats—For Cats and Their Humans
http://allcatz.tripod.com/
Cat advice, stories, photos and links

AllCritters.Com . . . Experience It!
http://www.allcritters.com
Directory to thousands of pet sites.

Allpets
http://www.allpets.com/flash/mainflash.htm
An ezine for pet owners of all types, including exotics, with events and chat.

Amby's Cat Information Site
http://amby.com/cat_site/
Information and links on cat health and care.

American Ferret Association, Inc.
http://www.ferret.org/
News, articles and advice on keeping ferrets.

American Miniature Horse Association-Official Site
http://www.minihorses.com/amha/
Organizational website with hundreds of pages on minature horses.

Anapsid.organization—Reptile and Amphibian Information Collection
http://www.anapsid.org/
Comprehensive site on the care and feeding of reptiles.

Animal Network
http://www.animalnetwork.com/
A site representing a number of print and online magazines for owners of all types of pets.

Animal Network
http://www.aquariumfish.com/
Extensive directory of pet sites and information.

Animal-Related Links and Submit Page
http://www.members.goldrush.com/~groomer
/me.html
Extensive links to thousands of pet pages sorted by animal type.

Aquaria and Tropical Fish
http://www.thekrib.com/
Fish, food, tanks and hardware, diseases, filtration, and more.

Aquariumsite
http://www.aquariumsite.org/
Links, fish, shopping, directory, and more.

ARK Online
http://www.arkonline.com/ark_online.html
This site provides information on animal shelters, animal abuse and animal news.

ASPCA
http://www.aspca.org/
Organizational site on caring for and protecting animals.

Beware of Cat!
http://www.geocities.com/Heartland/Meadows/
6485/
Directory of many cat-related sites. Huge cat graphics collection and virtual cat postcards!

BirdCLICK
http://www.geocities.com/Heartland/Acres/9154
Advice and information on training your bird.

Bow Wow Meow—Pet Names with Personality
http://www.bowwow.com.au/
View the top 20 names, find out what your pet's name
means, or check the popularity of a possible pet name.

Bullfrogs
http://www.bullfrogs-louisiana.com/
Site on the care and feeding of bullfrogs.

Cat Bytes
http://meowsandpurrs.homestead.com/
Health and grooming tips, links and cybercats.

Cat Fanciers' Association (CFA)
http://www.cfainc.org/
Information and photos on fancy cat breeds.

Cat Owner
http://www.catowner.com/
Information on different cat breeds, cat health, kittens,
pet supplies, cat newsgroups, cat poetry, and cat humor.

Cat-E-corner.com
http://www.cat-e-corner.com/
Information, advice and links on cats.

Cavy Hutch
http://cavyhutch2000.tripod.com/main.htm
Comprehensive site on guinea pigs.

Chinchilla Information Guide
http://www.geocities.com/Petsburgh/Park/6920/
Basic information and advice about chinchillas.

Choosing the Perfect Dog
http://www.choosingtheperfectdog.net/
Trivia, how much time, how much money, how much stuff,
and other information about the perfect dog for you.

Complete Hamster Site: Hamsters
http://www.hamsters.co.uk/
Basic information and news on hamsters as pets.

CritterHobbyist.com
http://www.critterhobbyist.com/
Links to many sites on small pets.

Critters Corner
http://www.critterscorner.com/
This site is from a supplier of exotic hand-fed baby birds, fish, reptiles, and small animals.

CyberPet
http://www.cyberpet.com
Includes guides for breeders and owners of cats and dogs. Information on pet selection, training, health care, rescue, products, and more.

DogGone
http://www.doggonefun.com/
This newsletter discusses issues and concerns relating to traveling with your dog. Subscription is required; details are provided.

Exotic Pets—Homepage
http://exoticpets.about.com/
Advice on selecting and keeping exotic pets.

Exotic Pets—Keen.com
http://looksmart.com/cgi-bin/go/adname=0:1 | 60024671;adfield=redirect;ref=1///www.keen.com/web/ pp.asp?PLID=585&URL=/web/categories/ categorylist.asp?Category=207
Iguanas, bearded dragons and tree frogs are among the pets which you can get information about.

Family.com: The Family Pets Site from Disney's Family.com
http://family.go.com/Categories/pets/
General information on finding and keeping a pet.

Ferret Net Homepage
http://www.ferret.net/
Directory of ferret sites for the beginner and expert.

FindaPet.com-Pet Names Directory
http://www.findapet.com/petnames.htm
Discusses the most popular pet names, including those in different categories.

Fishgeeks.com
http://badgerstate.com/JAWS/
Advice, tips and links on setting up and keeping an aquarium.

Freshwater Tropical Fish Keeping
http://www.tropicalfishkeeping.com/
Comprehensive tropical fish site for beginners and experts.

Frogland
http://allaboutfrogs.org
Frog information, advice, games and more.

Gerbil Information Page
http://users.bart.nl/~fredveen/gerbiluk.htm
Information and links on many gerbil varieties.

Happypets.org
http://happypets.addr.com/
Homepage for pets and the people who love them. Pet tips, information and links.

Horse Breeds—Horse World Data
http://horseworlddata.com/breed.html
This site provides a large alphabetical listing of breeds, registry information, general descriptions, and information about publications.

Horses
http://www.animalnetwork.com/horses/default.asp
News, calendar of horse events, and photos.

Horses, Horses and More Horses
http://www.horses.co.uk/
Over 1,000 horse photos.

House Rabbit Society
http://www.rabbit.org/
Care, behavior and health advice on pet rabbits, with an adoption service, too.

How to Love Your Dog
http://www.geocities.com/~kidsanddogs
A kid's guide to dog care, poetry, riddles, stories, dogs, and more.

In Memory of Pets
http://www.in-memory-of-pets.com/
A site where you can find support and and guidance after losing a pet.

Index of Famous Dogs, Cats, and Critters
*http://www.citizenlunchbox.com/famous/
animals.html*
Thousands of famous pet names.

InsectHobbyist.com
http://www.insecthobbyist.com/
Directory of sites on keeping insects and spiders as pets.

K9 Country- Your New Internet Guide to Man's Best Friend
*http://www.k9country.com/k9country/
dogMain.pl*
News, stories and links about dogs.

K9web
http://k9web.com/
This site features Cindy Tittle Moore's FAQ section, as well as lists of dog breeders and related businesses.

Kingsnake
http://www.kingsnake.com/
Reptile and amphibian directory of sites and resources.

Koi Vet
http://www.koivet.com/
A large library on the care and treatment of koi and goldfish. An online fee-based consultation service can also be used.

Llama Uses
*http://www.webcom.com/~degraham/Uses/
Use.html*
Discusses different uses for llamas, from assisting in carrying items to golfing.

P

Master Index of Freshwater Fishes
http://www.webcityof.com/mifftitl.htm
Large directory of aquarium resources.

Monkey Maddness
http://www.monkeymaddness.com/
Comprehensive site on all things to do with pet monkeys.

Mouse@horns
http://www.horns.freeserve.co.uk/mouse.htm
Advice on the care and feeding of pet mice.

MSN Web Communities—Pets
http://communities.msn.com/pets
Features areas where you can post pictures, participate in discussions, and get information. Requires membership, but an application form is provided.

Net Pets
http://www.netpets.com/
A site for pet lovers, with healthcare tips, an image gallery, and products.

One Fish, Two Fish.
http://members.xoom.com/onefish/index.htm
Beginners' aquarium site.

Pet Care at DoItYourself.com
http://www.doityourself.com/pets/
News and tips on caring for your pet.

Pet Channel
http://www.thepetchannel.com/
Provides guidance for finding lost pets, veterinary information, and products.

Pet Finder
http://www.petfinder.org/
Search shelters for your next pet by zip code or breed, and view a found pets section.

Pet Planet
http://www.petplanet.com/
Comprehensive pet information site.

Pet Project
http://www.thepetproject.com/
Extensive links, tips, and pet news.

Pet Rodent Homepage
*http://www.webcom.com/lstead/rodents
/rodents.html*
Fundamental information on hamsters, gerbils, mice and
more.

**Pet Selection: Take Care in Choosing an Animal that Suits
Your Needs**
http://www.learnfree-pets.com/pick/
How to pick the right pet for you.

Pet Station
http://petstation.com/central.html
This directory covers contact information for animal
care centers located throughout the United States, Canada and the United Kingdom.

Petbugs.com
http://www.petbugs.com/
Features and information on keeping pet bugs.

PetHobbyist
http://www.pethobbyist.com/
Search engine and links to many pet sites.

Pets and Vets
http://www.petsandvets.com/
Healthcare advice from pet experts.

Pets Forum
http://www.thathomesite.com/forums/pets/
Share information and learn from other pet owners.

Pets Forum and Live Chat
*http://isnerbunch.community.everyone.net/community/
scripts/community.pl?ClientID=53379&NodeID=48742*
This site includes chats and message boards for all types
of pets.

Pet's World

http://www.info-s.com/pets.html

Provides links to other sites on dogs, cats, horses, exotics, and endangered species. Links to zoos are also available.

PetShelter Network

http://www.petshelter.org/

Visit this adoption site to view the pet of the week and gain information about available animals and shelter locations, including a Lost and Found section.

PetTracker.com—Serving Pets and Pet Owners Worldwide

http://www.pettracker.com/

Online help for reuniting lost pets and owners.

PigPals

http://members.tripod.com/~PigPals/

Photos, stories and links on pet pigs.

Planet Mouse!

http://www.homestead.com/whiskerisland/index21300.html

All about pet mice.

Rabies—What You Need to Know

http://www.cfainc.org/articles/rabies.html

Cat Fanciers' associations site detailing precautions to take to avoid rabies.

Reptile and Amphibian Magazine

http://www.petstation.com/herps.html#TOP

Review the latest magazine issue, find books, classifieds, and other items. Features a calendar of upcoming events.

Reptile World

http://www.vertical.freeserve.co.uk/

Advice, information and links on keeping reptiles as pets.

Squeaks Page

http://members.aol.com/Squeakpig/Squeakpig.html

Links and information on caring for guinea pigs.

Tame Beast
http://www.tamebeast.com
This site includes links and reviews of pet sites on the Internet, including organizations.

Tarantula Planet
http://www.tarantulaplanet.org/
Fact and picture filled site on keeping tarantulas as pets.

Turtletopia
http://www.turtletopia.com/index.htm
Turtle facts, turtle photos, turtle news.

Portal Sites

A New You
http://www.tagnet.org/anewyou
A site emphasizing the Bible, Bible study, prophesy, seminars and sermons, Christian clip art, links, and more.

All in One Christian Index
http://www.allinone.org/
Search directory listing and rating search engines, indices, resources, regional language, and topical, including Bible search chat rooms, newsgroups, software, webmasters, apologetics, best award sites, churches, jobs, music, theology, and youth.

Alpha Omega Portal
http://www.start-page.net/
Web directory, Bible search, news and a lot more.

P

Atrevete
http://atrevete.com/
Portal site and search engine for Spanish speaking Christians.

Belief.net
http://www.beliefnet.com/
A large and comprehensive multi-faith e-Community.

Best of the Christian Web
http://www.botcw.com/index.shtml
The home of the award of Best of the Christian Web with links to all the winners. Also has real time chat features.

BibleWeb
http://www.bibleweb.com/
News, weather, search tools, free email and discussion boards.

BST Links.com
http://www.bstlinks.com
A site with links to other Christian websites, prayer requests, testimonies, stories, music, and more.

Calsplace Christian Directory and Hosting
http://calsplace.hypermart.net/
Features links to a variety of Christian websites, including the Y.L.T.G., Christian youth site.

Center Pew
http://members.aol.com/tamjensen/pew.html
A site for all family members, offering daily devotional, bible study, youth group, teen study, games for youth, prayer group at the Chapel, and growing every day.

Christ4U
http://www.helicon.net/christ4u/
A family-friendly site with a wide variety of topics to surf through. Everything from miscellaneous listings, devotionals, Christian helps, midi and music, and personal testimony.

Christian Index
http://www.christian-index.com/
Search over 20,000 Christian websites, organized by category.

Christian Interactive Network
http://www.gocin.com/
CIN is the home of many Christian ministries.

Christian Portal Homepage
http://www.christianportal.com/
News, commentary, search feature and numerous links to Christian sites on the web.

Christian Start Network
http://www.christianstart.com/
Gateway to many Christian resources on the web.

Christian World
http://www.christianworld.com
Christian web portal and search engine designed to be
the Internet starting point for the Christian community.

Christianity
http://www.allspiritual.com/Christianity.php3
Comprehensive directory of Christian websites organized
by category.

Christians Online
http://conline.net/
Prayboard, news, penpals, links and many more features.

ChristWeb.com
http://www.christweb.com/
ChristWeb single goal is to further the ministry of Jesus
Christ on the web, featuring online NIV Bible, daily devotionals and Scriptures, and articles from pastors, games,
etc.

Colu.net: Christians Online Unite
http://www.colu.net
Lists of Christian chatters, prayer requests, safe links, answers, online Bible, and Bible topics, chat rooms, and
more.

Committed to Christ
http://members.spree.com/ctc1/ctcmain.htm
Chat, links, page, email penpals, ICQ, poetry, and much
more, Committed to Christ newsletter.

Crosshome
http://www.crosshome.com
Christian portal featuring chat, discussion groups, devotionals, free email, music, news and shopping.

Cybergrace Christian Network
http://www.cybergrace.com/
One of the most comprehensive Christian resources on
the Internet.

P

FaithAvenue.COM
http://www.faithavenue.com

An online Christian community with inspirations created in Flash, e-cards, live Christian TV, free online training in Flash, Photoshop, html, and RealVideo streaming technologies, and more.

Finding the Way
http://www.findingtheway.com/index.php3

Christian gateway to the internet with rated websites in many categories.

IExalt
http://www.iexalt.com/

A global Christian online network with news, features, prayer network and more.

PoiemaNet
http://www.poiema.net/

Chistian email, webspace, chat and more.

Rob's Christian Links and Search Engine
URL: www.robslinks.com/

A Christian portal with a detailed Christian index of Christian websites and over 5000 Christian links in search engine.

Salvation.com
http://salvation.com/

Links to devotionals, electronic books, online Bible studies and much more.

Siervo
http://siervo.com/

Spanish language Christian portal site and search engine.

Sigueme
http://www.sigueme.com.ar/

A comprehensive Spanish language web gateway with a wide variety of topics.

United Christian Network
 http://www.unitedchristians.com/
 A vast directory of links to Christian sites on many subjects.

other sites of interest

AmericanNet
 http://www.americannet.com/
 A family-friendly gateway to the Internet.

Open Here
 http://www.openhere.com/
 A comprehensive and well organized gateway to the web.

Pocket
 http://www.thepocket.com/
 A wonderful way to sample all the things the Internet
 has to offer.

Via Family Online
 http://www.rated-g.com/
 News, shopping, email and links in a family friendly atmosphere. Kids' and teen pages, too.

Pregnancy and Childbirth

Above Rubies
 http://aboverubies.org/articles.html
 Articles about motherhood, childbirth and breastfeeding
 from a Christian perspective.

America's Crisis Pregnancy Helpline
 http://www.thehelpline.org/
 Counseling advice, information and referrals on pregnancy issues.

Answers About Life Before Birth
 http://www.ChristianAnswers.net/life/home.html
 Answers about life before birth.

Bible and Abortion
 *http://www.geocities.com/Athens/Acropolis/4824/
 abortf.htm*

Abortion is the killing of the unborn infant. What does the Bible teach about little children and abortion?

Birth and Breastfeeding
http://members.aol.com/shndoa/birth.html
Extensive list of Christian articles and links on homebirth and breastfeeding.

Care-Net
http://www.care-net.org/
A non-profit organization linking churchs, pregnancy care centers and concerned Christians.

Childbirth Links
http://www.crosswinds.net/~ilonaeee/chilinks.html
Large directory of links to informative sites on pregnancy and childbirth.

Christian Baby Center
http://www.ilovejesus.com/baby/baby.html
Links to dozens of Christian and secular sites on pregnancy and childbirth.

Christian Childbirth
http://www.christianchildbirth.com/
Providing quality information to expecting parents from a Christian perspective.

Crisis Pregnancy Ministry
http://www.family.org/pregnancy/
Strengthening families through support of crisis pregnancy centers.

Gentle Christian Mothers Message Board
http://pub11.ezboard.com/bgentlechristianmothers
Share advice and experiences with other expectant and new Christian mothers.

Lutherans for Life
http://www.lutheransforlife.org/bible/index.htm
Welcome to the collection of Bible references for Lutherans For Life. The foundation of this prolife ministry is the foundation of the world; apart from it the efforts of love and healing are in vain.

Rock of Inspiration

http://www.rockofinspiration.org

Catholic ministry to young adults. Its aim is to bring people to personal relationship with Jesus and maintain a firm pro-life stance.

Single Christian Parent's Place

http://www.angelfire.com/nc/scp/index2.html

Links for those who want to meet Jesus or find advice about being single and pregnant. Also, links to Christian websites and bookshelves, homeschooling information, teen pages, kids' pages, and rest and relaxation!

other sites of interest

Anne's Baby World

http://www.annegeddes.com

Beautiful photos of babies, by Anne Geddes.

Babies Online

http://www.babiesonline.com/

Dedicated to new and expectant parents.

Baby and Child Safety

http://www.babyandchildsafety.com/

A practical guide for preventing childhood injuries.

Baby Corner

http://www.thebabycorner.com/

Online magazine for expectant and new parents.

Baby Go to Sleep

http://win-edge.com/BabyGoToSleep.shtml

How to quiet a crying baby.

Baby Names—Their Origin and Meanings

http://www.geocities.com/Heartland/Meadows/2151/

Find out the meaning of baby names.

Babybag

http://www.babybag.com/

Articles, parenting tips, shopping links, etc.

Babycenter
http://www.babycenter.com/
Articles on pregnancy and birth, shopping links, etc.

Babylane
http://www.babylane.net
Extensive list of links to baby sites!

Breastfeeding.com
http://www.nursingmother.com/
Breastfeeding information and support.

Childbirth.org
http://www.childbirth.org/
Pregnancy and childbirth information.

Coby's Collection of Baby Freebies
http://www.angelfire.com/hi/CobysCollection/
heybaby.html
Extensive links for free items for new parents.

drpaula.com
http://www.drpaula.com/
Free online pediatric advice.

Fetal Development—Photos
http://www.w-cpc.org/fetal.html
Fascinating photos showing the development of the child
week-by-week.

Genius Babies
http://www.geniusbabies.com/genius-babies/index.html
Great gifts for the baby!

Heartbeat International
http://www.heartbeatinternational.org/
Dedicated to creating an environment where every human heart is cherished—both in the womb and within
strong families.

Interactive Pregnancy Calendar
http://www.olen.com/baby/
A customized calendar detailing the development of a
baby from before conception to birth.

Kidz Are People Too
http://www.geocities.com/~mykidzmom/
A resource of gentle parenting from conception through the toddler years.

La Leche League
http://www.laleche.org/
Homesite of the largest organization dedicated to mothers who breastfeed. Tips, information, support.

Lisa's Parenting Resource
http://www.geocities.com/Heartland/Meadows/8570/ index.html
Lots of links to parenting and birth sites.

Maya's Natural World
http://www.geocities.com/Heartland/5358/
Great information on the various stages of pregnancy, birth, and the first years after birth.

Motherhood Place
http://members.aol.com/mempenny/mothers.html
A page dedicated to mothers!

Natural Beginnings
http://www.naturalbeginnings.org/
Want an easier, shorter birth? Hire a doula!

Nursing Mother Supplies
http://www.nursingmothersupplies.com/
Information about breastfeeding.

Online Birth Center
http://www.moonlily.com/obc/
Information on midwifery, pregancy, birth, and breastfeeding.

Parents Place
http://www.parentsplace.com
Links to information on fertility, pregnancy, health, family, and much more.

Pregnancy and Baby
http://www.women.com/pregnancy/
Useful information during pregnancy and birth.

P

Pregnancy Calendar
http://www.pregnancycalendar.com/
An interactive pregnancy calendar—customized for you!

Pregnancy Centers Online
http://www.pregnancycenters.org/
Help and information for women in a crisis pregnancy.

Pregnancy Today
http://www.pregnancytoday.com/
The online journal and community for expectant parents.

Pregnancy Website Reviews
http://www.abcparenting.com/index.cfm?cat=124
Hundreds of sites organized by subject matter. A great
place to start looking for information.

Storknet
http://www.storknet.org/
A community site, with information, discussion area, parenting tips, etc.

Tip of the Week for Moms!
http://www.geocities.com/~boocat1/momtip.html
New tips every week for mothers around the world.

Ultimate Baby
http://www.ultimatebaby.com
A community for expectant and new parents, with chatroom, message boards, shopping links, etc.

Waterbirth Website
http://www.waterbirthinfo.com/
A beautiful site about giving birth in water.

Publications—Online

Boundless
http://www.boundless.org/
A "webzine" focusing on issues of interest to young
Christians.

Christian Computing Magazine
http://www.gospelcom.net/ccmag/
Online columns, game reviews, download software, inspirational thoughts, "Best of the Christian Web," and more.

Christian Homeschool Journal
http://members.nbci.com/hmschooljrnl/page8.html
Practical advice to making homeschooling effective. Full of fun and ready-to-use ideas.

Christian Mirror
http://christianmirror.com/
A "webzine" specifically for the Christian Woman.

Connection
http://www.connectionmagazine.org/current/contents.htm
A free online and print magazine giving glory to Jesus. News, opinion, reviews and sports coverage.

Current Thoughts and Trends
http://www.navpress.com/ctt.asp
A monthly magazine on what is happening in the Christian and secular worlds.

First Things
http://www.firstthings.com/
A magazine of Christian opinion, commentary, news and reviews.

Forthright
http://forthright.org/
An Internet and email magazine for people who are looking for new treasures from God's storeroom.

Just for Fun
http://www.geocities.com/EnchantedForest/Tower/9438/currentissue.html
An electronic magazine with a Christian focus for kids.

LatterReign
http://www.latterreign.com/
A journal of creative expressions of faith in God.

Light Ezine—Stories of Global Scripture Ministry
http://www.light-magazine.org
Light Ezine from the International Bible Society tells in stories and photography the truth of Jesus Christ in everyday lives and of theScripture ministry of Christians educating the world with God's Word.

New Jerusalem News
http://www.njcnews.org/
Free magazine featuring Bible truths that will strengthen, empower, and lead believers to a new relationship with Jesus Christ! Enlightening audio (no player or plugin required) and video.

Online Magazines
http://www.gospelcom.net/features/zines.shtml
Links to hundreds of Christian-oriented magazines.

other sites of interest

Best Magazines—A Special Report
http://www.1000magazines.com/best.htm
A report on the best magazines for consumers.

Classical Net
http://www.classical.net/music/links/publink.html
Links to a variety of online magazine sites, including classical music sites.

Computer Magazines
http://www.internetvalley.com/top100mag.html
The collection of links to the top 100 computer and software WWW magazines and journals.

ElectricBook Links to Online Books, Newspapers, Magazines
http://www.electricbook.com/
An Internet guide to online books, newspapers, magazines and electronic publishing.

Gravity
http://www.newsavanna.com/
An electronic magazine of black history and culture.

Internet Magazines
http://www.webreference.com/internet/magazines/
internet.html
What's new today on Internet.com's vast network of Internet-oriented sites and online magazines.

Just for Kids Electronic Magazine
http://www.geocities.com/EnchantedForest/
Tower/9438/currentissue.html
Monthly Christian magazine for children.

KidWorld
http://www.bconnex.net/~kidworld/
From Tandem House, artwork, writing, and ideas by and for kids.

Magazines
http://www.eduplace.com/kids/links/kids_4.html
Chickadee Net is an electronic supplement to the fun science and nature print magazine, Chickadee, which is designed for kids.

Magazines Online
http://www.thepaperboy.com/magazines/
The ultimate guide to the world of online magazines. Browse through a wide selection of magazines on subjects from news to gardening.

Outer-Net Links for Kids
http://www.outer-net.com/~software/kidsmags.htm
Outer-net links for kids. Ezines and magazines. These listings were culled from a variety of sources, including search engines, magazines, etc.

Sports Illustrated for Kids
http://www.sikids.com/
The youth edition of the well-known magazine, with articles, features, columns, and more, written with youth interests in mind.

Sports Parents
http://www.sportsparents.com/
From *Sports Illustrated for Kids,* this online magazine features articles for parents whose children are participating in sports activities.

P

Web Wombat
http://www.webwombat.com.au/magazines/
Links to hundreds of online magazines, including ones for the home, family, small businesses, hobbies, entertainment, and more.

World Kids Network
http://worldkids.net
Run mostly by kids, for kids. Includes chat, clubs, mailing lists, news, and school service.

Yeah! Sports Magazines
http://www.yeahsports.com/dir/magazines/
Articles on all types of sports, including football, basketball, hockey, etc.

Yak's Corner
http://www.yakscorner.com
News magazine for kids, with topics like animals, "yaktivities", games, and more.

Publications—Print

Beyond Magazine
http://www.beyondmag.com/
A magazine about God and life. View back issues, subscribe to the magazine, online discussion forums, volunteer options, and more.

Christian Century
http://www.christiancentury.org/
Dedicated to keeping the reader informed on the issues that define religious life today.

Christian Reader
http://www.christianity.net/cr
Christian history magazine located on the Christianity.net website. From *Christianity Today, Inc.*

Focus Magazine
http://www.focusmagazine.org/
A journal dedicated to the study and practical *application* of the truth found in God's Word.

Maranatha Christian Journal
http://www.mcjonline.com/

The purpose of the Maranatha Christian Journal is to report newsworthy events and activities affecting today's online Christian.

Touchstone—A Journal of Mere Christianity
http://www.touchstonemag.com/

A conservative ecumenical Christian journal of news and opinion.

Visions of Glory Magazine
http://www.visionsofglory.org/

Dynamic true-life stories, testimonies and biblical dramatizations offering hope, encouragement, and inspiration for this hour.

Well, The
http://www.thewellministries.org/well/

A free monthly Christian publication of inspirational and encouraging stories.

other sites of interest

Discover Magazine
http://www.discover.com/

Current issues and archive, science, gallery, ask *Discover*, and more.

Home Education Magazine
http://www.geocities.com/Heartland/Acres/9395/schedules.html

One of the oldest, most respected and informative magazines on homeschooling.

Kiplinger
http://www.kiplinger.com

A page of business information including stocks, funds, and the *Kiplinger* magazine.

World Magazine
http://www.nationalgeographic.com/media/world

Mailbag, articles, stories, and more from this *National Geographic* publication for kids.

ZDNet

http://www.zdnet.com/pcmag/stories/reviews/
0,6755,2394453,00.html

Reviews, chat, search, reference, and other articles of interest from *PC Magazine*.

Radio

Air-1 Radio Network

http://www.air1radio.com/

The first alternative/rock/contemporary Christian music station broadcasting live on the Internet.

Amen Corner

http://www.mp3.com/stations/amencorner

An online radio station featuring strictly Christian music, that promotes the name and message of Jesus Christ.

American Christian Network

http://www.acn-network.com/

Brings you the finest Bible teachers in the world 24/7 with RealAudio.

Back to the Bible

http://www.backtothebible.org

Practical counsel for applying God's Word to daily Christianity through media with RealAudio.

Baptist Hour

http://www.familynet.org/radio/baptisthour/
BaptistHour.htm

Programs of Christian music and thoughtful teachings over the web.

Blessing Music Radio

http://www.bmradio.net/

Bilingual (English-Spanish) Internet Christian music broadcasts.

Bug Radio

http://www.lightsource.com/

A "mother-approved" radio station designed for children.

Christian Pirate Radio
http://www.cprxtreme.com/
The best in popular Christian music on the Internet, 24 hours a day.

Christian Radio Internet Start Panel
http://www.terrycom.net/crisp.htm
Christian radio Internet tuner is now available as a free download.

Christian Tuner
http://www.christiantuner.com/Default.asp
Over 500 Internet Christian radio stations; music, talk, sports and more.

ChristianRadio.com
http://www.christianradio.com/
The Internet source for Christian radio stations, Christian radio shows, Christian music artists, and Christian radio resources.

Digital Stream Webcasting
http://www.digitalstream.net
Sharing the Christian message via webcast live and on-demand sermons, lessons, and music using RealAudio and RealMedia.

Family Life
http://www.familylife.com/
Daily radio broadcasts aimed at strengthening the family from the Campus Crusade for Christ.

Gigabase
http://www.active-ss.com/gigabase/webtv_netradio.html
Links to thousands of Christian radio, TV and music sites on the Internet.

Good News from the Bible
http://www.worshipradio.com/
GoodNewsFromTheBible.htm
Clear Bible message to search the Scriptures everyday, resulting in a return to the foundation Jesus left to the church.

Gospel Media Network
http://www.gospelmedia.com
Internet only radio taking lifegiving preaching and teaching of the Word of God and the Gospel of Jesus Christ.

HitVault Radio
http://www.lightsource.com/
Classic Christian music hitmakers of the '70s and '80s. Click to listen and let the memories roll.

Holy Hip Hop
http://www.holyhiphop.com/
Musically taking the Gospel to the streets. Online audio, news, chatrooms and more.

John Hagee Today
http://www.lightsource.com/
A faith-filled broadcast anchored not only to traditional values but to old-fashioned gospel preaching.

K-Love Radio
http://www.klove.com
A listener-supported, non-commercial contemporary Christian music station broadcasting across the United States and over the Internet at KLOVE.com.

Love Worth Finding
http://www.lightsource.com/
Listen to Dr. Adrian Rogers present a love worth finding in these chaotic times we live in. Learn biblical keys to understanding true love.

MasterControl
http://www.familynet.org/radio/MasterControl/Mastercontrol.htm
Family friendly radio show with segments on travel, business, entertainment and more.

NetRadio.com
http://www.netradio.net/
Online music provider with over 120 channels of streaming music.

OnePlace.com
http://www.oneplace.com/
Links to dozens of top Christian radio broadcasts available online.

Positive Alternative Radio FM Network
http://www.parfm.com/
An online source for Christian music, concert dates and information, contests, etc.

Praise in the Night
http://www.pitn.org
Radio revival heard coast to coast, border to border, and live on the World Wide Web.

Radio Station KFSG-FM
http://www.kfsg.com
Site offers classic Christian music and programs 24-hours a day. Broadcast live over the Internet, via Real-Player.

Rays of Glory
http://www.worshipradio.com/RaysofGlory.htm
The best in bluegrass, family style, quartet music, plain and simple Bible teaching to lift up and encourage.

Rhythm-N-Prayze
http://www.lightsource.com/
Check out this gospel music program and enjoy inspirational, contemporary, and traditional gospel music.

Soul2Soul
http://www.s2sradio.com
Weekly, syndicated one hour Christian artist feature that airs on radio stations both domestically and internationally. Interviews via RealAudio.

Sunlite Radio
http://www.sunlite-radio.com
Internet radio featuring gospel music, classic hymns, and urban gospel.

Voice of Wilderness Ministries
http://www.voiceofwilderness.com
Listen to RealAudio messages in Hindi and in English.

WBGL
http://www.wbgl.org
A contemporary Christian music station airing music
and programming 24/7, featuring RealAudio webcast.

WGCR Global Christian Radio
http://wgcr.org/default.htm
Gospel music and Christian talk radio.

WWJD Christian Radio Online
http://www.talkwire.com/wwjd
WWJD Christian music and praise online featuring
Christian rock, Bible study, prayer and more.

Zola Levitt Presents
http://www.worshipradio.com/zola.htm
Hear not only the current weekly program, but also past
programs.

other sites of interest

MIT List of Radio Stations on the Internet
http://wmbr.mit.edu/stations/list.html
A worldwide listing of all radio stations. Search by call
sign or location.

Top Radio
http://www.topradio.com
Links to stations around the world.

U.S.A.Radio Network Channel
http://www.usaradio.com/
Syndicated talk shows, music programs, etc.

Recipes

(see also Cooking)

Anita's Recipe Oasis
http://members.xoom.com/recipe_oasis
Favorite family recipes.

Christian Chefs Fellowship
http://www.christianchefs.org/links/Culinary/Recipes/

Links to dozens of recipe sites collected by the fellowship of Christian cooks and chefs.

Christian Classifieds—Recipes
http://www.christian-classifieds.com/recipes.htm
Time and taste-tested favorites from Middle Tennessee.

Christian Mirror—Recipes
http://christianmirror.com/recipes.htm
Recipes collected by the leading Christian Women's webzine.

Christian Moms—Recipe Box
http://www.uci.net/~cotton/recipe.htm
A directory of links to dozens of great recipe sites.

Cooking with Friends Across America
http://www.friendsacrossamerica.com/indexa.html
Recipes, links, advice, and tips.

Feast Day Cookbook
http://www.ewtn.com/library/FAMILY/FSTDAY.TXT
An online cookbook of special menus and recipes for Christian holidays.

other sites of interest

1st Traveler's Choice Internet Cookbook
http://www.virtualcities.com/ons/recipe.htm
3,000 recipes from innkeepers, restaurateurs, and other cooking professionals.

AccuChef
http://www.pc-recipebox.com/
Award-winning recipe software for Windows(tm).

All Delicious Recipes
http://www.culinary.com/link/jump.cgi?ID=963
Recipes from around the world.

All Recipes.com
http://allrecipes.com/
Recipes for appetizers, beverages, desserts, ethnic food, seasonal dishes, special diets, and more.

R

Betty Crocker
http://www.bettycrocker.com
Betty's recipes online as well as shopping and baking hints.

Breads by Category
http://breadrecipe.com/cat/category.asp?keyw=1
Bread recipes for everything from wheat to strawana smoothie bread.

Busy Cooks
http://www.culinary.com/link/jump.cgi?ID=789
A complete index of recipes, organized by category.

Cookie recipe.com | Recipes
http://www.cookierecipe.com/
Recipes for all kinds of cookies, plus links to other recipe sites.

Cooking Light
http://www.cookinglight.com/
Food, healthy living, recipe finder, customer service, store, talk, and more.

Culinary Connection
http://www.culinary.com/
Search for over 73,000 recipes in 53 categories.

Food Network's FoodTV.Com
http://www.foodtv.com/
Recipes of the day, world cuisine, tips from chefs, and much more.

Global Gourmet
http://www.globalgourmet.com/
Recipes from all around the world.

Grandma's Vegetable Dishes
http://www.b4uby.com/granny/collect.htm
Holiday, cookie, Native American, vegetable, and other recipes.

Ichef Recipe Archive
http://www.ichef.com/ichef-recipes/index.html
Browse or search over 30,000 recipes.

Inquisitive Cook
http://www.inquisitivecook.com/
Cooking tips, baking tips, cooking and baking chat, recipe ideas.

Links4Recipes.com
http://members.amaonline.com/nrogers/Kitchen/
Links to many categories of recipes.

Mimi's Cyber Kitchen
http://www.cyber-kitchen.com/
Cookbooks, weblinks, recipe exchange board, and much more.

Nabisco Recipes
http://www.nabiscorecipes.com/
Recipe search and meal planner from Nabisco.

Practical Kitchen Recipes
http://www.practicalkitchen.com/dir/Recipes/
Over 20 categories of recipes to choose from.

Recipe Center.com
http://www.recipecenter.com/
100,000+ recipes, software, games, quiz, and poll.

Recipes by Simply-Recipes
http://www.simply-recipes.com/
Hundreds of recipes divided by category: crock pot, Christmas, pork, ethnic, pasta, breakfast, etc.

RecipeXchange for Favorite Recipes and Cooking Secrets
http://www.recipexchange.com/recipexchange_cfmfiles/recipes.cfm
Share your recipes, search for recipes, or request a recipe on this website.

SOAR: Searchable Online Archive of Recipes
http://soar.berkeley.edu/recipes/
Recipes for everything from breakfast dishes to Thanksgiving, from oils to Moroccan food.

Southern U.S. Cuisine
http://southernfood.miningco.com/
About.com's Southern US Cuisine page with recipes for everything southern.

R

StarChefs
http://www.starchefs.com/Recipesearch.html
Recipe search engine. Searches the recipes of chefs and cookbook authors.

Top Secret Recipes on the Web
http://www.topsecretrecipes.com/
Recipes created from restaurant food, like McDonald's breakfast burrito or Outback Steakhouse's Bloomin' Onion.

True Southern Family Recipes
http://www.aheb.com/cookbook/frames.html
Recipes for appetizers, barbeques, brunches, cakes and frostings, tailgating, and other southern events.

Reference and Information

Apostles, Saints, and Holy Persons
http://www.apostles.com/
Links to biographies, discussions, creeds, and other sites.

Christian Reference Tools and Documents
http://www.geocities.com/Athens/Oracle/2566/
A extensive site featuring a search feature on a number of Bibles and basic reference works.

Christian Shareware and Reference Materials
http://shareware.crosswalk.com/ReferenceMaterial
Find a list of reference materials to download, utilize study tools, find Bible translations, play Christian games, and much more!

Creeds of Christendom
http://www.creeds.net/index.htm
A broad selection of creeds from numerous Christian denominations.

Glossary for Judaism, Christianity and Islam
http://ccat.sas.upenn.edu/~rs2/glossopt.html
Extensive glossary of religious terminology.

Historic Church Documents
http://www.reformed.org/documents/documents.html
Numerous fundamental texts and documents from the
Center for Reformed Theology and Apologetics.

Internet Libraries for Christian Reference
http://private.fuller.edu/dakim/online/library.htm
Links to the top Christian references sources available
online.

Methodist Archives and Research Center
http://rylibweb.man.ac.uk/data1/dg/text/method.html
Extensive online resources on Methodist history and
thought, including manuscripts and pictures.

Religious and Sacred Texts
http://davidwiley.com/religion.html
An extensive directory of links to sites containing basic
texts from many of the world's religions.

other sites of interest

10,000-Year Calendar
http://calendarhome.com/tyc/index.shtml
Print 10,000 years of calendar pages.

1001 Best Internet Tips
http://www4.zdnet.com/pccomp/besttips/
This informative site provides valuable tips on browsers,
search engines, the Internet, operating systems, and more.

American School Directory
http://www.asd.com/
Find vital school information on all 108,000 k-12 schools
in America.

American Universities
http://www.clas.ufl.edu/CLAS/
american-universities.html
With one page per university, this site provides phone
numbers for admissions, student life events, news,
sports, academics, etc.

AMTRAK on the Web
http://www.amtrak.com/
Here you can find schedules, fares, reservations, tickets, arrival status, and more.

Anyday
http://www.scopesys.com/anyday/
Choose any day of the year and find out who was born on that day, who died, what holidays occur, and more fun facts.

AnyWho Toll-Free Directory
http://www.tollfree.att.net/tf.html
Find any toll-free number searching by name or category. Maps, directions, white and yellow pages are also available.

Area Code / Country Code Look-up
http://www-cse.ucsd.edu/users/bsy/area.html
An area code listing by number for the U.S.A.

Ask an Expert
http://www.askanexpert.com/
A site that provides an expert's answer to even the toughest questions.

Ask Jeeves
http://www.askjeeves.com/
Here, Jeeves will answer the question posed to him on the subject you choose.

ATM Locator
http://www.visa.com/atms/
Find the location of an ATM in any region of the world. Also, this site offers information on commerce cards, debit cards, consumer questions, and much more.

Bank Rate Monitor
http://www.bankrate.com/
Find advice on anything from student loans to starting a small business. Information provided on rates, taxes, investing, and more.

Bartlett's Familiar Quotations
http://www.columbia.edu/acis/bartleby/bartlett/
A collection of passages, phrases and proverbs, traced to
their sources in ancient and modern literature.

**Better Homes and Gardens Home Improvement
Encyclopedia**
http://www.bhglive.com/homeimp/
Provides a guided tour of plumbing, wiring, decks, etc.,
plus tools and guides, discussion groups, help center, and
more.

Biography.com
http://www.biography.com/
More than 25,000 personalities to research. Includes magazine articles, trivia, links, and a weekly "Top Ten Bios."

Canadian Postal Code Lookup Service
http://www.westminster.ca/cdnlook.htm
An American and Canadian postal code lookup service
with other services such as national change of address information.

Card Games
http://www.netlink.co.uk/users/pagat/
Provides rules and information about card games from
all parts of the world.

Census Bureau Data Maps
http://www.census.gov/datamap/www/index.html
Provides state and county demographics, economic profiles, and country FIPS codes.

College and University Homepage—Worldwide
http://www.mit.edu:8001/people/cdemello/univ.html
This list has over 3,000 entries with a geographic listing
as well as alphabetical listing of schools.

Common Weights and Measures
*http://www.cchem.berkeley.edu/ChemResources/
Weights-n-Measures/index.html*
Common U.S. and metric equivalents, metric prefixes
and mathematic notation for orders of magnitude.

Company Profiles
http://www.hoovers.com
Look up a company and find out various facts about its different aspects. A great site with links to other sites, news center, business travel and much more!

Complete Home Medical Guide
http://cpmcnet.columbia.edu/texts/guide/
Guide to using your health care system, first aid and safety, treatment of disease, etc.

Consumer Price Index
http://stats.bls.gov/cpihome.htm
Inflation calculator, CPI revision, news releases, data, and more.

Convert It!
http://microimg.com/science/
Use these conversion tables to convert just about any-thing to anything.

Countries of the World
http://www.yahoo.com/Regional/Countries/
Current information on countries of the world. Just click on the country of your choice.

CyberStats
http://www.fas.org/
A comprehensive guide to Internet-related statistics and sources.

Daily Almanac
http://www.dailyalmanacs.com/
Organized by date, information about birthdays, events, and other dates of importance.

Date and Time Gateway
http://www.bsdi.com/date?US/Pacific
View timezone databases for countries all over the world.

Dictionary, Thesaurus, and Desk Reference Tools
http://www.acns.nwu.edu/world/desk-reference.html
Links to dozens of online references.

Driving Directions
http://www.mapquest.com/cgi-bin/mqtrip?link=/
TripQuest-Main&uid=u1mi1embgn9ac5jt:
2al6bngf8&random=803
This site provides directions, maps, traffic reports, hotel rates, and more helpful traveling tools.

E-Conflict World Encyclopedia
http://www.emulateme.com
The Internet's best source of country data. Includes country flags, current weather, national anthems, etc.

EDGAR Database of Corporate Information
http://www.sec.gov/edgarhp.htm
A database for retrieving data, searching, planning, and learning SEC procedures.

Electronic Library
http://www.elibrary.com/
A site that allows you to search for a topic, providing results from magazines, books, newspapers, maps, pictures, and radio.

Elements of Style
http://www.bartleby.com/141/index.html
This page is a helpful writing aid, concentrating attention on the rules of usage and principles of composition most commonly violated.

Encyclopedia.com
http://www.encyclopedia.com/
Sleuth center, company, sports, jobs, entertainment, shopping, reference, and more.

R

Ethnologue
http://www.sil.org/ethnologue/
A site for languages of the world with maps, 682 bibliographical references, 6,703 language descriptions, and more

Fast Facts
http://gwu.edu/~gprice/handbook.htm
A directory of links to sites with information on numerous subjects, including nations of the world.

FedNet
http://www.fednet.net/
Provides access to numerous facets of the U.S. government, as well as fast-breaking news on Capitol Hill.

FindOut
http://www.nytimes.com/partners/findout/
A personalized research "help desk" to answer queries quickly and effectively.

Free Internet Encyclopedia
http://www.encyclopedia.com/
The premiere free encyclopedia on the Internet, with more than 14,000 articles.

Funk and Wagnalls Free Encyclopedia
http://www.funkandwagnalls.com/
A great site with world news, a world atlas, thesaurus, dictionary, encyclopedia, plus current events, and quick links.

General Reference Links
http://www.peak.org/~bonwritr/ref.htm
Includes *American Demographics, National Libraries of Europe, Publisher's Weekly, Library of Congress* and much, much more.

Global Yellow Pages, The
http://www.globalyp.com/world.htm
A collection of phone directories from around the world. Find a number anywhere in the globe at this site.

GO Translator
http://translator.go.com/
Translate webpages by entering the URL, and other translation tools.

How Far Is It?
http://www.indo.com/distance/
Enter two places on this site and find the distance between them.

Human Anatomy Online
http://www.innerbody.com/
Study the anatomy of the human body at this site. Each topic has animation, hundreds of graphics, and thousands of descriptive links.

Information Please
http://www.infoplease.com
Search engine, news, games, sports, entertainment, and more.

International Affairs Resources
http://www.etown.edu/vl/
A well organized directory of links to information about the world around us.

International Directories
http://www.wayp.com/
The international white and yellow pages for queries on names, addresses, telephone numbers, and fax numbers.

International Telephone Directories
http://www.infobel.com/
Here you may find anyone anywhere in the world, just by selecting a country and entering certain information.

Internet 800 Directory
http://inter800.com/
Find the 800 number of any product, service, or company through this resource.

Internet Public Library
http://www.ipl.org/
This organized and informative site has many resources for teens, youth, adults, and librarians. Provides magazines and serials, newspapers, online texts, and more!

iTools
http://www.iTools.com/research-it
Research site searches for reference materials such as dictionaries, thesauris, and translations.

Kelley Blue Book
http://www.kbb.com/
A great guide for the car buyer, with car pricing, used car values, motorcycles, insurance information, reviews, and more.

Kid's Almanac
http://kids.infoplease.com/
Almanac, dictionary, encyclopedia, searches, and more.

Knowledge Adventure Encyclopedia
http://www.letsfindout.com/
From this site you may access information on a variety of subjects. Acts as a great homework helper.

Law and Politics Internet Guide
http://www.geocities.com/CapitolHill/Lobby/5011/
A one stop source for legal research with law books and reviews, journals, research, and more topics.

Learn2.com
http://www.learn2.com
Links for everyday learning, corporate learning, news, and more.

Library of Congress Homepage
http://lcweb.loc.gov/
A site packed with information that contains a catalog to search, exhibitions online, news and events, forms and information about copyrights, plus more general information.

MapQuest!
http://www.mapquest.com/
Here you can find maps, driving directions, live traffic reports, guides, and much more!

Martindale's Reference Desk
http://www-sci.lib.uci.edu/HSG/Ref.html
This huge reference desk has information on anything from gardening to radiology. A must-see!

Measurement 4 Measure
http://www.wolinskyweb.com/measure.htm
A collection of interactive sites on the web that estimate, evaluate, calculate, and translate measurements for you!

Measurements Converter
http://www.mplik.ru/~sg/transl/
Provides conversions for weight, capacity and volume, length, area, speed, and pressure.

MedicineNet
http://www.medicinenet.com/
A great site with information about diseases and conditions, procedures and tests, medication, health news, cholesterol, and much, much more!

Merck Manual
http://www.merck.com/!!seFMm3Qb0seFMm3Qb0/pubs/mmanual/
Provides a manual for diagnosis and therapy with a search feature, table of contents, health infopark, and more.

Merriam-Webster Online Dictionary
http://www.m-w.com
Online dictionary for research or homework help. Includes games, books, maps, and more.

My Facts Page
http://www.refdesk.com/facts.html
A great index of subjects including government, libraries, history, dictionaries, and much more! Also has a virtual encyclopedia and virtual newspaper.

My Homework Helper
http://www.refdesk.com/homework.html
Provides help from Grade 1-College. You can ask the experts, do research, or get connected to other homework links.

National Address Service
http://www.cedar.buffalo.edu/adserv.html
Site server allows users to submit U.S. postal addresses

R

and receive a postscript or GIF file of the address for printing, including barcode.

National Center for Health Statistics
http://www.cdc.gov/nchswww/
Surveys and data collection systems, initiatives, research and development, fast stats, data warehouses, news releases, and more.

NetClock
http://events.yahoo.com/
Find out events occurring on the web, local events, movie showtimes, TV listings, and much more.

Netdictionary
http://www.netdictionary.com/
A reference guide to technical, cultural and humorous terms related to the Internet.

Old Farmer's Almanac
http://www.almanac.com/
An online almanac with many pages to view and great links to almanac products. Reports on crop growth, weather, the moon, and more.

OneLook Dictionaries
http://www.onelook.com/index.html
Search for online dictionary websites, browse dictionaries, view FAQs, and more.

Online Calculator
http://www.naveen.net/calculator/
An online stack calculator that is JavaScript enabled.

Periodic Table
http://www.shef.ac.uk/uni/academic/A-C/chem/web-elements/web-elements-home.html
The first periodic table on the web, with a printable table, element names, FAQs, and much more!

Peterson's Guide to Colleges
http://www.petersons.com/
At this information site you can search and find colleges,

rams, private schools, summer
more!

.com/

arizes the most reliable prod-
sources.

k.com/index.html

ce, reference site of the day, fact of the
advice, just for fun, current news, and in-
ries.

ce.com

p://www.reference.com/

An online ad service and management system with information on advertisers, web publishers, corporate information, and more.

Research It!
http://www.itools.com/research-it/
Search language tools, library tools, geographic tools, financial tools, shipping and mailing tools, etc.

ResearchPaper.com
http://www.researchpaper.com/
A guide to getting the most out of your time researching
online, with a writing center, idea directory, chatroom,
and search engine.

Reverse Lookup(1)
*http://pic1.infospace.com/_1_4P93UJE085NOY__
info.go2net/reverse.htm*
Do a reverse search by typing in a phone number, address, or email address to find a person, or enter an area
code to find the area it covers. Classifieds listed, as well
as Personals, and Yellow and White pages.

Roget's Internet Thesaurus
http://www.thesaurus.com/
Do a search, browse the thesaurus, do a crossword puzzle, or look up the definition of a word.

RxList

http://www.rxlist.com/

The Internet drug index where you may search medical dictionary, and generally educate yours various drug issues.

Search Systems

http://www.pac-info.com/

Here you will find over 1,500 searchable public reco databases with states listed alphabetically.

Social Security Death Index Search

http://www.ancestry.com/search/rectype/vital/ssdi/main.htm

This site offers census, marriage, military records, and more great tools to help you locate your ancestors.

Soyouwanna

http://www.soyouwanna.com/

Information on how to do all those things "you didn't learn in school."

Statistical Abstract of the United States

http://www.census.gov/stat_abstract/

A site with United States statistics in brief, frequently requested tables, state rankings, profiles, and other statistical reference products.

Sunrise/Sunset Computation

http://tycho.usno.navy.mil/srss.html

This site shows the times of sunrise / sunset, moonrise / moonset, the current phase of the moon, and other astronomical data.

Swissinfo: Worldtime

http://www.swissinfo.net/cgi/worldtime/

This is an import-export bulletin board with international trade leads, offers to buy and sell, and business opportunities.

Symbols

http://www.symbols.com/index.html

An encyclopedia of graphic symbols. Searchable by meaning or shape.

Thomas: Legislative Information on the Internet
http://thomas.loc.gov
A site that includes congressional records, committee information, bills in the news, web links and more legislative information.

Today in History
http://www.440.com/twtd/today.html
This interesting site lists famous historic events that occurred on each day of the current week. Includes links to other sites.

Today's Calendar and Clock Page
http://www.ecben.net/calendar.shtml
This provides today's date hundreds of different ways as represented by various cultures and religions.

TRIP.com
http://www.thetrip.com/
A complete guide to trip planning, with guides for travel, newsstand, marketplace, flighttracker, car and hotel information, and many more helpful tools.

U.S. Census Bureau
http://www.census.gov/
Extensive resources on all sorts of census data and news.

U.S. National Debt Clock
http://www.brillig.com/debt_clock/
Shows the current outstanding public debt with news articles on the subject and links to related sites.

R

U.S. Population Clock
http://www.census.gov/cgi-bin/popclock
Displays the current resident population of the United States, along with frequency of births, deaths, and migrants.

U.S. Postal Service
http://www.usps.gov/
Here you can order, locate, mail, or pay for packages, track your package on its course, and much more!

Ultimate Collection of News Links
http://pppp.net/links/news/
A site where you can read newspapers from other countries. A very useful site with a great layout and content.

Ultimates
http://www.theultimates.com
Site contains Yellow and White pages for finding phone numbers as well as a trip planner and more.

Universal Shipping Calculator
http://www.intershipper.net/
A great information guide for your shipping needs. Will gather information from eight different shipping companies so you can spot the best rates.

Virtual Human Project
http://www.nlm.nih.gov/research/visible/ visible_human.html
A site where you can find complete, anatomically detailed, 3-D representations of the normal male and female bodies. Links, health information, library services, and more.

Virtual Reference Desk
http://thorplus.lib.purdue.edu/reference/
Links to dictionaries, thesauri, information technology, maps and travel information, phone books, area codes, and other reference sources.

Weights and Measures
http://www.refdesk.com/factmeas.html
A facts page with dozens of links to pages about weights and measures.

West's Legal Directory
http://www.lawoffice.com
A site that provides information for dealing with legal affairs free of charge. You can find a lawyer, learn law tools, and roam the legal marketplace.

WhitePages.com
http://www.whitepages.com/
This site helps you find a person, area code, zip code, website, toll free number, links, and more information.

WhoWhere
http://www.whowhere.com/
The way to find anybody on the web, whether it be a
friend, celebrity, or professional.

World Directories
http://www.worldpages.com/global.html
Search business and people directories around the world.
Contains helpful links, resources/ tools, etc.

World Time Zones
http://tycho.usno.navy.mil/tzones.html
A site that provides a map of world time zones, U.S. law
on standard time zones, and explanation of time zones
by an expert.

Worldwide Holidays and Events
http://www.holidayfestival.com/
A site that provides national holidays for different countries, with links and information on countries and religions.

WWW Virtual Library
http://www.w3.org/vl/
A library with a variety of topics to choose from. Search
the web for a topic of your own.

WWWebster Dictionary
http://www.m-w.com/dictionary
An online collegiate dictionary and thesaurus with a
search engine, word games, books, CDs, and more.

Yahoo's Index of Reference Tools
http://www.yahoo.com/Reference/
An index of tools to help you find information you need,
with search engines and great links.

ZipFind
http://link-usa.com/zipcode/
Find the distance between any two zip codes at this helpful finder.

R

Science

10,000-Year Calendar
http://calendarhome.com/tyc/index.shtml
Print 10,000 years of calendar pages.

Center for Theology and the Natural Sciences
http://www.ctns.org
Promoting the creative mutual interaction between contemporary theology and the natural sciences.

Christian Geology Ministry
http://www.kjvBible.org
Uses science, logic, and the KJV Bible to interpret the Genesis narratives and the Earth's geology.

Christian Reference Tools and Documents
http://www.geocities.com/Athens/Oracle/2566/
Site with a broad range of articles and documents dealing with science and Christianity.

Christians in Science
http://www.cis.org.uk
Applying biblical principles to science and technology, including God's work in creation, and encouraging concern for the environment.

Creation SuperLibrary
http://www.ChristianAnswers.Net/creation/home.html
A multilingual creation megasite providing answers, articles, special features and more.

Does God Exist?
http://www.doesgodexist.org
Geology and biology from a Christian perspective. Newsletter, seminar schedules, more.

Evidence for God from Science
http://www.godandscience.org/
Provides evidence for the existence of God and the reliability of the Bible from scientific studies.

Faith and Reason
http://www.pbs.org/faithandreason/
Resources on the interaction between religion and science.

Faith and Science
http://www.cco.caltech.edu/~newman/sci-faith.html
A collection of writings on issues of faith and science
from a Catholic perspective.

God and Evolution: A Convergence of Science and Religion
http://www.scientific-religious.com
Built on the thesis that the purpose of evolution is the development of human beings; for this to occur, a God is
necessary.

Institute on Religion in an Age of Science
http://www.iras.org/
Working for a dynamic and positive relationship between
religion and science.

Jason Project
http://www.jasonproject.org
Year-round scientific expedition designed to excite and
engage students in science and technology.

John Ray Initiative
http://www.jri.org.uk
Bringing together scientific and Christian understand-
ings of the environment.

Mike's Origins Resource
http://www.creation-science-prophecy.com/
A molecular geneticist creationist uses science and the
Bible to investigate our origins. Sites include creation science topics, pseudogenes, ancient DNA, biological time
clocks, Carbon 14, flood geology.

Science and Christianity
http://www.dimery.com
Articles, book reviews and links, looking at the engagement of science with Christianity, both historically and
in the present.

Science and Christianity Resources
http://www.rjdimery.freeserve.co.uk/science.html
Resources for the study of science and faith, including es-
say articles and in-depth book reviews.

S

Science and Faith
http://solon.cma.univie.ac.at/~neum/sciandf.html
Extensive links to information on science from a Christian perspective. Biographies of Christian scientists, too.

Science and Religion
http://home.earthlink.net/~rlphen/index.html
Using the methods of process theology, it is possible to explore boundary questions of science and religion. This includes brief overviews of ecology and evolution.

Vatican Observatory
http://clavius.as.arizona.edu/vo/
Homepage for one of the oldest astronomical research centers in the world.

other sites of interest

3000 Year Perpetual Calendar
http://members.home.net/sedford/cal/main.html
International and British versions, as well as links to other calendar sites.

Amazing Space Web-Based Activities
http://oposite.stsci.edu/pubinfo/education/amazing-space
Galaxies galore, star light-star bright, solar system trading cards, astronaut challenge, and more.

Astrobiology Web
http://www.reston.com/astro/index.html
An online guide to the living universe.

Astronomy Links
http://www.rpi.edu/dept/phys/Astro/ObsAstro/links.html
Links to agencies, organizations, space probes, journals, images, and other links.

Bill Nye
http://nyelabs.kcts.org/openNyeLabs.html
Demo of the day, teacher's lounge, TV guide, home demos, ask Bill Nye, and more.

Cells Alive
http://www.cellsalive.com/
Fascinating site about the basic building blocks of all living things. Don't miss the cell-cams!

Chem4Kids!
http://www.chem4kids.com
Links to matter, elements, atoms, math, reactions, and more.

Comets and Meteor Showers
http://comets.amsmeteors.org/
Links to comets now visible, periodic, sungrazers, information, meteor shower calendar, and more.

Discovery
http://www.discovery.com/
Animals, history, and TV listings can be found on this site. Directories to scale models, fun and games, and more.

Dr. Karl Kruszelnicki
http://www.abc.net.au/science/k2
Ever wondered 'What Eats Bacteria?", ''Why is yawning contagious?" or ''What is happening when we crack our knuckles?" The good Doctor shares his answers from his radio show about subjects that affect real people in their normal life.

Earth and Moon Viewer
http://www.fourmilab.ch/earthview/vplanet.html
View a map of the earth or view the earth from the sun, moon, or the night side of the earth.

EurekaAlert!
http://www.eurekalert.org/
Your global gateway to science, medicine, and technology news.

ExploreScience.com
http://www.explorescience.com/
Great interactive site with activities to teach young and old about scientific principles.

S

Geology Link
http://www.geologylink.com/
A geology news service, glossary, virtual field trips and more!

High Moon
http://eclipse.span.ch/
Worldwide eclipse photos, news and schedules.

Invention Dimension!
http://web.mit.edu/invent/
Find out who invented what and when.

Kennedy Space Center
http://www.ksc.nasa.gov/ksc.html
Contains information about the center and shows dates for important events.

Mars Global Surveyor
http://barsoom.msss.com/moc_gallery/index.html
View images of the planet Mars.

Mineral and Gemstone Kingdom
http://www.minerals.net/
Explore the world of rocks, minerals and gemstones on this beautiful and comprehensive site.

NASA
http://www.nasa.gov
Educational resources, information, history, see a launch, and much more.

Natural Science Pages
http://web.jjay.cuny.edu/~acarpi/NSC/index.htm
Site is an interactive journey through the wonders of natural science. Designed to use animation and experimentation to enhance learning.

Naturesongs.com
http://www.naturesongs.com/
Provides free samples of various natural sounds.

Neuroscience for Kids
http://faculty.washington.edu/chudler/introb.html
Explore the brain and spinal cord, drug effects, common questions, and more.

Nine Planets for Kids
http://planets4kids.com/
Students' introduction to the solar system.

Questacon
http://sunsite.anu.edu.au/Questacon
Australia's National Science and Technology Center's on-line interactive museum.

Quite Amazing
http://sln.fi.edu/qa96/amyindex.html
Video games, the Hubble telescope, kite flying, amazing women, and more. Each of these articles contain related links.

spaceKids.com
http://www.spacekids.com/
A virtual tour of the solar system with puzzles, games and lots of space information.

Star Child
*http://starchild.gsfc.nasa.gov/docs/StarChild/
StarChild.html*
A learning center for young astronomers with links to the Solar System, space stuff, other questions, and more.

Thinking Fountain
http://www.sci.mus.mn.us/sln/tf
A to Z index of ideas, like how to grow orange mold.

Volcano World Starting Points
http://volcano.und.nodak.edu/vw.html
Links to current eruptions, volcanoes, adventures, and much more.

Welcome to the Planets
http://pds.jpl.nasa.gov/
Introduction to the solar system with NASA photos.

Whelmers Science Activities
http://www.mcrel.org/whelmers
Hands-on science activities like fire sandwich, density balloon, straw oboes, liquid rainbow, and more.

Windows to the Universe
http://www.windows.umich.edu
Science facts for kids, parents, and educators.

Wonderful World of Trees
http://www.domtar.com/arbre/english/start.htm
A year in the life of a tree, uses for trees, action and protection, formidable forms, and more links about trees.

World Climate
http://www.worldclimate.com/
Contains over 85,000 records of world climate data (historical weather averages) from a wide range of sources.

Zoom Dinosaurs
http://www.EnchantedLearning.com/subjects/dinosaurs
Comprehensive online hypertext book about dinosaurs, news, information, printouts, and more.

Search Engines

Active Christian Search Engine
http://www.active-ss.com/
Connect to tens of thousands of Christian sites on many subjects through here.

Bible Gateway
http://bible.gospelcom.net/
Search ten versions of the Bible by passage or single word.

Catholic Online Search
http://www.catholic.org/search/
Catholic community worldwide search engine.

CatholicCity
http://www.catholicity.com/
Email discussion groups, messages, audio, free books and tapes, links to Catholic sites.

Christian Link
http://www.Christianlink.com/
An online Christian community and search engine.

Christian WebCrawler
http://www.Christianwebcrawler.com
Christian website directory and search engine.

ChristianLife.com
http://www.Christianlife.com/
A Christian search engine with news, online magazines,
weather service, website hosting and design, chat, shopping, entertainment listings, games, forums, conference,
event listings, and more.

Christians Unite
http://www.Christiansunite.com/
A Christian search engine containing a variety of links
to sites related to various aspects of Christianity, including Bible study and devotional resources, classifieds,
business resources, singles, home schooling, clipart, Internet services, prison ministry, and more.

ChristSites.com
http://www.christsites.com/
Fast and extensive Christian search engine and rating
site.

Cross-Search
http://www.crosssearch.com/
Wonderful search engine for Christian sites (over 8,000
listed), categorized by topic to make searching easier.

Family Life Trusted Links
http://www.familylife.com/community/links.asp
Links to ministries and organizations, media, references
and resources, student links, forums and chat, and other
links.

Goshen.net
http://www.goshen.net/
Find any subject in their directory or the whole web.

Koinonia House—Blue Letter Bible
http://www.khouse.org/blueletter/
Powerful Bible search engine with cross-referencing and graphics.

Rated G Online
http://www.ratedg.com/
Search the web, family, shopping, education, news, travel, Christian links, sports, computing, business, and other links that are family safe.

Search the Bible
http://www.thechristian.org/
Search the Bible in several languages and versions.

Top 100 Christian Search Engines
http://www.active-ss.com/topsearchengines/topsites.html
A worldwide directory of the best Christian search engines.

other sites of interest

4freestuff
http://4freestuff.hypermart.net/pages/
Site features search engine and links to free stuff, coupons, home and living, fun and games, software, sports and leisure, catalogs, and other free trials, along with free webmaster resources.

700+ Great Sites
http://www.ala.org/parentspage/greatsites/amazing.html
Site for parents, caregivers, teachers, and others who care about kids.

About.com
http://www.about.com
Features information with an intelligent twist, since all sites are managed with the human touch. Bulletin boards, chat rooms, email newsletter, events calender, search engine, and pre-screened links.

Alenka
http://www.alenka.cz
A search site for hundreds of search engines.

All-in-One Search Page
http://www.allonesearch.com
Topical search engine for a variety of subject areas—from general Internet to people to news and technical reports.

AltaVista
http://www.AltaVista.com.
A search engine, and media, and ecommerce network offering an array of web portal services including maps, free email, chatrooms and online shopping.

Ask Jeeves for Kids
http://www.ajkids.com
A search engine and information site for children. Site includes tours, advice, Net-mom picks, Brain Box TV and more information for education and fun.

Bess, The Internet Retriever
http://www.bess.com
Search engine for kids. Bess retrieves subjects like politics, arts, sports, and more.

Debriefing
http://www.debriefing.com
Meta search engine that allows users to choose search engines and other options.

Dogpile
http://www.dogpile.com
Web directory, meta search engine, downloads, web portal.

Family Internet
http://familyInternet.about.com/entertainment/familyInternet/mbody.htm
Articles, email, Internet filtering, safety, software, wallpaper, entertainment, books, family resources and more!

Family-Friendly Sites
http://www.virtuocity.com/family/Index.cfm
Directory of sites that are family-friendly, membership available, and you may add or edit sites.

FAST Search
http://www.alltheweb.com
Search engine offering a database of 300 million web-pages. Also allows FTP and MP3 searches, along with picture and music databases.

GO Network
http://www.go.com
Large search engine linked to sites such as ABC, ESPN, and others.

Information Please
http://www.infoplease.com
Search engine contains news, games, sports, entertainment, and more.

Inside the Web
http://www.insidetheweb.com/
Search engine with categories such as arts and entertainment, health and fitness, recreation, culture, travel, and more.

Kids Click
http://sunsite.berkeley.edu/KidsClick!/
Created by librarians specifically as a search engine for kids. Hundreds of categories.

Mamma.com
http://www.mamma.com
Search everything from insurance quotes to auctions, to dating and travel.

MSN.com
http://www.msn.com/
Links to hotmail, search, shop, money, chat, and more from Microsoft.

New Websites
http://www.webwizards.net/useful/newweb.htm
This site helps you keep up with the web as it grows—lists the most recent additions to the World Wide Web.

Pandia
http://www.pandia.com
An all-in-one meta search page, search tutorial, web directory and more.

Planet Good
http://www.browsesafe.com/
Links to BrowseSafe, PlanetGood, support, news and information, press, and more.

QPL Search Page
http://www.rsa.lib.il.us/public/public.htm
Megasearch engine site.

Search Engines
http://www.grandisland-cs.k12.ny.us
School-based search engines with links to a variety of search engines.

Search Engine Showdown
http://www.searchengineshowdown.com/
Which search engine works best? This site tests them all.

Search Page
http://www.accesscom.com/~ziegler/search.html
A search directory of over 200 listings for people who don't know where to start in their search.

Search Tools
http://www.arttexnet.com
A list of search engines and online directories.

StudyWeb
http://www.studyweb.com
A search engine and Internet database of over 100,000 research quality sites.

Super-Kids
http://www.super-kids.com/
Multiple searchable links on kid-related topics.

Surfing the Net with Kids
http://www.spokane.net/kids.asp
The best the web has to offer, kid-reviewed, rated, and organized by topic.

Surfing the Net with Kids
http://www.surfnetkids.com/
A nationally-syndicated newspaper column of site reviews for kids and families.

W3 Search Engines
http://cuiwww.unige.ch/meta-index.html
Lists of links to powerful search engines.

WebCrawler
http://www.webcrawler.com/
Site features search, channels, auctions, yellow pages, maps, product finder, and more.

Yahooligans
http://www.yahooligans.com/
A website guide for kids—full of links.

Senior Adults

Seniors Christian Radio
http://www.wiredseniors.com/christianradio/home.htm
Links to radio stations with descriptions.

other sites of interest

50 Connect
http://www.50connect.com
An interactive portal for the 50-plus community with thousands of links to useful resources.

50 Up Community
http://www.matesearch.net/50UP.htm
A community for the 50+ active adult. Free email, personals, discounts, travel, shopping, savings, financial, and more.

50SomeThing
http://www.50something.net
A fun infomative site for the over fifty, but not over the hill crowd.

AARP: American Association of Retired Persons
http://www.aarp.org/
Health and wellness, life transitions, computers and technology, and more.

Age 50 and on!
http://www.50on.com
50on.com is to help guide you to an enriched lifestyle, with information on staying healthy—physically, mentally, and financially.

Age of Reason
http://www.ageofreason.com
Senior Citizen resource center with over 5,000 Links to sites of interest to the over 50+ age group. Provides senior with practical information relative to seniors lifestyles.

AgeNet.com
http://www.agenet.com
Health and drug information specific to seniors including online senior drugs reviews of commonly prescribed drugs for the elderly.

AgeVenture News Net
http://www.demko.com
Health and wellness, lifestyle features, age smart quiz, travel adventure, active aging, and more.

Aging with Success
http://www.agingwithsuccess.com
Advice and access to gerontology, geriactrics, nursing homes, health care, and financing assembled by the Carroll Group through a newsletter and products.

Alzheimer's Homepage
http://www.alz.org/
This is a guide to a wealth of information, with a search utility, physician and health care professionals, media, and more.

American Hospital Directory
http://www.ahd.com/
Hospital characteristics, financial reports, free services, custom data services, and more.

AmericanSelect Senior Services Directory
http://www.marketfinder.com/amselect/services.html
Senior services registry, directory, bulletin board, and more.

Autobiography and Literary Services
http://www.autobiography.cc
Guides to preparing your autobiography so that you can pass on the wonders and details of your life and your family's history to the generations to come.

Boomer's Information Kiosk
http://kenrussellassociates.bizland.com/boomers.htm
A concise guide for information regarding new sites to explore, free classified ads, and weekly information from FiftyPlus.net.

CCSeniors
http://www.ccseniors.bizland.com
A computer help site primarily for seniors. Live help chat, how to files, tips and tricks, and much more.

ClassicCitizen.com
http://www.classiccitizen.com
This is an interactive site that offers news, information, and motivation for individuals age fifty plus. Turning senior years to Classic years.

Computer Skills and Internet Help for Seniors
http://www.secretsof.com/computertips
Computer and Internet help for seniors and beginners. Step-by-step instructions for Windows and the Net. Learn to download and unzip files, gain computer skills.

Confident Living
http://www.confidentliving.org
Confident Living addresses the concerns of individuals in the middle stage of life by providing a biblical perspective for the complex issues they are facing.

Double Nickels
http://www.doublenickels.com
Senior information: travel, home and garden, medical and health, financial, Alzheimer's, cooking and recipes, retirement, elderhostel, books and museums, scams, computers and the web, and much more.

Duke of Url: Site for Older Eyes
http://www.kirk-white.com/duke
After years of reviewing sites for the 50+ Friends club,
the Duke offers these entertaining pages for all senior to
learn to surf the easy way.

Family Chronicle Magazine
http://www.familychronicle.com/
Written for family researchers by people who share their
interest in genealogy and family history.

Fifty Something
http://www.fifty-something.co.uk
A UK site dedicated to those of us over the age of 50.
We'd like your to get your voice heard on ANY topic that
you'd like to raise.

Fifty-Plus News
http://www.fiftyplusnews.com
News, information, discussion, gardening, lifetsyle tips,
poems, short stories for seniors.

Fifty-plus.net: Canadian Association of Retired Persons
http://www.fifty-plus.net/
Making fifty-plus the best time of your life.

For My Grandchild
http://www.mygrandchild.com/
A website to celebrate that special relationship between
grandparent and grandchild. With stories, ideas for pass-
ing on memories, message forum, etc.

For Seniors Who Wish to Go Beyond
http://www.savvy-seniors.org
This site is designed for seniors who want a few handy
tools, to help them sample more of the good stuff the
web has to offer without putting themselves at risk.

Friendly4Seniors Websites
http://www.Friendly4Seniors.com/
A web directory specializing in sites of interest to seniors, including topics such as housing, travel, health issues, insurance, legal information, etc.

Globewide Network Academy
http://www.gnacademy.org/
An extensive catalog of distance learning opportunities worldwide.

Go60.com
http://www.go60.com
Site offers research information on aging, society, and the growing population of senior adults. Includes computing helps, travel tips, talk forum, finances, myths about aging, and more.

Golden Fifty Directory
http://www.goldenfifty.com
An informative resource for all individuals age 50 plus.

Grand Times
http://www.grandtimes.com
A unique weekly magazine published for active older adults. Controversial, entertaining and informative, it celebrates life's opportunities and examine life's challenges.

HealthWorld Online
http://healthy.net/
A guide to staying well, with tips for "healthy aging," insurance, alternative medicines, information links, a free newsletter, etc.

Healthy Ideas
http://www.prevention.com/
Homepage for one of the best-known health magazines, with information on diet, fitness, alternative medicine, community issues, etc.

iGrandparents
http://www.igrandparents.com
A site for those who interact with seniors on a regular basis—i.e. their children and grandchildren. Site contains chat rooms, health and safety information, travel helps, tough subjects, values and traditions, technology lessons, photo contests, etc.

Independent Senior
http://www.maturus.com
For 50+ readers who want to be informed and entertained. Updated daily with news, views and portal tours by subject matter.

Laterlife.com
http://www.laterlife.com
UK-based site aimed at making life more enjoyable for the over 50s. Wealth of lifestyle and lifetime information from planning a wedding anniversary to taking up new hobbies.

Less Alone . . . Senior Friends and Neighbors
http://www.less-alone.com
Using the Internet to bring seniors together. Pen pals, chatrooms, links, etc.

Life After55
http://www.after55.com
A site designed to address the needs and interests of the seniors in a format that features large print and an uncluttered design.

MatureConnections.com
http://www.matureconnections.com
An Ezine for mature people providing information and ideas about travel, health and fitness, relationships, antiques, entertainment, and other areas of interest.

Middle Age Canada
http://kenrussellassociates.bizland.com/midage.htm
A great place for middleagers to surf the net with news, site of the day, search, and interesting websites including sailing, theatre, non-urban living, baby boomers info, golfing, baseball and outdoor lifestyles

MyPrimeTime
http://www.myprimetime.com
Your personal trainer for life: Tips on money and finance, work and jobs, health and fitness and travel and culture for baby boomers.

National Senior Citizens Law Center
http://www.nsclc.org/
Advocates nationwide to promote the independence and well-being of low-income elderly individuals.

New Choices
http://www.newchoices.com
Readers Digest—New Choices: Living Even Better After 50 online community. Here you'll find some of the magazine's best articles from past issues, plus special features created just for this website.

Next50.com
http://www.next50.com/
A gateway to living online: education, community, content and commerce for active Americans in their post children rearing years. Site filled with articles and links from health to finance to lifestyles and the arts.

Off Our Rockers
http://www.sonic.net/thom/oor/
Information of grandparents becoming parents again.

Prostate Cancer and Health Resources
http://www.prostate90.com
Comprehensive resource for avoiding and curing prostate cancer and other prostate problems.

Rememory.com
http://www.rememory.com
A place where people from all over the world can read, write and share their unique experiences with others. It is a melting pot for the funny, sad, unusual and downright weird memories of the world.

Retire Refire
http://www.retirerefire.com
This site was designed with the aim of "Improving the Lives of Seniors". A very active chat community and a special course for seniors makes it worth a visit for any senior looking for a good, safe, clean senior site.

Saturday Evening Post
http://www.satevepost.org/
Cartoons, archives, excerpts from current issues.

SCORE: Service Corp. of Retired Executives
http://score.org
A national non-profit organization partnered with the
Small Business Administration.

Senior Celebration
http://www.seniorcelebration.com
A complete on-line store featuring products dedicated to
the enjoyment of life after 50.

Senior Citizen Topics and Resource Links
http://members.tripod.com/~hall9000/
A wealth of information useful to both seniors and aging
professionals.

Senior Citizens Bureau
http://seniors.faithweb.com
Provides networking, entertainment and educational opportunities for senior adults. Many programs that help seniors to create long lasting friendships and relationships.

Senior Island
http://www.seniorisland.com
This site attempts to be the One Stop for all senior information, fun, education, and mature issues.

Senior Law Homepage
http://www.seniorlaw.com/
Website dedicated to making legal knowledge accessible
to elderly people concerned about Medicare, Medicaid,
and more.

S

Senior Net
http://www.seniornet.com
The nonprofit SeniorNet site provides adults 50 and over
access to and education about computer technology and
the Internet to enhance their lives and enable them to
share their knowledge and wisdom. Because it is non-
profit, site offers little commercial.

Senior Square
http://seniorsquare.com
Original, laugh-out-loud buzz from park bench wide
enough for width of all 50-Plus-R-Us.

SeniorCom
http://www.senior.com
Site concentrates on the interests of senior adults. Includes search engine, travel information, history forums,
opinion polls, chat, game room, medical care information, news, faith, finances, relationships, insurance
needs, prizes, and much more.

Seniors Information Resource Center
http://www.seniorssearch.com
Forums, chat, categories of info especially for seniors.

SeniorSite—For the Young at Heart
http://www.seniorsite.com
Online community for mature seniors 55 and over and
their families.

SeniorSites
http://www.seniorsites.com/
Search for a facility, making the "not for profit" choice,
senior resources.

Senior-Spirit
http://www.senior-spirit.com
E-Zine for 50+ Women where senior women can find information, inspiration, and ideas for healthy living.

Shopping for Seniors
http://www.shoppingforseniors.com
This site is an online catalog targeting seniors in assisted
living or nursing homes. Buy gifts and clinical items for
friends and family.

Sites for Silver Surfers
*http://ourworld.compuserve.com/homepages/SMilne6/
silv.htm*
List of elder friendly sites for those of us who will not
see 50 again.

Solutions for Life Beyond55
http://www.beyond55.com
Self-help tips and ideas for the elderly and their caregivers on geriatric healthcare advances, computer use, web services and tactics to extend independent living.

ThirdAge.com
http://www.thirdage.com
A senior's portal. A guide to free online fun and frills, from great downloads to online shopping.

TodaysSeniors.com
http://www.todaysseniors.com
Seniors site with local, regional and national news on finance, travel, relationships, issues, activities.

Too Young to Retire
http://www.2young2retire.com
Offers information, links and inspirational profiles of productive seniors leading productive lives.

University of the Third Age
http://www.tased.edu.au/tasonline/uni3age/
The University of the Third Age-Nepean Blue Mountains Inc., an educational resource for Seniors.

Weretired
http://pub4.ezboard.com/bweretired.html
Message boards for older adults, featuring health, finance, lifestyle and humor.

Wisecity
http://wisecity.com
Wisecity is devoted to making your time on the Internet easier and more productive—the premier site for people 45 and better.

Sewing

Christ Mums Sewing Room
http://www.christmums.com/sewing_room.html
Sewing tips from the online ministry for motherhood.

Educational Sewing Patterns
http://www.edupatterns.com
Free Bible lesson, Bible story mat, Bible cover pattern, Bible action figures, and links. Patterns to create supplies to use in Sunday School or other Christian education settings.

other sites of interest

Bette Gant Designs
http://www.bettegant.com
Machine Sashiko designs, supplies, batiks, Wearable Art Patterns by Bette, costume and sale patterns.

Butterick
http://www.butterick.com/
Shop online for patterns for all purposes.

Carol Price's A Stitch In Time—Embroidery
http://home.att.net/~carolcp
Free and for sale designs available. Tutorial for sale for the PE-Design V3 with a free sample video to download.

Classact Designs
http://www.Classact.bigstep.com
Every sewers site for fitting, designing and patternmaking using the dressform double.

Cotton Pickin' Quilts
http://www.cottonpickinquilts.com
A premier site for quilters featuring an online interactive fabric calculator and Secret Pal shopping.

CyberDressForms, Inc.
http://www.cyberdressforms.com
Computer generated dress forms. A refined process to accurately reproduce symmetrical dress forms.

Designs by Judy
http://home.att.net/~diggy2
Custom embroidery, personalized baby blankets and bib. Embroidery designs for sale and free.

Fabrics to Dye For
http://www.FabricsToDyeFor.com
Hand painted fabrics, thousands of books, notions, fabric paints, and more all discounted.

Ginger's Needleworks and Quilting
http://www.quiltknit.com
Large online catalog of quilting fabrics, patterns, books, notions, templates, redwork, batting, quilt frames, and supplies.

Hemming Away
http://www.hemmingaway.com
The sewing site for the savvy seamstress.

Home Sewing Association
http://www.sewing.org/
Free project, kids page, tips and trends, learn to sew, links, discussions, and more.

HouseNet—Sewing and Crafts
http://www.housenet.com/sw/main.asp?CategoryID=5
Projects, chatrooms, tips, newsletter, contests, and more.

Louwana Albury Embroidery Designs
http://www.laedesigns.com
Embroidery design sets, freebies, and also quality blank clothing and accessories.

Mary Elizabeth Anne Creations
http://members.aol.com/meacreate/index.html
Machine embroidery designs to inspire creativity! Many free and "for sale" designs.

Niti Design
http://www.nitidesign.com
Embroidery threads and supplies, freebies, quilting threads, and more.

Posidelki
http://www.posidelki.hotmail.ru
A journal for women, embroidery, free designs, design sets, knitting, patchwork, cooking.

Secret Workshop
http://www.secretworkshop.com
Full service online quilt shop, free monthly newsletter, plus Thimbleberries, Moda, Jinny Beyer, Debbie Mumm, KP Kids, and more.

Sew 'n' Sew
http://www.lubbockmetro.com/sewnsew
Simplify sewing with this unique collection of patterns, online sewing classes and tips from the newsletter, "Sew 'n' Sew."

Sew City
http://www.sewcity.com/index1.html
Links to sewing, quilting, crafting, fashion, interior design, wedding, hobbies, needlework, software, upholstery, patterns, and more.

Sew What's New
http://www.sew-whats-new.com
Fun site for sewing and quilting, projects, tips and a free weekly newsletter.

Sewing Homepage
http://sewing.about.com/hobbies/ sewing/mbody.htm
Alterations, fabric care, crafts, bulletin boards, hat making, applique, pattern index, and more.

Sewing Rummage
http://www.jps.net/cfield/rummage
Sewing yard sale, machines, notions, etc, gently used but still usable.

SewMommy's Sewing Tip Exchange
http://www.SewMommy.com
A sewing tip exchange where you can come and take a sewing tip or leave a sewing tip—updated weekly. Archives of past tips.

Simplicity Pattern Company
http://www.simplicity.com/
Shop online for dress, kids, men, home, and costume patterns.

Singer Sewing and Vacuum
http://www.singersewing.net
Sewing and embroidery supplies, threads, designs, accessories, etc.

Vogue Patterns Online
http://www.voguepatterns.com/
Shop the catalog of designer patterns, join the mailing list, and more.

Shopping

Active Spirit
http://www.activespirit.com
Site offers men's and women's casual apparel in colors and styles for everyday inspiration in walking with Christ.

Awesome Christian T-shirts
http://www.choicemall.com/greatideas
T-shirt creations proclaim your faith in Jesus Christ! Also offers t-shirts (up to 4X), sweats, ball caps, and other gift ideas.

Beautiful Time for Shopping
http://www.nunavut.nu/shop/christian.html
Where to buy children's Christian videos, games, and software.

Catholic Store
http://www.catholicstore.com/
Thousands of Catholic books, Bibles, gifts and more.

Christian Expressions
http://www.christianexpression.com/main/index.html
Online Christian "superstore" offering a tremendous selection of goods.

Christian Fun Store
http://store.yahoo.com/christianfun/
Bible games, t-shirts, toys and more.

S

Christian Shopping
http://www.christian-shopping.co.uk/shop/wccc.html
One stop online shopping spot in the UK for Christian books, music and much more.

ChristianShoppingZone
http://www.christianshoppingzone.com/
A wide variety of merchandise. A portion of all sales go to local outreach missions.

Claramente Cristiano
http://www.claramente.com/cgi-bin/SoftCart.exe/
sitepages/vida_cristiana.html?L+scstore+
xbtp3946ff832e83+986706232
Online store featuring a wide variety of Spanish language Christian books, videos and CDs.

Gospel Super Center
http://www.gospelsupercenter.com/
Bargains on books, music, computers and more.

Great Info
http://www.greatinfo.com
Shopping made easy for today's Christian, including books, mailing and financial services, people search and business articles, current news, Bible studies, and more.

Impact Online
http://www.impact-online.co.za/
Distributing the best in Christian books, music and merchandise in South Africa and around the world.

Life Checks
http://www.lifechecks.com
Personal checks, matching labels and genuine leather checkbook covers that preserve integrity for your transactions and savings.

More Than Words
http://www.morethanwords.net
Messages of faith, hope, and love through products of t-shirts, poetry, animations, funnies, tech help and other inspirations. Free animation gallery, online greetings, Veggie Tales, and children's resources.

MyCSN
http://www.mycsn.com/home/index.asp
Christian shopping site donating 5% of all purchases to
the church of your choice.

Noah's Ark Christian Store
http://www.noahsarkchristianstore.com/
Noah's Ark Christian store—Featuring collectibles and
gifts for everyone! Featuring angels, nativity, crosses,
wwjd, books, music, kids items, home items, garden, and
more, with secure online ordering.

Shop4Acause
http://www.shop4acause.com/
A Christian online mall where your purchases are tithed
to selected charities.

United Christian Network—Christian Shopping Mall
http://www.unitedchristians.com/shop/
Links to dozens of merchandise sites organized by category.

other sites of interest

A to Z Deals
http://www.a2zdeals.com/
Coupon codes, coupons, and online shopping deals.

Autobytel
http://www.autobytel.com/
Options such as car care and pricing are available on
this online car sales page.

BabyCenter.com
http://www.babycenter.com
Select products and services for new and expectant parents. Providing reliable information backed by medical
professionals and consumer health experts.

Bargain Dog
http://www.bargaindog.com/
Browse bargains in a variety of categories: hobbies, apparel, computing, cooking, pets, movies, and more.

S

Blue Fly
http://www.bluefly.com
Shop for name brand designers at discount prices.

Bottom Dollar
http://www.bottomdollar.com/index.html
Comparison shopping for home, fun, office, auctions, entertainment, lifestyle, and more.

Buy for Kids
http://www.buyforkids.com/index.htm
Site offers newborn and infant clothing and accessories, including baptism christening clothing, plus crib bedding.

Buy.com
http://www.buy.com
Sells through seven speciality sites for books, computers, videos, DVD, music, games software and outlet for bargain hunting.

Carsmart
http://www.carsmart.com
Buying, leasing, and other options are found on this online car dealership.

Christian Shopping
http://www.hallelujahkids.com/index.html
Links to games, gifts, books, links, values, and more.

Deal Time
http://www.dealtime.com/main.asp?AID=26859 &eb=yes
Get deals on appliances, home and garden, pet supplies, computers, music, flowers, video games, and much more.

Especials—Best of the Web
http://www.especials.com/
Hundreds of links to shopping sites, with featured sites, information resources, special offers, and more.

IKEA
http://www.ikea.com
Product guide, local stores, catalog, customer service, careers, and more affordable solutions for better living.

Living.com
http://www.living.com/?
Shop for home products by room or department, newsletter, magazine, and more.

LLBean
http://www.llbean.com/
Searches for parks and information about parks for the planning of trips and getaways.

Netmarket
http://www.netmarket.com/
Online shopping with directories to deals of the day, gift lists, and more.

Office Max
http://www.officemax.com/max/solutions/nav/home.jsp
Browse supplies, furniture, technology, order online and more.

Priceline
http://www.priceline.com/
Name your own price and save on gas, groceries, mortgage, cars, airline tickets, and hotels.

Public Eye
http://www.thepubliceye.com/
Extensive links to safe shopping sites.

Surprise.com
http://www.surprise.com/
Search for gift ideas by person, occasion, and hobbies.

Ultimate Outlet
http://www.ultimate-outlet.com/
Shopping online for fashion and home.

Singles and Dating

Access Christian Matchmaker
http://www.accessmatchmaker.com
Features thousands of profiles of Christian singles from around the world seeking Christian singles. Dedicated to singles with dating resources, chat, and pictures.

Adam Meet Eve
http://www.adammeeteve.com
Meet Christian singles for penpals, dating, marriage.
Free matchmaker dating personals.

Big Church for Christian Singles
http://BigChurch.com/go/p1030f
A community of people building their faith and inter-
acting with others. A community and dating service with
thousands of active church members. The site has a
searchable Bible, Bible emails, chatrooms, and more.
Free listing service.

Christ Love—Christian Singles Community
http://www.ChristLove.com
Site contains over 9000 names of Christian singles, and
growing. Links to make new Christian friends in member's area and places to stay to make new Christian
friends while traveling.

Christian Connection Matchmaker
http://www.Christian.email.net/
Christian singles site with photos, postcards, chat, user
profiles, and private email boxes.

Christian Date
http://www.christiandate.com/
Free Christian matchmaking site with photos and chat
rooms.

Christian Dating Services
*http://www.nowomenallowed.com/christian_dating_*
services.htm
A free site for posting and reading personal ads from
Christian singles around the country.

Christian Dating Tips
http://www.geocities.com/Heartland/Plains/8218/
dating.html
Advice on preparing for and finding the right relationship.

Christian Single Online
http://www.Christiansingle.com/
Entertainment, single parents, past issues, profiles, articles, and more.

Christian Singles Connection
http://www.cybergrace.com/html/singles.html
Christian singles profiles, photos and an auto-matching service.

Christian Soulmates
http://www.Christiansoulmates.com
Site where Christian singles correspond using chat, email, profiles with photos, instant messaging. A network for friendship, dating, and long-lasting relationships.

ChristianFriendship.com
http://www.Christianfriendship.com
Christian adult singles find friends, companions, penpals, partners, relationships, mates, love, romance, chat, classifieds, dating services, email, matchmaking, personals, photos and profiles.

Covenant Singles.com
http://www.covenantsingles.com
Christian romance connection site features full size webpage listing's with pictures, free listings, free replies, free email and more.

Equally Yoked
http://www.equallyyoked.com/
The largest and most respected club for Christian singles in the US.

Koinonos
http://www.cy-bear.com/koinonos/
Site is free and open to all Christian singles, 18 years of age or older, who wish to use it for the purpose of meeting other Christians, having fellowship, and building friendships.

Matchmaker.com
http://www.Christian.matchmaker.com
The Christian Connection is an online community serving the Christian community for fun, fellowship, and growing in the Body of Christ.

S

Single Parent Online Retreat
http://www.singleparent.org/
A place to browse and relax. Features links, articles on dating, finances, etc.

Singles Christian Network
http://www.singlec.com/
A community site, featuring articles, information links, a chatroom, ads, news, a free newsletter and more.

other sites of interest
Single Parenting
http://singleparentresources.com/singleparenting_548.html
A list of single parenting sites, chatrooms, and newsgroup.

Single Parents Support Group
http://www.singleparents.net/
A place for parents to ask questions, find information and resource links, chat, place personal ads, etc.

Soloparent
http://webprojex.com/singleparent/
An extensive informational site with articles about health, romance, parenting advice, finances, etc.

Spanish Language Sites
Aleluya
http://aleluya.com/
A site featuring news from around the world of interest to Spanish speaking Christians.

Atrevete
http://atrevete.com/
Portal site and search engine for Spanish speaking Christians.

Chat Cristiano
http://espanol.geocities.com/peonline2001/pechat.htm
A directory of Spanish language Christian Chat rooms.

En Voz de Gracia
http://cristo.org/index1.html
Bible history, Bible study courses, Christian books, music and more.

Oramex
http://www.oremex.org/Videos/espanol.htm
Bible study video programs in Spanish.

Siervo
http://siervo.com/
Spanish language Christian portal site and search engine.

Sigueme
http://www.sigueme.com.ar/
A comprehensive Spanish language Christian web gateway with a wide variety of topics.

Spanish Channel
http://www.christiantuner.com/channels/genre.asp?g=53
A directory of Christian Internet radio stations broadcasting in Spanish.

Supermercado Espiritual
http://216.55.34.99/supermer/
A Spanish language Christian portal site with chat, free email and more.

Sports

Athletes in Action
http://www.ccci.org/aia/
Developing athletes into into Christ-centered leaders.

CCA Online—The Home of Christian Cheerleaders of America
http://www.cheercca.com/
Tips, events, and spiritual help.

Christian Bowhunters of America
http://www.christianbowhunters.org/
A non-profit, non-denominational Bible centered ministry to the American bowhunting community.

Christian Cycling Club
http://www.jps.net/iccc
Homepage for the International Christian Cycling Club.

Christian Database Sport
http://www.active-ss.com/gigabase/sport/sport.htm
An extensive directory of links to Christian sports related sites on the Internet.

Christian Motorsports
http://www.christianmotorsports.com
Homesite of *Christian Motorsports Illustrated* online, with links, past issues, etc.

Christian Sport Bike Association
http://www.christiansportbike.com/
A gathering place for Christian bike enthusiasts.

Christian Sports
http://www.servehim.com/sports.html
Award-winning sports site.

Christian Sports Flash
http://www.gospelcom.net/gci/sf/
Sports news, interviews and athletes' testimonies from Gospel.net.

Christian Sports Minute
http://www.christiansportsminute.com
A broadcast heard on more than 70 radio stations, the goal is to use sports and well-known sports figures as a vehicle to share the gospel of Jesus Christ.

Fellowship of Christian Athletes
http://www.gospelcom.net/fca/index.shtml
An influencing ministry using sports as its platform.

Goal, The
http://www.thegoal.com/
A ministry showcasing world class athletes who make a positive difference in our world.

God's Rods
http://www.godsrods.com/
With a desire to help spread the Good News of Jesus Christ, through an interest in automobiles, this site offers links, testimonies, and news of upcoming events.

Pendak Silat Ratu Adil
http://www.ratuadil.com/
An Indonesian martial arts form with a Christian foundation.

Racing for Jesus
http://www.racingforjesus.org/
Spreading the good news of the gospel to the world
through auto racing.

other sites of interest

1stserve Tennis Homepage,
http://www.1stserve.com/
News, schedules, profiles, links, tips.

Aarons Baseball Links
http://www.aaronslinks.com/
Links to baseball sites about all levels of play.

ABA BMX—The World's Largest BMX Sanctioning Body
http://www.ababmx.com/
Event schedules, news, tips.

ABC Sports Online
http://www.ABCsports.com
Up to the minute coverage of what's happening in the
world of sports. Including: news, recruiting coverage, an-
nouncers, promos, press releases, affiliates, ask abc
sports, Monday night football online, bowl championship
series online and much more.

About Kendo
*http://www.sfn.saskatoon.sk.ca/sports/kendo/
about.html*
A introduction to Kendo.

Absolute Authority on Pro Basketball
*http://www.absoluteauthority.com
/pro_basketball/*
Search engine, statistics, links.

AikiWeb Aikido Information
http://www.aikiweb.com/
News, tips and links on Aikido.

All in 1 Sports—Golf news
http://www.allin1sports.com/gf/index2.htm
News, statistics and links.

Allexperts Water Sports—Sailing QandA
http://www.allexperts.com/getExpert.asp?
Category=1650
Ask an expert about sailing.

AllSports (tm)—Boxing (WBA, WBO, IBA)
http://www.allsports.com/boxing/
Up-to-date news from the world of boxing.

Altered Skateboarding
http://www.camsk8.com/
Tips, news, pictures and links on skateboarding.

Amateur Wrestler
http://www.amateurwrestler.com/
News, tips, training, interviews.

American Track and Field
http://www.runningnetwork.com/atf/
News, tips, calendars, results, links.

Archery Information Service, Home of the Archer's Retreat!!
http://www.archery-info.com/
News, equipment reviews, tips.

Athletics Site
http://www.athletix.gr/
Extensive coverage of world track and field events.

ATLAS F1
http://www.atlasf1.com/
Comprehensive coverage of Formula 1.

Badminton Information Site DDS
http://www.anitavandijk.nl/bad_index.html
Information, instruction, news.

Baseball America Online
http://www.baseballamerica.com/
Comprehensive resource on minor league players and teams.

Baseball Links
http://www.baseball-links.com/main.shtml
Links to the major leagues, minor leagues, college teams, amateur teams, youth, international, players, parks, and much more.

Basketball Hall of Fame
http://www.hoophall.com/
Official homepage of the Basketball Hall of Fame.

BASS on HOOK Total Fishing Resource
http://www.bassonhook.com/
News, links, tips.

Beach Volleyball Authority
http://www.scs.ryerson.ca/~m3ross/bva.html
Photos, news, links.

Beginner's Guide—Windsurfing
http://www.windsurfer.com/beginners/index.html
Instructions for the new windsurfer.

Better Water Search
http://www.watersportfun.bizland.com/
Extensive links to boating and all watersports sites.

Bicycling—Homepage
http://bicycling.about.com/
News, articles, links.

BMX and BMX RACING
http://www.bmxracing.net/
News, race results, links.

Boating Channel
http://www.boatingchannel.com/
News, links and information on all aspects of boating.

Bo-Fish Bowling News: The Positive Source for Bowling Worldwide
http://bowling.hypermart.net/
News, links, tips on bowling.

Boxing Fight Page—The Boxing source
http://www.netcolony.com/members/boxing/
Rankings, news, events.

BskBall's Hoopsworld
http://www.bskball.com/
News, team reports, statistics.

BuckShots Links
http://www.geocities.com/vanchap/links.html
Links to many rodeo sites.

CBS SportsLine
http://www.sportsline.com
Fast facts on news, standings, schedules, statistics,
teams, players, fantasy and more.

Celebration of Wheels
http://lenmac.tripod.com/
An introduction to wheelchair sports.

College Basketball—Homepage
http://colbasketball.about.com/sports/colbasketball/
mbody.htm
Articles, interviews, news.

College Football Hall of Fame
http://www.collegefootball.org/
Homepage of the college football hall of fame.

College Ice Hockey—Homepage
http://collegehockey.about.com/sports/collegehockey/
News, rankings and links on college hockey.

Combat Fishing Homepage
http://www.combat-fishing.com/index.html
Features, tips, anglers' resources.

Complete Bowling Index
http://www.bowlingindex.com
News and shopping, links to pro shop, instruction, tour-
naments, who's who, and more.

Cruising World and Sailing World Magazines
http://www.sailingworld.com/
News and articles on sail and powerboating.

Cycling: How-to Tips and Tutorials
*http://www.knowledgehound.com/topics/
cycling.htm*
News, repair and maintenance, links.

Deadpoint
http://www.thedeadpoint.com/
News, interviews, photos on climbing.

Dirk Feige: Karate Links
*http://webrum.uni-mannheim.de/math/feige/
martweb.htm*
Extensive list of karate links.

Divernet
http://www.divernet.com/
Articles and links to hundreds of diving sites.

ESPN Network
http://www.espn.com
Coverage of Sports from A-Z featuring: video/audio high-
lights, tv listings, ESPN radio, chat, message boards, arcade games.

FANSonly—Your Ticket to College Sports
http://www.fansonly.com/
All college sports; links, articles, news.

Field and Stream and Outdoor Life Online
http://www.fieldandstream.com/
Online edition of the hunting and fishing magazine.

Fishtheworld.com!
http://www.fishtheworld.com/
Reports, conservation, news.

**Fly Fish America Magazine: The Fly Fishing Angler's
Choice**
http://www.flyfishamerica.com/
Tips, articles, and links for the fly fisherman.

Football Search Engine
http://footballsites.com/
Links and search engine for football fans.

Football Soccer Futbol
http://www.bobcommon.co.uk/
World soccer news, links.

Formula1.com—The Definitive Formula One Website
http://www.formula1.com/
News, events, photos, links.

FOXSports.com—The Biggest Name in Sports
http://www.foxsports.com/
Homepage for comprehensive sports coverage online.

General Taekwondo Information
http://www.barrel.net/
History, photos and links.

Giantfish.com
http://www.giantfish.com/
Focus on American freshwater gamefishing.

Goal.com
http://www.thegoal.com
The heart and soul of the world of sports.

GolfChannel.com—Home
http://www.thegolfchannel.com/
Events, news, statistics, links.

GoSki.com
http://www.goski.com/home.htm
Links to ski resorts around the world.

Gravitygames.com
http://www.gravitygames.com/
Broad site for boards, bikes, skates and other extreme sports.

Gymnastics—Homepage
http://gymnastics.about.com/index.htm
News, links, profiles.

Hockeynews.com
http://www.thn.com/servlet/thn
News on pro, amateur and collegiate hockey.

i-Glow.com
http://www.i-glow.com/html/index.cfm
Site designed for girls' sports.

iLAXx.com—YOUR "One Stop" Lacrosse Site!
http://www.ilaxx.com/
News, articles, product reviews.

InfoSports—Youth Soccer on the Web
http://www.infosprts.com/soccer/index.html
Links to organizations and events.

Inline Hockey Central
http://www.inlinehockeycentral.com/
News, photos and links.

International Wheelchair Basketball Federation
http://www.iwbf.org/
Homesite for the international organization; news and links.

ISHOF-International Swimming Hall of Fame
http://www.ishof.org/
Homepage for the Hall of Fame.

Karate Resources Online
http://www.ryu.com/karate.html
Karate links sorted by subject.

Kick!—Complete guide to Running, Jogging and Racing
http://www.kicksports.com/
Articles, tips, training and links.

LACROSSE NETWORK
http://www.laxnet.com/
High school, college and pro news, articles and links.

Ladies Professional Golf Association
http://www.lpga.com/
Official LPGA site. Tournament coverage, news, scores, history, hall of fame, and more.

Locker Room
http://members.aol.com/msdaizy/sports/locker.html
Links to volleyball, hockey, soccer, basketball, baseball, football, gymnastics, diving, running, field hockey, tennis, bowling, and more.

Martial Arts Resource
http://www.martialartsresource.com/index.html
General links on many forms of martial arts.

Motorcycle Online
http://motorcycle.com/
News, events and product reviews.

NASCAR Online
http://www.nascar.com/
Homepage for auto racing organization; news, events,
links.

National Baseball Hall of Fame
http://baseballhalloffame.org/index.htm
A virtual tour of Cooperstown; photos, stories and more.

National Basketball Association
http://www.NBA.com
The official site of the National Basketball Association.
Featuring: news, statistics and schedules, teams, players,
sights and sounds, chats and mailboxes, global basketball, history and NBA store.

National Football League
http://www.NFL.com
Official NFL sites. On the field news, standings/teams,
players, statistics, chats, tv and radio. Off the field. NFL
Shop, kids, QB club, coaches club, international, fans
and NFL insider.

National Hockey League
http://www.NHL.com
The official site of the National Hockey League including all leagues, news, games, history, kids, insider information, shopping and community.

**North American Whitetail Deer Magazine and Hunting
Guide!**
http://www.whitetail-deer.com/
News, information, hunters' resources and links.

Number One Hang Gliding and Paragliding Resource
http://www.web-search.com/myhom13.html
Links to many sites on hang gliding and parasailing.

Official Soccer Site
http://www.drblank.com/soccer.htm
Links to women's FIFA, women's world cup, 1998 men's world cup, soccer bookstore, rules, contests, and Hall of Fame.

Olympic Museum
http://www.museum.olympic.org/
Revisit the great world athletic competitions from Athens to Sydney.

RacingOne.com
http://www.racingone.com/
Extensive coverage of National Hot Rod Association news.

Runner's World Online
http://www.runnersworld.com/
News and articles; focus on training and tips.

SearchSport—THE Sports Directory
http://www.searchsport.com/
Thousands of links to sport sites.

Skating.com—The Skater's Online Magazine
http://www.skating.com/
News, reviews, many links.

SkiCentral—Skiing and Snowboarding Index and Search
http://www.skicentral.com/
Links and search engine for all snow sports.

Swim Info: Homepage
http://www.swiminfo.com/
News, articles, results, links.

Swim.net
http://www.swim.net/
Comprehensive swimmers resources on the net.

Tennis Online—Official Website
http://atptour.com/frameset.html
News, events and statistics from the pro tennis tour.

S

Tennis.com
http://www.tennis.com/
Articles, events and schedules for all levels of play.

Total College Sports Network
http://www.totalcollegesports.com
Site features conference pages with stories, team statistics, scores, game logs and more.

Total Sports: Front Page
http://www.totalsports.net/
News, articles and links on all sports.

Track and Field News
http://www.trackandfieldnews.com/
News, results, links.

U.S. Diving Online
http://www.usdiving.org/
News, results, calendar, links.

United States Golf Association
http://www.usga.org/
Homepage for the USGA, includes virtual tour of the museum.

USA Football!
http://www.usafootball.com/
Comprehensive site on pro, college and high school football.

USA Hockey InLine
http://www.usahockeyinline.com/
News and links, league information.

Volleyball.org
http://www.volleyball.org/
News, tips and links.

Welcome to Basketball News
http://www.basketballnews.com/
Extensive coverage of college and pro games and players.

Windsurfer.com
http://www.windsurfer.com/
News, photos, and links.

WNBA.com
http://www.wnba.com/index.html
Homesite of the womens' pro league.

Xoutdoors.com—Everything for the Outdoors Enthusiast!
http://www.xoutdoors.com/
Articles and product reviews for the hunter and fisherman.

Youth Sports Network
http://www.ysn.com/
Central site for youth sport leagues.

Television

Benny Hinn Ministries
http://www.bennyhinn.org
Schedules, news and articles.

Billy Graham
http://www.billygraham.org/home/
News, schedules and downloads of Billy Graham.

Breakthrough with Rod Parsley
http://www.breakthrough.net/tele.htm1
TV and Internet broadcast schedule.

Christian Streaming Media
http://christian-worldwideweb.com/
Live church service video broadcasts from around the world.

Christian Television
http://www.christiantv.org
Directory of sites on Christian TV and radio.

Christian.TV
http://www.gospelmedia.com/
Live and archived Christian television programs from a number of ministries.

Eternal World Television Network
http://www.ewtn.com/
Internet home of the Global Catholic Television and Radio Network.

T

FamilyNet
http://www.familynet.org
Southern Baptist Radio and TV resource directory.

Hour of Power
http://www.hourofpower.org
Homepage of the ministry of Dr. Robert Schuller.

In Christ's Image
http://www.inchristsimage.org/Television_Gen.asp
Internet and satellite broadcasts from the ministry of
Francis Frangipane.

It Is Written
http://www.iiw.org/index.html
Seventh Day Adventist TV and radio ministry resources.

Living Way Ministries
http://www.livingway.org
Homepage of the ministry of Pastor Jack Hayford.

Preview Family Movie and TV Review
http://www.gospelcom.net/preview/
A site with reviews and ratings of over 1,800 films and
TV shows. A great family resource.

Re-versed Lyrics
http://www.ultranet.com/~mari/
Rewritten Chirstian lyrics to popular TV themes and
many other songs. Write your own and submit them.

Sportsweek
http://www.ctv.org/sportsweek/week.html
Homepage for Christian outdoors show.

Sure Foundation, The
http://www.tsfs.org/
Daily streaming webcasts with interactive chat feature.

Television for Teens
http://christianteens.about.com/teens/christianteens/
msub21.htm
Directory of US Christian TV outlets.

Three Angels Broadcasting Network
http://www.3abn.org
Inspirational TV and Internet broadcasts.

Trinity Broadcasting Network
http://206.83.163.246/
Homepage for the Christian broadcasting company.

Video on Demand
*http://www.livingway.com/radio_tv_files/
video_on_demand.htm*
Televised inspirational messages available online from
Living Way Ministries.

other sites of interest

AandE.com
http://www.aetv.com
Cable channel homesite.

ABC.com
http://www.abc.com
Homepage for TV network.

Academy of Television Arts and Sciences
http://www.emmys.org
Official site of the Academy of TV Arts and Sciences.

Animal Planet
http://animal.discovery.com
Schedules and articles about wildlife cable outlet.

Bravo
http://www.bravotv.com
Articles and listings for cable entertainment channel.

Cartoon Network
http://www.cartoonnetwork.com/index.flash.html
Homepage for cable channel with new and old cartoons.

CBS.com
http://www.cbs.com
Network homepage.

T

CNBC.com
http://cnbc.com
Cable business channel, with stock quotes.

CNN.com
http://cnn.com
The TV cable news channel online.

Country.com
http://www.country.com
Homepage for The Nashville Network, CMT and more.

Court TV Online
http://www.courttv.com
Homepage for cable channel featuring trials and legal
news.

Discovery.com—Tools for Everyday Adventures
http://www.discovery.com
Science and history homepage.

Disney Channel
http://disney.go.com/DisneyChannel/zoog.html
Directory and homepage for children's programming
channel.

ESPN.com
http://espn.sportszone.com
Homepage for leading cable sports channel.

Food Network's FoodTV.com
http://www.foodtv.com
Schedules, recipes and features from the cooking network.

Fox.com
http://www.fox.com/
Broadcast network homepage.

Free TV Studio Audience Tickets
http://www.tvtickets.com
How to find the shows you can see live.

FXNetworks
http://www.fxnetworks.com
Cable sports, entertainment and movie channel page.

Game Show Network
http://www.gameshownetwork.com/index2.html
Cable channel featuring new and classic game shows.

History Channel
http://www.historychannel.com/home
Homepage for cable channel focusing on history.

Lifetime Online: Where Women Click
http://www.lifetimetv.com/cgi/home.cgi
Homepage for cable channel focusing on women's interests.

Mister Rogers' Neighborhood Homepage
http://www.pbs.org/rogers/
The long-time children's favorite homepage.

MSNBC
http://www.msnbc.com/
Up-to-date news and features from cable news channel.

NBC.com
http://www.nbc.com
Network homepage with news and features.

Parents Television Council
http://www.parentstv.org
News, links and guidance for parents about TV.

TBS Superstation
http://www.superstation.com/index.htm
Homepage for superstation; news, movies and more.

TLC—The Learning Channel
http://tlc.discovery.com
Schedules and articles on science and society cable channel.

Travel Channel
http://travel.discovery.com
Cable channel focusing on exotic destinations.

TV Guidelines
http://www.tvguidelines.org
Reference site for parental guidelines for TV.

T

UPN
http://www.upn.com/intro.html
Cable network homesite.

USA Network
http://www.usanetwork.com/homepage.html
Homepage for cable sports and entertainment channel.

Warner Brothers Online
http://www.wb.com
Cable network homesite.

Toys

Christian Games
http://sr5.xoom.com/FreeChristianDownloads/gam.htm
Links to many sites containing Christian games to download or play online.

Christian Toy Box
http://www.homestead.com/christiantoybox/index.html
Giving children and families the opportunity to have fun with God.

Download Christian Games
http://www.homestead.com/jczone/downloadgames.html
Educational arcade-style games to download to your computer teaching about God and the Bible.

Heavenly Toy Store
http://members.truepath.com/hiddenmanna/
gift_toystore.htm
Over 10,000 Christian toys, games and children's software all at one site.

Precious in His Sight—Toys
http://www.preciousinhissight.com/toys.html
Promoting Christian values through some of the best original Christian toys and apparel available.

Toys for the King's Children
http://www.doorposts.net/ToysForKings.htm
Simple make-at-home Bible related toys for children.

other sites of interest

4 Toy Safety
http://www.toy-tma.org/consumer/parents/
safety/4toysafety.html
This site is made available by the Toy Manufacturers of
America (TMA) which represents over 250 manufacturers and importers of toys. Questions are answered
about specific toys, tips on safe play, as well as advice
concerning what toys are suitable for what age group. Ordering instructions for free brochures on safe and fun
play.

Big Red Toy Box, The
http://bigredtoybox.com/
Toy encyclopedia, buy/sell/trade, online store, links, reviews, etc.

Discovery Toys
http://www.discoverytoysinc.com/
The premier educational toy company. Products arranged by age and developmental benefit.

Fisher-Price
http://www.fisher-price.com/
Fun-filled toys to enhance imaginations and encourage
developing skills.

Fun Play, Safe Play
http://www.toy-tma.org/industry/publications/fpsp/
fpsp.html
Includes and age appropriate guide to buying toys as
well as choosing toys for children with disabilities.

Hasbro, Inc.
http://hasbro.com/
Great toys and games such as: Star Wars, Furby, Trans-
formers, Scrabble, Batman, Monopoly, Pokemon, G.I.
Joe, Play-Doh and more.

I'm Safe Network, The
http://www.imsafe.com/smartsteps/toys.html
How to tell safe toys from their unsafe counterparts.
Also, informative articles and toy recalls.

T

KB Kids
http://kbkids.com/
Thousands of toys and collectibles, video games and software titles at great prices. Don't miss the online Outlet department. Find the KB toy store nearest you.

K'NEX Industries
http://knex.com/
This company was born when Joel Glickman was tinkering with some straws at a crowded, noisy wedding. His dabbling gave way to the popular Rod and Connector building system, now with the option to add wheels, pulleys, gears, and motors. Easy-to-follow, color-coded instructions included in every set.

Lego Group, The
http://lego.com/
Facts and updated information about LEGO products, history, and family attractions, as well as a guide to child development and tips for using LEGO toys to encourage children's skills and creativity. Join the LEGO web club—it's fun and free.

Matchbox
http://matchboxtoys.com/
This site is for the avid Matchbox fan featuring a collector's showcase, rarities, FAQ, history, games, contests, and more.

Mattel, Inc.
http://mattel.com/
Toys that "touch the child in everyone." Some of the companies in Mattel's "family" include: Cabbage Patch Kids, Barbie, Hot Wheels, Matchbox, Tyco R/C, American Girl, Disney, Fisher Price Pooh, Sesame Street, Nickelodeon, to name a few.

National Lekotek Center
http://www.lekotek.org/
Promoting learning-oriented play for all children.

National SAFEKIDS Campaign
http://www.safekids.org/
Product recalls, health/safety links, FAQ, and more.

Playmobil
http://www.playmobil.com/

Safe, colorful figures and sets encourage your child's physical and emotional development through hours of un-structured role play. Facts (approximately 3 million indi-vidual pieces are produced daily!), company information, products, Playmobil Fun Parks, games, and online shop-ping.

Radio Flyer, Inc.
http://radioflyer.com/

Wagons, bikes and trikes, preschool toys, ride-on toys, etc.

Smarter Kids
http://smarterkids.com/

Smarterkids.com's mission is to help children learn, dis-cover, and grow. Site includes "My Kid's Store," educa-tional tools, teacher-reviewed selection, guides for gift-giving, parent-friendly information and outstanding shopping options.

Toys R Us
http://toysrus.com/

The ultimate website for toys. Shop by age, brand, cate-gory, or character/theme. Store finder, career opportuni-ties, gift registry, and links.

Zany Brainy
http://zanybrainy.com/

Extraordinary toys for extraordinary kids! The first mul-timedia educational superstore. Biggest and best selec-tion of safe, high-quality toys in an environment that's interactive and exciting. Shop online for toys, books, mu-sic, software, and videos.

Travel and International Information

Agency of Christian Tourism "Pilgrim"
http://act.yaroslavl.ru

Missionary tours in the European part of Russia.

Catholic Travel Club
http://catholictravelclub.com/
A free membership club offering discounts on cruises, pilgrimages and tours.

Christian House Exchange Fellowship
http://www.thisengland.co.uk/pw.htm
Exchange your house with other Christians—safely through CHEF.

Christian Outdoor Recreation & Adventure Travel
http://www.fisher-of-man.com/
This outdoor adventure guide for Christians features outdoor recreation links, destinations and information.

Christian Travel Study Programs, Ltd.
http://www.ctsp.co.il/index.htm
Special group travel programs and courses to enhance and illuminate your faith.

Fellowship Travel International
http://www.fellowship.com/
Christian group tour and discounted airfare specialists.

FourWinds Travel—The Christian Tour Hotels
http://www.fourwindstravel.com/christian_hotels.html
A listing of Christian hotels for tour groups visiting Tel Aviv, Jerusalem, Israel, Tiberia, and others.

Leading Source
http://www.leadingsourcetravel.com/lsi_2.htm
A Christian Travel Agency, full service with cruises, discount travel, Christian Travel, etc.

Travel and Recreation Christian Pages
http://www.bstlinks.com/christian/travel/
Traveling and recreation from a Christian point of view.

other sites of interest

1Travel
http://www.1Travel.com
Offers its registered users reduced-cost bookings of up to

70 percent savings on airline tickets, car rentals and cruise packages.

Airlines on the Web
http://www.4airlines.com/
Online airfare, reservations, hotel information, car rentals, vacations, and more.

Airlines Toll-Free
http://www.princeton.edu/Main/air800.html
An extensive list of toll-free numbers and websites for airlines.

AMTRAK on the Web
http://www.amtrak.com/
Schedules and fares, arrival status, special offers, fun and games, and more.

Backyard's Community of Cities
http://citywideguide.com/backyard/cities/cities.htm
A guide to cities, with classifieds, recreation, shopping, entertainment, search engine, and more.

Bali Travel News
http://www.bali-travelnews.com/Batrav/Batrav02/index.html
Complete information about news, art, culture, society, and tourism in Bali, Indonesia

Big Fare Cut Index
http://www.air-fare.com/allsav.htm
Discover big fare cuts on dozens of different cities, special deals, travel links, and more.

BizTravel
http://www.biztravel.com/
Travel planner, travel toolkit, news and views, testimonials, and membership, plus more.

Caribbean Destination Interactive Magazine
http://www.bviwelcome.com
The official site for Tortola and the British Virgin Islands, with dining, lodging, services, and more.

T

CDC Travel Information
http://www.cdc.gov/travel/index.htm
Reference materials, outbreaks, diseases, vaccinations, visitor survey, and more.

City Directories Online
http://www.citydirectories.psmedia.com/
Genealogical archives online where you can search for names, street addresses, churches, schools, businesses, and more.

Citysearch
http://www.citysearch.com
Search engine designed to give information about desired city.

Delta Airlines
http://www.delta.com/home/index.jsp
Make reservations, links to travel, sky miles, programs and services, customer care, arrival and departure information and more.

Driving Directions
http://www.mapquest.com/cgi-bin/mqtrip?link=/ TripQuest-Main&uid=u1mi1embgn9ac5jt: 2al6bngf8&random=803
Map out your vacation with very specific directions or more generally with a city-to-city route for long trips.

E-biztrip
http://www.e-biztrip.com/
Extensive information on travel to Indonesia and the Far East.

Expedia.com
http://www.expedia.com/
Book travel flights, hotels, cars, packages, cruises, plus links to destinations and maps.

Farebeater
http://www.flifo.com
Travel site that finds lowfare tickets for people wanting to fly.

Flight Discount
http://www.flightdiscount.com
Discount tickets are available through this site.

Flight Tracking
http://flight.thetrip.com/flightstatus
This site tracks the path of any flight using the flight
number and cities to track it.

Guide to Airport Rental Cars
http://www.bnm.com/rcar.htm
A complete guide to car rental for all ages in any city, nationally or internationally.

Hotel Discount
http://www.180096hotel.com/
Guaranteed lowest rates for national and international
cities.

Infohub Specialty Travel Guide
http://www.infohub.com/
Offbeat vacation ideas from around the world.
Searchable by interest and budget.

Maps on Us
http://www.mapsonus.com
Site dedicated to making maps for travelers or researchers.

MapBlast
http://www.mapblast.com
An atlas site that promises to find anything, Includes
maps and directions.

MapQuest
http://www.mapquest.com
Driving directions, maps, and more can be found on this
atlas site that even includes live traffic reports.

National Scenic Byways Online
http://www.byways.org
Maps, resources, and pictures are all on this site for the
traveler in need of information.

T

New England.com
http://www.Newengland.com
Yankee magazines guide to New England includes maps and reviews.

Official City Sites
http://officialcitysites.org/country.htm
Links to city guides, chambers of commerce, travel information for the major cities of the world.

Passport Services
http://travel.state.gov/passport_services.html
A list of passport services, how to, press releases, and more.

Pets on the Go
http://www.petsonthego.com
Hints and tips for traveling with pets. Includes listing of accomodations that accept pets.

Priceline.com
http://www.priceline.com
Bargains on air, car, loans, and more at priceline.com. Also includes groceries and garage sales.

Rent-a-Holiday
http://www.rent-a-holiday.com/scripts/
HomePage.asp?lg=en
Database of thousands of properties available for holiday rentals.

Surfsun.com
http://www.surf-sun.com/
Travel tips on finding and getting to the best beaches in the world.

Travel Zoo
http://www.travelzoo.com
Low prices on plane fares, vacation packages, lodging and more.

Travelocity
http://www.travelocity.com
Finds low fares for flights, rental cars, hotels, and more.

Travelwizard.com
http://www.travelwizard.com/
Worldwide travel and vacation guide, with links to specific countries and a trip planner.

Travlang
http://www.travlang.com/
Travel services and the most important words and phrases to learn in the local language.

TRIP.com
http://www.thetrip.com/
Flight, travel, car, trip planner, and hotel information for all your travel needs.

Universal Packing List
http://www.henricson.se/mats/upl
All purpose packing list for weekends away or hiking trips that will take many months.

US Airways
http://www.flymetrojet.com
Airline site advertises promotions, services, and news.

US Resort and Cottage Registry
http://lodging.org/
Vacation resorts, mountain cabins, condominiums, bed and breakfasts, guest ranches, and more.

USA City Link
http://www.usacitylink.com.
A comprehensive listing of U.S. cities offering information on travel, tourism and relocation.

Virtual Voyages
http://www.virtualvoyages.com/usa/us_city.sht
Travel resources, a destination directory, and a newsletter to help with all your travel needs.

Zagat.com
http://www.zagat.com
Reviews of restaurants in many major US cities and some outside the US.

Trivia

Bible Challenge
http://www.gospelcom.net/bttb/challenge/
Bible trivia and Bible quizzes.

Bible Quizzes
http://www.hunter.net/~hunter/quest00.htm
Each quiz covers a basic theme.

Bible Trivia
http://www.bbcs.net/bible_trivia/
Quizzes on the Old and New Testaments and other subjects.

Bible Trivia
http://www.klove.com/fun/jokes/bible_trivia.asp
Trivia, jokes, articles, and fact sheets.

Bible Trivia
http://www.bethelwayofthecross.org/trivia.htm
Weekly quiz with chance to be listed in the Top Ten.

Bible Trivia—NSCS
http://www.nscschool.com/trivia.html
Monthly contest with prizes to test your Bible knowledge.

Bible Trivia for Kids
*http://www.skybusiness.com/leoswebsites2/
trivia.html*
Easy questions for kids.

Bible Trivia for Kids
http://www.stpaul-lcms.org/trivia.htm
Weekday Bible quiz for kids 12 and under.

Bible Trivia Questions
http://www.j30ad.org/BibleTrivia.htm
Fun quizzes with drop-down menu answers.

Bible Trivia Quiz
http://www.chattervalley.com/btrivia.html
Trivia quizzes by grade level. Word scramble and more!

BibleTriviaSite.com
http://www.jesuscaressite.com/jcsjoinusinchatnow.html
Games, puzzles, prayer requests, scripture quotations
and much more.

CrossDaily Bible Trivia
http://trivia.crossdaily.com/
50 questions to test your Bible knowledge.

Gladness.com
http://www.gladness.com/games/
Bible based knowledge and word games.

Ma Sherry's Bible Trivia
http://www.nlcfranklin.org/bibletrivia.htm
Bible trivia quizzes updated frequently.

Seek—Christian Resources: Bible Trivia and Quizzes
http://www.bright.net/~seek/triviaquizzes.html
A selection of challenging games to test your Bible
knowledge.

Weekly Bible Trivia Links on the Web
http://www.natcitychristian.org/bible.htm
Links to many Bible trivia, quiz, and game sites.

other sites of interest

4Trivia.com
http://www.4trivia.com/
Dozens of trivia games on one site.

A to Z Trivia and Puzzles for FREE at MindFun.com
http://www.mindfun.com/
Thousands of questions in multiple categories.

Cascoly Free Online Trivia Games
http://cascoly.com/games/triv/trivmain.htm
History, the Presidents and more.

ChatGames Live Trivia Games
http://www.chatgames.com/
Compete with others or by yourself in different trivia
games.

T

Cool Quiz
http://www.coolquiz.com/
Trivia, word and math games for the family.

CosmoQuiz—A World Trivia Contest
http://www.cosmoquiz.com/en/
Thousands of questions in dozens of categories.

FunTrivia Community Forums
http://www.funtrivia.com/forums/cgi-bin/
forumdisplay.cgi?number=3&action=topics
Need a quick answer? You should find it here.

Knowledge Chamber Trivia Question Game
http://www.mindfun.com/classic.trivia.game.htm
Three levels of play and dozens of categories in this general knowledge game.

MindProbes
http://www.mindprobes.net/
Join a worldwide online trivia tournament.

Music Masters Game
http://www.rcc.ryerson.ca/schools/rta/brd038/usr/
jbaker/game/ind_game.htm
A challenge game where the questions get harder with every right answer.

Professor Mim's Trivia Tutorial
http://home.earthlink.net/~currer/
A series of trivia quizzes, each one harder than the last.

QuizMatic—The Live Quiz!
http://www.quizmatic.com/
Go for a top score on this general knowledge quiz.

Take 5 Intro
http://members.aol.com/Adluvseh/take5intro.html
Hundreds of entertainment trivia categories to choose from.

This Week's Trivia Game from Cornerstone
http://www.triviahalloffame.com/newgame.htm
Weekly games on a variety of subjects.

Trivia Circus
http://homepage.calypso.net/~ci-11245/trivia.htm
A movie challenge for the experts.

Trivia Portal
http://trivia.lsds.com/
Large directory of trivia sites, with hundreds just for kids.

Trivia Quiz—The UselessKnowledge Challenge
http://www.uselessknowledge.com/quiz.shtml
Thousands of questions with weekly quiz updates.

Trivia Scavenger Hunt
http://www.hunting4treasure.com/
Search the web for clues to solve the puzzle and win a cash prize.

TriviaWars
http://www.triviawars.com/
Over 50,000 questions by category, with a special kids' section.

Web Trivia
http://aaagames.com/trivia.htm
Trivia games for all ages.

Your Portal to Trivia!
http://trivia.searchking.com/
A directory of hundreds of trivia sites.

Videos

Action Christian Videos
http://www.actionchristianvideos.com/
Christian videos featuring exciting extreme sports athletes. Clips available on line.

AMF Christian Videos
http://www.amfchristianvideos.com/
A wide variety of videos for the Christian family available at deep discounts.

V

C.M.L. Cafe
http://cmlcafe.cjb.net/
Extensive Christian music site with videos and concert videos.

Children's Christian Videos
http://www.christianchildren.com
Christian videos, games and software. Also provides secure online transactions.

Christian Family Home Video Superstore
http://www.kingdomquest.com/joeog/video.htm
Catalog of secular and Christian videos for sale with reviews.

Christian Movies.com
http://www.christianmovies.com/
A source for the best Christian videos and industry news.

Christian Video Collection
http://www.christianvideocollection.org/index/index2.htm
A comprehensive source of inspirational, educational and entertaining videos from around the world.

Christian Videos Etc.
http://www.christianvideoetc.com/index.htm?577
A broad selection of Christian videotapes and DVDs organized by category.

Christian Videos for Adults
http://www.internationalbibles.com/Videos/Adults/videos_for_adults.htm
A broad range of videos to enlighten and entertain are available here. Links to kids' videos, too.

CITV.com
http://www.citv.com/broadcast/musicvideos/
Top Christian music videos viewable online.

Crown Video
http://www.crownvideo.com
Over 1000 Christian videos in many different categories.
Veggie Tales, Gary Smalley, Neil Anderson, Ken Davis,
Gaithers, Steve Bell, and all your other favorite Chris-
tian videos are available here.

Family Music and Video Classics
http://www.mountcarmel.com/index.htm
Providing the best price for the best in Christian classics.

GospelMusic TV
http://www.gmtn.com/
Watch live performances on the Internet.

Guiding Light Video
http://www.guidinglightvideo.com
Lighting the way with children's Christian videos,
games, and software.

Music Video—Homepage
*http://musicvideo.about.com/entertainment/
musicvideo/mbody.htm*
General music video page with links to Christian music
sites.

NCCB/USCC—Movie Reviews
http://www.nccbuscc.org/movies/videoall.htm
Catholic reviews of films and videos for families.

PraiseTV
http://www.praisetv.com/
Live TV, streaming videos.

Videos 2 Inspire
http://www.videos2inspire.com/
Entertainment "with a purpose" to inspire and aid in
Biblical education.

What Parents and Teachers Should Look For
http://www.users.bigpond.com/rdoolan/kidsvids.html
Tips on selecting Christian videos for children.

V

World Christian Video Directory
http://www.gospelvideos.com/
A compilation of dozens of sites offering Christian videos in many languages.

Worship Music
http://www.worshipmusic.com/
Secure online shopping for the best in Christian videos, music, etc.

other sites of interest

Family Classics
http://store.yahoo.com/familysafemedia/famvidclas.html
Catalog of movie and music videos suitable for the family.

Family Video Catalog
http://www.familynet.org/products.htm
Extensive catalog of family and children's videos.

Family Wonder
http://www.familywonder.com/
Reviews and store for age-appropriate videos.

Kids and Family Video
http://www.thegrid.net/dakaiser/books/releases/vidkid99.htm
Reviews of hit videos and films for parents.

Movie Mom
http://www.moviemom.com/nav/video.cfm
A mother's review of new and classic movies and videos.

Sandstar
http://www.familyfilms.com/
Catalog of reviewed family videos.

Volunteering

Best Bets for Volunteering Abroad
http://www.cie.uci.edu/iop/voluntee.html
Links to dozens of Christian and secular volunteer programs around the world.

Christian Relief Services
http://www.christianrelief.org/
Empowering local volunteers to help those in need in
their own communities.

Christian Volunteers
http://www.christianvolunteers.com/
An on-campus Christian witness to college students.

Maranatha Volunteers International
http://www.maranatha.org/
Spreading the Gospel throughout the world as it con-
structs urgently needed buildings.

Recruiting Volunteers for Christian Service
*http://www.moody.edu/ED/GS/Servant/jan-feb00/
recruit.htm*
Advice on how to find, motivate and keep volunteers
from one minister's experience.

Time for God
http://www.timeforgod.org/volunteers.htm
A UK based charity offering opportunities to serve others around the world.

Volunteers in Medical Missions
http://www.innova.net/~vimm/page1.htm
Ministering to the spiritual and physical needs of children and adults in developing nations around the world.

other sites of interest

America Reads Challenge
http://www.ed.gov/inits/americareads
Information about training opportunities, questions and
answers, legislation, the President's Coalition for the
America Reads Challenge, federal work-study, publications, and research.

America's Promise: The Alliance for Youth
http://www.americaspromise.org
Dedicated to organizing volunteers to help youth grow
into healthy and well-rounded and personally successful
adults.

V

City Year
http://www.cityyear.org
Launched in 1988 with private funding, this youth service corps is now part of the AmeriCorps national service network, providing its service with help from the federal government, corporations, foundations and individuals. Corps members serve as teachers aides, run after-school programs, conflict resolution workshops, and more.

Community Volunteerism
http://www.fremontpublic.org/volunteerism.html
Puts interested people in touch with the MLK Vista program, JustServe AmeriCorps, and the Washington Reading Program.

Do Something
http://www.dosomething.org/
A nationwide network for young people eager to help make a better world.

Habitat for Humanity International
http://www.habitat.org
This page will answer your questions on how to get involved, where the houses are built and how the program works. Fact sheets describing Habitat's progress are available for each country in which Habitat is working.

Healing Hands
http://www.healinghandsproject.com/
Devoted to providing reconstructive surgery and support to men and women with facial disfigurement.

IdeaList
http://www.idealist.org
This site from Action Without Borders lists 14,000 nonprofit organizations from 125 countries. Services, volunteer opportunities, job openings, internships, upcoming events and publications.

Literacy Volunteers of America
http://www.literacyvolunteers.org
A national network of 366 locally based programs, supported by state and national staff. Its mission is to change lives through literacy.

Locks of Love
http://www.locksoflove.com/
Providing hairpieces to financially disadvantaged children suffering from long-term medical hairloss.

Project America
http://www.project.org/
Inspiring people to make positive steps in their communities by creating partnerships between volunteers and organizations that need them.

Project Sunshine
http://www.projectsunshine.org
A nondenominational, not-for-profit organization, which provides numerous free programs and services to children with cancer, AIDS, and other life-threatening illnesses.

Reaching Out to the World: Volunteering to Create a Global Neighborhood
http://e.usia.gov/millennium/index.htm
A site dedicated to individuals who freely and voluntarily give of their time, talent, and effort on behalf of visitors from other nations.

Virtual Volunteering
http://www.serviceleader.org/vv
A guide for agencies and volunteers who wish to offer their aid and services online. Especially geared toward people for whom normal volunteer activies would be impossible.

Volunteer Match
http://www.volunteermatch.org
An arena for nonprofit organizations and potential volunteers to match opportunities for service with those interested in serving. Nationwide opportunities.

Weather

Bible Weather Station, The
http://my.homewithgod.com/bibletruths/BibleWeather.html
Weather news and information combined with Biblical insights.

W

Christian Weather Net
http://www.cweathernet.com/
Combining the latest scientific data with a strong Christian witness.

other sites of interest

AccuWeather
http://www1.accuweather.com/adcbin/index?partner=accuweather
Customize your online weather forecast for your location and your sport and recreation interests.

Atlantic Tropical Weather Center (Blake)
http://www.atwc.org/
Meteograms, forecasts, buoy and ship data, satellite pictures, and more.

Australian Weather News and Links
http://ausweather.simplenet.com/
News about Australian weather, and the most comprehensive list of Australian weather links available.

Canadian Hurricane Center
http://www.ns.ec.gc.ca/weather/hurricane/index_e.html
A great satellite picture of Hurricane Bonnie, weather, pollution, search, links, and more.

Central Pacific Hurricane Center, Honolulu
http://www.nws.noaa.gov/pr/hnl/cphc/pages/cphc.shtml
Information on cyclones, hurricanes, hurricane safety, tropical cyclone advisories, and more.

CIMSS Tropical Cyclones
http://cimss.ssec.wisc.edu/tropic/tropic.html
Storm coverage, cool images of the week, storm tracks, winds and analyses, and more.

CNN Storm Center
http://www.cnn.com/WEATHER/storm.center/
Hurricane tip center, weather maps, allergy report, tornado and thunderstorm update, and more.

Dr Gray's Annual Hurricane Forecast (CSU)
http://typhoon.atmos.colostate.edu/
FAQs, forecasts, tropical weather, and more.

Earth Watch Weather on Demand
http://www.earthwatch.com/
Weather headlines, stormwatch, forecasts, satellite and radar, and more.

FEMA
http://www.fema.gov/hu98/hurinfo.htm
Hurricane background and preparedness information.

Hurricane Basics
http://www.usatoday.com/weather/huricane/whur0.htm
Tropical weather news, forecasts, satellite images, latest storms, and more.

Intellicast
http://www.intellicast.com/
Weather reports for active lives, lifestyle weather, seasonal weather, and more.

Joint Typhoon Warning Center
http://www.npmoc.navy.mil/jtwc.html
Current bulletins, warning graphic legend, current tropical systems, and more.

National Hurricane Center
http://www.nhc.noaa.gov/
Active cyclones, forecasts, imagery, glossary, acronyms, storm names, and more.

National Weather Service
http://www.nws.noaa.gov/
Weather data, warnings, forecast products, weather maps, storm prediction, marine weather.

National Weather Service Interactive Weather Information Network (IWIN)
http://iwin.nws.noaa.gov/iwin/graphicsversion/bigmain.html
Current national warnings, great satellite images, world weather, great links, and more.

W

Rain or Shine Weather Weather Reports
http://www.rainorshine.com/
Hurricane watches, radar and maps, weather cams, current weather, ski reports, and more.

Stormchase Online
http://www.stormchase.com/
Links to radar and satellite, weather maps, and weather information. This site is for storm chasers—not a daily weather report.

Tornado Project Online
http://www.tornadoproject.com/
Tornado videos, books, storm shelters, tornado safety, and more.

Travel Forecast—Weather—Net Links
http://www.weather.about.com/medianews/weather/ msubtrav.htm
Weather, travel, from your About.com Guide.

Tsunami Research Program
http://www.pmel.noaa.gov/tsunami/
Field observations, modeling and forecasts, events and data, mapping efforts, and more.

Weather Education from the National Weather Service
http://www.nws.noaa.gov/er/btv/html/ wxeduc.html
Storm reports, climatology, forecasts, links, and more.

Weather Links National Hurricane Center
http://www.hurricanehunters.com/wx_links.htm
The Weather Channel's tropical update. Frequently Asked Questions (HRD), homework help, a hurricane hunter's photo album and more.

Weather Network
http://www.theweathernetwork.com/
Information in French, instant weather maps, seasonal reports, and more.

Weather Underground
http://www.wunderground.com/
Current conditions and forecasts: temperature, humidity, pressure, conditions, and warnings.

Weather: The Atmosphere for Learning from the Weather Channel
http://www.weather.com/education/index.html
Weather maps, forecasts, news, storm watch, and lesson plans for teachers.

WeatherNet Connecting You to the World of Weather
http://cirrus.sprl.umich.edu/wxnet/
Weather maps, fast forecasts, travel, other weather sites, warnings, and more.

Weddings

Bible Readings for Weddings
http://www.bible-reading.com/wedding-readings.html
Selected Old and New Testament verses for wedding ceremonies.

Christian Couples Wedding Guide
http://www.crosssearch.com/cgi-bin/bounce/83438
A forum and chatroom where engaged Christian couples can exchange tips and ideas on wedding planning.

Contemporary Christian Wedding Songbook
http://www.musicbookstore.com/
Item available through online resource.

Wedding Vows
http://www.bible.org/docs/pastor/weddings/vows.htm
A selection of sample vows from NET Bible.

other sites of interest

All About Showers
http://www.allaboutshowers.com/bridal/
Hosting details, shower games, special touches, decorations, themes, and more.

W

Alt.weddings Collected Information Resources
http://showcase.netins.net/web/wedding/indexx.htm
A directory of sites with information on showers, gifts, ceremonies and more.

Ask the Newlyweds
http://www.ultimatewedding.com/newlyweds
Here you can read questions and responses all about weddings and honeymoons, with a search engine, shopping information, and more.

Bridal Links
http://www.bridal-links.com
Search engines, coupons, tips, books, travel, shopping, prizes, and more.

Bridal Show Online
http://64.65.35.41/planning.shtml
Checklists and helpful articles on planning a wedding.

Bridal Shower Games
http://www.blissezine.com/library/games.asp
Listings of over 100 games to play at bridal showers.

Bride-to-Bride Classifieds
http://www.ultimatewedding.com/classifieds
The bride-to-bride connection where one can sell bridal items to future brides.

Brides and Grooms.com
http://bridesandgrooms.com/
Online wedding planning resource.

Country Weddings
http://www.countryweddings.com/
Information and links about country weddings.

Destination Weddings
http://ultimatewedding.com/destination/
Articles, locations, coordinators, bookstore, and more planning tips for your destination wedding.

Favors, Favors!
http://www.ultimatewedding.com/favors
Dozens of ideas for favors for shower hosts and guests.

ForeverWed
http://www.foreverwed.com
A wedding planning resource including accessories, bridal stories, planning tips, articles and more.

Fun Facts about You!
http://www.ultimatewedding.com/polls
Fun facts and polls regarding wedding planning.

Get Away Vehicle
http://www.ultimatewedding.com/articles/pot117.htm
An article on the get-away vehicle, and how to prepare for pranks from friends.

Honeymoon Information and Packages
http://honeymoon.excite-travel.com/
Links to vacations in USA, Mexico, Caribbean, Bahamas, and more.

JS Online
http://www.jsonline.com/lifestyle/weddings/
Links to information and articles on marriage and weddings.

Kiss the Bride
http://kissthebride.com.au/
Tips and advice on all aspects of getting married.

Making Your Own Veil
http://www.ultimatewedding.com/articles/pot114.htm
Tips and ideas on making your own veil.

Marriage and Wedding Book Store
http://bridesandgrooms.com/bookstore
Marriage, wedding, honeymoon, engagement, anniversary and more book store .

Martha Stewart Weddings
http://www.marthastewart.com/weddings/
Links for the bride, groom, bridal party, and all the necessary wedding elements.

Modern Bride.com
http://www.modernbride.com/
Links to local resources, honeymoon spots, wedding resources, and more.

W

New Bride Legal Name Change Kit
http://lawfirm.webjump.com/
Name change forms online, or have them mailed to your home for a small fee.

Online Discussion Board
http://www.weddingchat.com/board/Forum2/HTML/ 000772.html
A discussion on engagement and pre-engagement.

Planning a Wedding
http://www.tetranet.net/users/stolbert/wedding/ wedindex.html
A helpful timeline, plus suggested music and Bible readings.

Planning Article Database
http://www.ultimatewedding.com/search
Search for planning articles or choose from one of the many categories.

Pre-Wedding Parties
http://www.ourmarriage.com/html/bridal_ showers.html
Articles and ideas for bridal showers, bridesmaids' luncheon, bachelor party, and more.

Soc.couples Wedding Page
http://www.wam.umd.edu/~sek/wedding.html
A large directory of links to helpful web resources on many aspects of weddings.

The Knot
http://www.theknot.com
Planning, real weddings, proposals, fashion, beauty, groomsmen, bridesmaids, moms, honeymoons, and more.

Ultimate Bridal Shower Guide
http://www.ultimateshower.com
A complete list of games, party ideas and favors—everything for planning the perfect shower.

Ultimate Wedding Guide
http://www.ultimatewedding.com
One of the most extensive sites on the web for wedding planning. Features resources, shopping links, music, poetry, vows, sample planners, etc.

Ultimate Wedding Song Catalog
http://www.weddingromance.com/songs/
Suggestions on musical selections for the ceremony and the reception.

UltimateWedding.com Community
http://www.weddingchat.com
Chatroom and message boards discussion all aspects of wedding planning.

Vows & Ceremonies
http://www.ultimatewedding.com/vows
An extensive list of traditional, non-traditional, and specialty vows.

Way Cool Weddings
http://www.waycoolweddings.com/home.htm
Links to wedding resources, registries, and much more.

Wedding 411
http://www.wedding411.com/
default.cfm?passcode=99vk3d2zr1&group_id=0&new_pc=1
To do list, guest manager, budget, photo album, website, and more.

Wedding Cam
http://www.discovery.com/cams/wedding/
wedding.html?ct=395d54c5
Information about weddings at a little chapel in Las Vegas, with a wedding cam to view live weddings.

Wedding Channel
http://www.weddingchannel.com
Fashion, planning tools, articles, shopping, registry, travel, advice, and more.

W

Wedding Circle
http://www.weddingcircle.com/
A centralized source for advice and ideas on weddings and honeymoon planning, too.

Wedding Gazette
http://www.weddinggazette.com/
Shower and wedding ideas and tips on attire, flowers, music and more.

Wedding Information & Resources
http://www.ultimatewedding.com/articles
Planning information and articles on a variety of wedding topics.

Wedding Poetry
http://www.world-wideweddings.com/Poetry/index.htm
Links to romantic pieces of literature to choose from for readings at your wedding.

WeddingChoice.com
http://www.weddingchoice.com
Online wedding resource, including information onf Christian wedding ceremonies.

Weddings Online—Officiants
http://www.weddings-online.com/off/
Links to wedding officiants in your state.

Weddings Poems
http://www.weddingromance.com/poems
More than 200 poems, each which will add a touch of love and romance to your wedding.

Who Pays for What?
http://www.ultimatewedding.com/articles/pot75.htm
A list of financial responsibilities for each member of the wedding party.

Women.com Weddings
http://www.women.com/weddings/
Tools, tips, and advice for the bride-to-be.

Women's Health

Christian Women Today
http://www.christianwomentoday.com/health/health.html
Health and fitness articles and tips.

Health News—News of Interest to Christians
http://news.christiansunite.com/health.shtml
A daily digest of worldwide health news from ChristiansUnite.com.

Healing Hands
http://www.healinghandsproject.com/
Devoted to providing reconstructive surgery and support to men and women with facial disfigurement.

Women's Health and Medical Info
http://www.cbull.com/health.htm
A directory of hundreds of Christian and secular websites dealing with women's health topics.

other sites of interest

Black Women's Health
http://www.blackwomenshealth.com/
Guides to specific diseases, nutrition, and mental health.

Breast Cancer.com
http://breast.cancer.com/
The latest news on breast cancer for the community.

Childbirth.Org
http://www.childbirth.org/
Lots of information on pregnancy and childbirth.

Early Menopause
http://earlymenopause.com/
A site for women who experience menopause at an early age.

Eating Disorders
http://www.mirror-mirror.org/eatdis.htm
All about eating disorders and how to overcome them.

W

Gilda Radner Familial Ovarian Cancer Registry
*http://rpci.med.buffalo.edu/clinic/gynonc/
grwp.html*
Registry for families with two or more members suffering from ovarian cancer.

Global Health
*http://www.pitt.edu/HOME/GHNet/
GHWomen.html*
Links to women's worldwide health resources.

Health Square
http://www.healthsquare.com/
Health news, medicines and drugs, dental corner, kids health, pregnancy, and more.

Health Web
http://healthweb.org/browse.cfm?subjectid=96
Devoted to general and specific resources for women's health.

Healthy Women
http://www.healthywomen.org/
Comprehensive information on women's health topics.

I Emily
http://www.iemily.com/
The website for health and wellness—just for girls.

Intellihealth
*http://www.intelihealth.com/IH/ihtIH?t=9103&p=
~br,IHW|~st,9103|~r,WSIHW000|~b,• |*
Resources and links from Harvard Medical School and Johns Hopkins University.

My Starting Point—Women's Health
http://www.stpt.com/category.asp?ID=4&cat=12
Medicine, nutrition, self-help links.

National Breast Cancer Center
http://www.nbcc.org.au/
Search, information, support, events, and more.

National Women's Health Information Center
http://www.4women.gov/
Your online source for health information and referrals.

On Health
http://www.looksmart.com/r?page=/dls/he/
he.html
Links to fitness, health, medicines, pregnancy, stress,
and much more.

Personal MD.com
http://personalmd.com/womenhealth.shtml
Links to information on women's health issues.

Power Surge
http://hometown.aol.com/dearest/intro.htm
Resources for women going through menopause.

WebMD Health
http://my.webmd.com/condition_center/whp
Health and wellness for women in mid-life.

Women First
http://www.womenfirst.com/
Focuses on over 50 topics of importance to women.

Women's Health & Sports
http://www.clark.net/pub/pribut/spwomen.htm
Info on sports injuries and related disorders and links to
other women's health issues.

Women's Health Interactive
http://www.womens-health.com/
Guidelines and resources for better personal health, nutrition, and lifestyle.

Women's Health Sites
http://aztec.lib.utk.edu/~shrode/wss_health.htm
Links to a large collection of websites for women's
health.

Women's Memory Quiz
http://www.womentodaymagazine.com/fitnesshealth/
memoryquiz.html
Tests your memory for studies in Alzheimer's disease.

W

Women's Pavillion
http://www.obgyn.net/women/women.asp
Provides resources for women's ob/gyn concerns.

Women's Issues

Bizy Moms
http://www.bizymoms.com/
News, links, articles, advice, shopping, community, and more.

Business Women's Network
http://www.bwni.com/
Lots of links to sites for working women and business concerns.

Christian Moms
http://www.uci.net/~cotton/cmhome.htm
Advice, information and inspiration for the Christian mother.

Christian Women's Ministry
http://www.bccwomensministry.org
Site based on Titus 2:3–5 encouraging Christian women to be all that Christ intended them to be. Information on organization, devotions, hospitality, writings by women, how to start a WM in your church, quiet time helps, and more.

Christian Working Woman
http://christianworkingwoman.org/
Daily radio broadcasts and a weekly email newsletter for the Christian woman in the workplace.

Girltech
http://www.girltech.com/index.html
A large site dedicated to girls' interests.

God's Word to Women
http://www.godswordtowomen.org
Help for women in their search to discover who God says they are.

Handmaidens
http://ionanet.com/women/499/ed.htm
A Christian women's webzine. Christian comedy, education, marriage, stewardship, poetry, and more.

Hearts at Home
http://www.hearts-at-home.org
Professional organization encouraging and supporting the professional mother at home with conferences and a monthly newsletter.

Independent Means
http://www.anincomeofherown.com/
Encouraging young women, and their mentors, to find an income of their own.

IVillage—The Women's Network
http://www.ivillage.com/experts/
Resident experts by topic: health and fitness, parenting, money, relationships, career, books, computing, and more.

Just MomsChristian Online Mother's Group!
http://www.JustMoms.com
We offer daily Bible studies, chats, online newsletter, message boards, and support groups.

Ladies of Sonshine
http://www.geocities.com/ladiesofsonshine/index.html
A Christian women's online group offering love, support, biblical counsel, as well as studies, fellowship, chat and friendship

LOOK
http://www.thelook.net
Learn, shop, and discuss everyday issues such as family, career, self-esteem, beauty, fashion, relationships, and investing.

Love@Home
http://www.loveathome.com/index.html
A monthly dose of encouragement online for Christian women.

Moms Helping Moms
http://www.geocities.com/Wellesley/Atrium/5562
A site for those of us who love the Lord and can reach out to help others.

ProverbWomen
http://www.geocities.com/Wellesley/Garden/5863/
For divorced and/or single women with prayer and e-letters offered, women's links, reference books, encouragement to renew self worth as God sees you.

Single Christian Woman
http://www.ilovejesus.com/memberpages/singlesisters/
Resources and fellowship for the single, Christian woman.

Sisters in Christ
http://www.tywebbin.com/faith/sisters/
A cyber-ministry for Christian women and network of Christian women and their websites.

Top Ten Women's Issues
http://www.cs.toronto.edu/~andria/reviews/NetWatch.html
The content here will be pertaining to women's issues, or the sites are run by women.

Women in Business Hotlist
http://www.sbaonline.sba.gov/hotlist/women.html
Links to women-run businesses and information on how to start one.

Women of Faith
http://www.womenoffaith.com/
Events, spiritual life, ministries, health and fitness, relationships, beauty and style, shopping, and other Christian links.

Women.com Network
http://www.women.com
Women.com is the smart network for women's content and community, includes Women's Wire, Beatrice's Web Guide, Prevention's Healthy Ideas, Stork Site, and

MoneyMode, plus community message boards and chat where our visitors take center stage.

Women's Cancer Network
http://www.wcn.org/
Great information site devoted to preventing, detecting and conquering cancer in women.

Women's Resources
http://www.cybertown.com/women.html
Links to all sorts of information and women's issues available online.

Women's White Pages @feMail.com
http://www.femail.com/
Links to topics from art to workplace issues.

Women's Wire
http://www.women.com/
Tips, links, shopping, contests, and lots more.

WWWomen:Women Online
http://www.wwwomen.com/
The premier search directory for women. Easy links to follow.

Young Women's Christian Association
http://www.worldywca.org/
Directory of National associations, projects, publications, policy statements, employment opportunities, and more.

Writing Resources
American Christian Writers
http://www.ecpa.org/ACW/index.html
Dedicated to locating, encouraging and motivating Christian writers.

Association of Christian Writers
http://www.christianwriters.org.uk
Site includes information, resources and inspiration, competitions, events, and writer groups.

W

Books for Christian Writers, Authors, Poets and Speakers
http://www.bluejaypub.com/win/books
Information on books, writers, authors, poets, speakers,
marketing advice, Internet, self-publishing, self-help,
writing, and more.

Christian Romance Writers
http://kanawha.lib.wv.us/ref/rolodex/ro-chrom.htm
Features works and resources of interest related to Christian romance writers.

Christian Writers' Group Homepage
http://members.truepath.com/CWG
Site offers 2000 resources and encouragement helps for
today's Christian writer.

Christian Writers' Market Guide
http://www.joypublishing.com/guide.htm
A guide sponsored by Joy Publishing has published dozens of spiritually enlightening books and Christian literature for many years.

Omnilist of Christian Publishing
http://members.aol.com/clinksgold/omnbook.htm
Links to dozens of sites on Christian writers and
writing.

Religion Publishers
http://acqweb.library.vanderbilt.edu/acqweb/pubr/rel.html
Links to many publisher's homesites.

Writing for Christian Markets
http://www.writerswrite.com/books/writers/relig.htm
Books on Christian writing and related books.

other sites of interest

4Writers.com
http://4writers.4anything.com/
Site offers support for professional and aspiring writers,
including information on conferences and artists' colonies, and creative writing programs.

Aylad's Writer's Group
http://www.publication.com/aylad/index.htm
An online writers group, with information, tips, etc.

Best in Science Fiction
http://www.sfsite.com/home.htm
With news, latest releases, writers resource links, reviews, and more.

Curmudgeon's StyleBook
http://www.theslot.com/contents.html
An online stylebook with a goal to ensure consistency, and to provide an alternative to, not a replacement of, the AP stylebook.

For Young Writers
http://www.inkspot.com/young/
Information and resources for writers under age 18.

Guide to Grammar and Style
http://andromeda.rutgers.edu/~jlynch/Writing/
These notes are a miscellany of grammatical rules and explanations, comments on style, and suggestions on usage.

Guide to Grammar and Writing
http://cctc.commnet.edu/grammar/index.htm
A detailed guide to grammatical rules, usage, hints, links, etc.

Inkspot: The Writer's Resource
http://www.inkspot.com/
A writer's community site with market information, advice, education, and workshops.

Poetry Pals Internet Poetry Publishing Project for K-12 Students
http://www.geocities.com/EnchantedForest/5165
Links to books, forms of poetry, free reign poetry, participants, project info, and more.

Storymania
http://www.storymania.com/
Find a community of creative writers and readers of all types of original works not published elsewhere. Short stories, poetry, novels, plays, and more.

W

Strunk and White's *The Elements of Style*
http://www.bartleby.com/141/index.html
The online text of one of the most valuable style guides for writers.

Writer's Digest
http://www.writersdigest.com/
Links to hot list, writer's guidelines, "Market of the Day" feature, magazines, books, contests, conferences, and more.

Writers.Net
http://www.writers.net/
An extensive resource for writers, with lists of publishers and agents, news, tips, information, etc.

Zoos

A Modern Noah's Ark
http://www.mfa.gov.il/mfa/go.asp?MFAH01up0
Article on the Tisch Family Zoological Gardens (Jerusalem) where creatures of the Bible have been collected.

other sites of interest

Audubon Institute Website
http://www.auduboninstitute.org/
Tours, information, education. Located in New Orleans.

Bronx Zoo!
http://www.bronxzoo.com/
Animal cams, tours, events.

Chicago's Shedd Aquarium
http://www.sheddnet.org/index.html
Exhibits, kids' page, news.

Dallas World Aquarium and Zoological Garden
http://www.dwazoo.com/
Manatee cam, exhibits, tour.

Lincoln Park Zoo
http://www.lpzoo.com/
Information, events, conservation. Located in Chicago.

Long Beach Aquarium of the Pacific
http://www.aquariumofpacific.org/
Exhibits, fish cams, online learning center.

Los Angeles Zoo
http://www.lazoo.org/
Facts, opportunities, animals, dates, conservation, and more.

National Aquarium in Baltimore
http://www.aqua.org/
Exhibits, news, information .

National Zoo Homepage
http://web2.si.edu/organiza/museums/zoo/nzphome.htm
Animal cams, news, exhibits. Located in Washington, DC.

San Diego Zoo
http://www.sandiegozoo.org/
Wild animal park, shop, membership, zoo, and more.

SeaWorld—Busch Gardens
http://www.seaworld.org/infobook.html
Animal information and fun facts database.

Vancouver Aquarium Marine Science Center Online
http://www.vanaqua.org/
Tour, exhibits, conservation. Located in Vancouver, British Columbia.

Wildlife Conservation Society—Zoos and Aquarium
http://www.wcs.org/zoos/
Central site for New York City zoos and aquarium.

Zoos Worldwide
http://www.zoos-worldwide.de/
Links to zoos and aquaria world-wide, full page of zoo cams.

ZooWeb
http://www.zooweb.com/
Your link to zoos and Aquaria on the web with hundreds of links.

Z